The Life and Music of

BOOKER "BUKKA" WHITE

American Made Music Series

The Life and Music of BOOKER "BUKKA" WHITE

Recalling the Blues

David W. Johnson

Foreword by Frank Matheis

University Press of Mississippi / Jackson

publication supported by a grant from
The Community Foundation for Greater New Haven
as part of the Urban Haven Project

Publication of this book was made possible in part by a generous donation from
Newberry Tanks and Equipment, LLC.

The University Press of Mississippi is the scholarly publishing agency of
the Mississippi Institutions of Higher Learning: Alcorn State University,
Delta State University, Jackson State University, Mississippi State University,
Mississippi University for Women, Mississippi Valley State University,
University of Mississippi, and University of Southern Mississippi.

www.upress.state.ms.us

The University Press of Mississippi is a member of
the Association of University Presses.

Manufactured in the United States of America
∞

Library of Congress Cataloging-in-Publication Data

Names: Johnson, David W. (David William), 1946– author. | Matheis, Frank, writer of foreword.
Title: The life and music of Booker "Bukka" White : recalling the blues / David W. Johnson ; foreword by Frank Matheis.
Other titles: American made music series.
Description: Jackson : University Press of Mississippi, 2024. | Series: American made music series | Includes bibliographical references and index.
Identifiers: LCCN 2024026613 (print) | LCCN 2024026614 (ebook) | ISBN 9781496817518 (hardback) | ISBN 9781496853448 (trade paperback) | ISBN 9781496853455 (epub) | ISBN 9781496853462 (epub) | ISBN 9781496853479 (pdf) | ISBN 9781496853486 (pdf)
Subjects: LCSH: White, Bukka. | African American musicians—Biography. | Blues musicians—United States—Biography. | Guitarists—United States—Biography. | Singers—United States—Biography.
Classification: LCC ML420.W475 J64 2024 (print) | LCC ML420.W475 (ebook) | DDC 782.421643092 [B]—dc23/eng/20240620
LC record available at https://lccn.loc.gov/2024026613
LC ebook record available at https://lccn.loc.gov/2024026614

British Library Cataloging-in-Publication Data available

Dedicated to Irene Kertchaval, Beulah Faye Anderson, Henrietta Williams, Kathy Williams, Sandra D. Marble, James Kertchaval, and all the children and grandchildren of Booker White.

CONTENTS

AUTHOR'S NOTE AND ACKNOWLEDGMENTS

THIS IS THE THIRD TIME I HAVE WRITTEN ABOUT BOOKER WHITE. IN 1976, I interviewed him in a Massachusetts hospital and wrote about the visit for my newspaper. The story ran on the front page with a photograph of Booker smiling from a hospital bed. I put aside my tape of the interview and possibility of writing more until 2010, when the journal *Southern Cultures* published a much longer article, "'Fixin' To Die Blues': The Last Months of Bukka White."

This book got its start in 2017 when I proposed to Craig W. Gill, director of the University Press of Mississippi, that the Press consider publishing a collection of Booker's interviews. Craig advised that the Press would be more interested in a traditional biography. As it happened, I had begun my research.

In the book's earliest stages, the late Sean Killeen, who was working on a biography of Leadbelly, encouraged me to do something similar with Booker White. In 1991, while working at Phillips Exeter Academy in New Hampshire, I applied for a grant from a fund that supported student-faculty collaboration. I was not a faculty member but received a hundred dollars from the Riordan Fund.

I sent the tape of my interview with Booker to the Center for the Study of Southern Culture at the University of Mississippi and used the grant money to pay for transcribing it. Blues authority William Ferris, the center's director at the time, put me in touch with graduate student Joel Nathan Rosen and Rosen's friend Linda L. Boulton. Quotations from their transcript bring Booker's voice to the narrative. Today Dr. Rosen is on the faculty of Moravian University in Pennsylvania, where he teaches a course that includes blues.

The Exeter student I collaborated with, LaKenya Houston, went home to Memphis on a school break and returned with a photocopy of Booker's obituary in the *Commercial Appeal* and a librarian's recommendation of *Tom Ashley, Sam McGee, Bukka White: Tennessee Traditional Singers*. When I later bought the book, I found that it contained a sixty-page biography of Booker written by University of Memphis professors F. Jack Hurley and David Evans.

In the acknowledgments in my 2013 book about two old-time country musicians, I wrote that it takes a community to write a biography. Now I am certain of it. I only could have completed this book with a great deal of support, understanding, and generosity from the following people and institutions.

In 2018, the MacDowell Colony gave me eight weeks of uninterrupted time to draft the early chapters. In 2022 and 2023, when I needed to revise much of what I had written, blues enthusiast David Little offered to read the manuscript and help me reorganize it. Dave's steady patience and informed perspective kept us on task through two revisions.

I am indebted to the members of Booker White's family for sharing their personal recollections: daughters Irene Kertchaval, the late Beulah Faye Anderson, and Henrietta Williams; grandchildren Kathy Williams and Sandra Marble; and cousins B. B. King and Jerry Fair.

I extend my gratitude to Chris and Rebecca Long, Newberry Tank & Equipment Company, for the generous gift that made it possible for us to purchase a number of excellent photographs; to Professor Bruce Jackson for his permission to listen to the tapes he recorded in April 1964 during Booker's visit to Boston and Cambridge; and to Judith Gray and Jonathan Gold of the American Folklife Center of the Library of Congress for digitizing the tapes and making them available to me.

I am grateful to Andrew Yale for sharing his September 1982 interview with Booker's partner Leola Morris at her home in Memphis. Without Andy's interview, I would not have been able to include Leola's personal recollections.

I owe much to John Shaw, T. DeWayne Moore, James E. Clark, the late Burt Feintuch, Larry Davis, Melanie Munlin, Jimmy Crosthwaite, F. Jack Hurley, the members of the Mississippi Blues Trail Writing and Research Team: Bob Eagle, Jim O'Neal, Scott Barretta, and Ed Payne, and Tina Robbins, executive director of the Aberdeen (Mississippi) Visitors Bureau.

While in Mississippi in July 2017, I did research in two county courthouses. In Chickasaw County, Chancery Clerk Tiffany Lovvorn introduced me to the records room, which Atty. Rex F. Sanderson helped me navigate. In Grenada County, Chancery Clerk Johnny L. Hayward directed me to his records room, where title researcher Dianne W.

Barnidge helped me find the relevant volumes of property transactions. I am indebted to each.

In West Point, Mississippi, Code Enforcement Officer Jeremy Klutts opened the Howlin' Wolf Blues Museum on a Sunday so that I could see the collection, then drove me to the deserted shell of an authentic roadhouse, the Roxy. Our next stop was a railroad track that runs through the adjacent community of White Station, where Chester Burnett (aka Howlin' Wolf) lived as a boy. Jeremy told me that Wolf wrote "Smokestack Lightning" based on his boyhood memories of smoke and flame from steam locomotives passing through Whites.

For sharing their deep knowledge of blues and the music business, I am grateful to Robert Gordon, Peter Guralnick, Gayle Dean Wardlow, Mary Katherine Aldin, Barry Melton, Claudio Guerrieri, TJ Wheeler, Luigi Monge, Frank Matheis, Linzie Collier Butler, Augusta Palmer, Barry Mazor, Fred J. Hay, Dick Waterman, John Battaglia, Wayne Shirley, and Bruce Pingree.

In the course of my research and writing, I referred often to Hurley and Evans's biography "Bukka White" in *Tom Ashley, Sam McGee, Bukka White, Tennessee Traditional Singers*; the biographical data in *Blues: A Regional Experience* by Bob Eagle and Eric S. LeBlanc; the invaluable listings of *Blues & Gospel Records 1902–1942* by John Godrich and Robert M. W. Dixon; and Robert Ford's *A Blues Bibliography: The International Literature of an Afro-American Music Genre*. For the itinerary of the American Folk Blues Festival tours, I often consulted Stefan Wirz's American Music Web site https://www.wirz.de/music/america.htm.

Helping me obtain photographs and research materials were Dr. Gerald Chaudron, head of Special Collections at the University of Memphis Library; Adele Heagney, librarian in the St. Louis Room of the St. Louis Public Library; the Reference Department of the Salem, Massachusetts Public Library; Rachel E. Lyons, archivist of the New Orleans Jazz & Heritage Foundation; Debbie Shaw, senior curator of archaeology at the Tennessee State Museum; Danielle Kovacs, curator of collections for the Robert S. Cox Special Collections and University Archives Research Center of the University of Massachusetts Amherst Library; Kristin Eshelman, archivist for the University of Connecticut Library and Special Collections; Sandra McCaulla, reference librarian at the Elizabeth Jones Library, Grenada, Mississippi; the Benjamin L. Hooks Central Library in Memphis; and blues scholar Tony Russell.

I am grateful for the collegial support extended to me by writer and historian Eric K. Washington and my fellow biographers who attended the Marginalized Lives workshops of the Biographers International Organization.

Allowing me to interview them by phone, email, FaceTime, and in person were Michael Taft, ED Denson, Barry Melton, B. B. King, TJ Wheeler, the late Ed Pearl, Bernie Pearl, the late Phil Spiro, Gayle Dean Wardlow, Dick Waterman, David Evans, John Battaglia, F. Jack Hurley, Richard Flohil, Fred J. Hay, Linzie Collier Butler, Paul Rishell, Dave Little, the late Alyce Guthrie, Mrs. Ellen Rogers, Arne Brogger, Councilman Lewis Johnson, Mayor Thelma Collins, Bo Prestidge, Bruce Jackson, Zorana Ivcecic Pringle, Attorney Barbara L. Dean, the late Chris Strachwitz, Mike Vernon, Tom Rush, Gary Atkinson, Mark H. Makin, Volker Steppat, and Arne Schumacher. I am indebted to Gary Atkinson and Document Records for sending me a number of out-of-print CDs for my research.

At the University Press of Mississippi, I owe a special debt of gratitude to director Craig W. Gill for his editorial direction and commitment to this book, and to executive assistant Katie Turner for her attention to detail and unfailing support. I am grateful to esteemed folklorist and series editor David Evans for responding to my many questions and sharing his unparalleled expertise. For the vibrant graphic design of the book's cover, I extend my gratitude to Todd Lape, assistant director/production and design manager. I am very grateful to fellow UPM author Frank Matheis for his insightful foreword, and to blues writer and guitarist Jas Obrecht for his expert guide to Booker White's guitar technique.

I extend my sincere thanks to Margaret Judge Pooley for her meticulous proofreading, and to Bill Wolf of Wolf Productions and Dr. Toby Mountain of Northeastern Digital for transferring and enhancing audio material.

Sharing their images and/or granting permission to publish them were Joe Stevens, Keith Perry, Amy van Singel (by Jim O'Neal), Jochen Mönch, Andrew Yale, Keith Perry, Dick Waterman, John Messina (by Rachel E. Lyons), R. Milan Sabatini, Peter Daniels, Luke Hobbs, Lydia Pitcher (by Frank Weston), Mitch Greenhill, and Melody Fahey. I am grateful for their generous assistance.

I am deeply grateful for the love and support of my two children, Matthew and Geoffrey Johnson, and encouragement and understanding from my friends John Kane, Gerry Priesing, Jeff Doran, Peter Coonradt, John Simon, Ellen Cederbaum, Lou Salome, and Larry Doyle,

My grandchildren Evan and Inga make my life more enjoyable every day.

FOREWORD

FRANK MATHEIS

DAVID W. JOHNSON HAS MANAGED TO WRITE THE MOST COMPLETE and fullest portrait of singer/songwriter Booker White, with a fresh and original approach to this important artist. His exhaustive research is a profound contribution to the blues annals and the history of Southern and African American culture.

It's an immense responsibility to guide the reader through someone's life and to do the subject justice, to show respect, and to bestow dignity—all while making it an enthralling and interesting read, page to page.

The writer frames the story. We know many great, respectable music writers and musicologists who have done it right. We tip our hat to them. Serious blues readers also know some biographies that are filled with the sensationalism, romanticism, and writer's delusion of self-importance. The list of pitfalls is long.

Conversely, a good biography lets us understand the life and times of the subject, to accurately depict who, what, when, and why—but never to overlook the essential humanity and dignity of the subjects. We want to understand how the artists lived, their trials and tribulations, but also how they felt and perceived the world around them, their *weltanschauung*—their point of view. This is hard enough when the writer collaborates with a living musician to tell their story. When the artist is long deceased, the task is even more difficult.

Journalist and biographer David W. Johnson has a strong success record in roots and blues writing. In 2013, the University Press of Mississippi published his biography of old-time country musician brothers Carter and Ralph Stanley: *Lonesome Melodies: The Life and Music of the Stanley Brothers*, which was nominated for awards from the Appalachian Studies Association and International Country Music Association, and a Virginia Readers' Choice Award.

David W. Johnson faced a difficult task in writing *The Life and Music of Booker "Bukka" White: Recalling the Blues.* He had some limited interactions with his subject, having interviewed him back in 1976, but that was not nearly enough to write a comprehensive biography. Starting in 1991, he bridged that gap by conducting extensive and thorough research of trusted sources who had previously published about the musician. One look at the bibliography shows that he did not leave a stone unturned in those thirty-two years of research. He also fact-checked comprehensively. The result is meticulous scholarship, worthy of publication in this prestigious publishing house.

Importantly, Johnson shows respect for his subject's artistry and humanity. Throughout the book, he juxtaposes White's life stages with the unjust and violent Jim Crow segregation era. We can understand the fear and apprehensions that White and his kin must have felt under the repressive racialism, fraught with violence, subjugation, and exploitation. *The Life and Music of Booker "Bukka" White* is not just filled with critical insights about the societal realities; the author leads us to a point of understanding White's essential humanness, as well as his musicality. There is no hero worship or romanticization. Here we get to know a real *mensch,* straight, no chaser, as good and simultaneously imperfect as any.

Sometimes it has been said that Booker White is underrated as a musician. Not hardly. Any blues fan interested enough to read a book about this riveting artist and slashing slide guitar player will surely already know the prowess of White's expressive and energetic music. His impassioned blues was as deep and organic as it gets, but also tender, sad, tense, and emotive.

Booker White told it like it was, using simple language to convey complicated laments. A song can be just as powerfully demonstrative as a painting. To draw a comparison, the visual artist Pablo Picasso's painting *Guernica* is widely considered to be among the greatest antiwar artworks, with its disquieting power and agony. Picasso depicted tragic brutality in a stark monochromatic palette of gray, black, and white. Like Picasso, Booker White's blues are equally dramatic and uncompromisingly honest, accentuated by his fiery guitar style, with rhythmic bass lines and percussive effects. White conveys personal experiences, the state of his inner life, as much as his world environment, just as Picasso did with his powerful symbolism in *Guernica*. Both artists are equally bold. Both are high art, except that one is accepted by the broad mainstream art world, whereas the other is celebrated by a much smaller but fervent audience of country blues fans.

While reading this manuscript, this writer revisited a few old albums by the bard. Booker White's transcendental and haunting slide guitar masterpiece "Jitterbug Swing" came up on one and Eric Bibb's fascinating lyric stanza from the song "Booker White's Guitar" kept coming into memory:

Booker's guitar's got a story to tell
Of hard-earned hope an' unshed tears
Booker's guitar rings like a bell
It's gonna keep on ringin' for a thousand years

Bibb's admiration for White comes through clearly, whereas the author of this biography maintained greater objective journalistic distance, never glorifying but aptly depicting the artist as a subconscious socio-critical documentarian. White's single line "Poor boy, I'm a long way from home" encapsulates the blues feeling most intensely.

To understand the harsh existentialism of a black artist in the South during the Great Depression and World War II eras, just listen to "Parchman Farm," a song penned by Booker White when he served time for murder in this notorious prison. His blues lyrics aptly convey the dehumanizing effects of post-slavery oppression, as well as his business dealings. W. E. B. Du Bois said, "the slave went free; stood a brief moment in the sun; then moved back again toward slavery." White was a blues existentialist, a simple but poignant poet.

As we get to know the intricacies of Booker White's fascinating but arduous life and times, it becomes clear that David W. Johnson approached the project as an objective scholar with sensitivity and with a true sense of curiosity and respect. Johnson's appreciation of the music, culture, and blues people come through clearly.

It's way more than an artist's biography. By the time the reader gets to the end of the story, an entire history of the blues has been unveiled.

It's a joyride of a read. That's big!

The Life and Music of
BOOKER "BUKKA" WHITE

Chapter One

MISSISSIPPI 1910

THE DISTANCE FROM MEMPHIS, TENNESSEE, TO HOUSTON, MISSISSIPPI, is 130 miles. Traveling southeast on I-22, Mississippi state road MS-15/30, and county road 515, a visitor today can drive the distance in a little over two hours; but in 1910, Memphis and Houston might as well have been in two different worlds. Memphis was the thriving commercial center at the top of the Mississippi Delta and its vast cotton plantations. Houston was a town located in a region of smaller farms, and one of two county seats in Chickasaw County. The other was Okolona, twenty miles to the east.

The county took its name from the Native American people who had been driven from their territory by European settlers, while the town was named in honor of a famous Texan. The Mississippi legislature formally established Chickasaw County on February 9, 1836, and then appointed a board of five commissioners to organize the county. Meeting "at an Indian House" north of the current city of Houston to choose a location for the seat of county government, the board argued for two days over different alternatives. Enter land speculator Joel Pinson, who stepped forward to offer a site for the new county seat that was made official on July 8.

As a young man, Pinson had been a good friend and rival in courtship to Sam Houston, who in 1836 had won the most decisive victory in Texas's battle for independence from Mexico. Like the town in Texas—and several weeks earlier—the new town in Mississippi was named in Sam Houston's honor. County surveyor Thomas Williams divided Pinson's land into lots, which soon sold. Income to the county from the sales covered construction of a brick courthouse on the town square (officially Pinson Square, but most often called Courthouse Square), and a jail one block north. The town of Houston was incorporated on May 9, 1837—fifteen months to the day after the process began.[1]

The first photograph in Harley Hill Floyd's *A Short History of Chickasaw County Mississippi* [*sic*] is of the county's new courthouse. Its domed tower is visible behind a row of tall trees. The photograph below is captioned "The First Grand Jury in New Houston Courthouse." Arranged in four rows, twenty-four men pose for the camera dressed in their Sunday-best coats and pants, some wearing ties and others wearing hats. At the edge of the picture, a casual interloper, wearing a brimmed western-style hat, sits on the low buttress next to the courthouse steps. He slouches against a column. Two men peek between two columns on the other side. All of the men are white.

The city of Houston has a claim to being the birthplace of Booker T. Washington White—the musician credited with making the last great country blues recordings prior to World War II. More accurately, Booker White's birthplace appears to have been a farm a couple of miles south of the crossroads community of Sparta, which is ten miles south of Houston.[2] Lack of certainty about exact age was not unusual among Black children born in Mississippi in the first decade of the twentieth century. In 1968, Booker told an interviewer, "In my time they didn't have too much of a thing with birth certificates, so I've never made too much discussion on that. When you come off the hook like that, you can say what you like because no one really knows. . . . I'm up in years and I thank the Lord that I'm here. But I believe I'm 67."[3]

Birth year remains one of a number of uncertainties in the life of Booker White. According to the 1910 United States Census, his age in the summer of 1910 was five. On his application for a Social Security account in 1940, he gave March 9, 1904, as his date of birth. In 1976, when I asked him when he was born, he replied without hesitation "November 12, 1909." Even the location of his birth is not certain. In a 1976 interview on Houston radio station WCPC, White told station manager Robin Mathis that he was born "about five miles south of Houston on the farm of Willie Harrington." The distance from Houston to the farm was double that, but the identity of the farmer seems to be correct. Washington's grandfather and grandmother were tenant farmers on Willie Harrington's farm.

In *Early Downhome Blues*, folklorist Jeff Todd Titon identifies three different types of tenant farming. "Black families worked the land as owners, as hired laborers, or in one of the forms of tenant farming: sharecropping, share renting, or cash renting. The landowning family almost always worked its own land."[4] Sharecroppers gave their labor and half the crop to the landowner in exchange for a shack (as the building was known), firewood, farm implements, work animals (often a mule), seed, and half the fertilizer used. At settlement time, the owner told sharecroppers how much their share of the crop was worth. A share renter gave one-fourth to one-third of his labor and crop to the owner in exchange for a shack and firewood. The share renter supplied his own farm implements and other necessities. A cash renter paid the owner a fixed price per acre of land to be farmed in exchange for the shack and firewood, but owned the crop. Both Black and white farm families hoped to improve their situations from sharecropping to one of the two forms of renting. Single Black men often worked as seasonal laborers.

After the Civil War ended in 1865, sharecropping proved to be an effective way for white landowners to keep Black laborers on the plantations and under their control. The system achieved its goal for decades. Southern Mississippi State University historian Neil R. McMillen writes that, from 1900 to 1940, "more than half of all of the Mississippi farms and some three-fourths of its tenant farms were operated by blacks. Roughly three in every four farm owners, however, were white. Although black land ownership was not inconsiderable, approximately 85 percent of all black operators in any given decade did not own the land they farmed."[5] A 1916 survey of the labor-intensive Delta region found that 94.5 percent of Black farm families were tenants rather than owners. A percentage of Black men and women found other kinds of employment. Booker's father, John White, became a fireman on the railroad while Booker's mother, Lula Davidson White, most likely worked in Willie Harrington's fields alongside her parents. In 1976, Booker told me that his father was a railroad engineer from New York, and his mother was born in Horse Nation—a community in Chickasaw County.[6]

As a boy, Washington White grew up looking forward to the wagon ride from the farm to the market in Houston. The trip was about fourteen miles by wagon. Wearing the short pants of a child, Washington would sit next to his grandfather Pomp Davidson on the hard wooden seat of the wagon that was pulled by a mule. Behind them on the wagon was a load of stove wood they had collected on the farm and among the trees that bordered the farm. The dirt road from Sparta to Houston would take them across the historic Natchez Trace, a trail blazed by generations of Native Americans.

Pomp Davidson was born a slave around 1859. His full name, Pompey, was a slave name from a time when owners gave classical Roman names, such as Augustus or Cassius, to their slaves. Pompey lived the life of a slave boy until the Union army's victory gave him his freedom at around the age of six. By 1910, the degree of freedom Pomp might have experienced during the early years of Reconstruction was now a fading memory. Since 1890, the white residents of Chickasaw County had pushed the Black population toward sharecropping and subservience. In Mississippi and other states in the Deep South, whites and Blacks were divided into two castes until Congress passed the Civil Rights Act of 1964.

Because of a provision made into law by Mississippi and South Carolina in 1920, Washington White would never be able to vote in Mississippi. Like other Black boys of his generation, he did not come from a bloodline of at least two generations of free men. While the "grandfather clause" did not withhold the vote completely from Black men, other laws put other obstacles in their way, such as poll taxes and literacy tests—and threats of bodily harm to the men and their families.

In 1891, Mississippi's poll tax made front-page news in the *New York Times*. Enacted in 1890, a new state constitution required men of voting age to pay the tax before February 1, 1891, "to be qualified for voting at any elections in 1891."[7] The *Times* gave this generalized explanation: "There are a great many young men . . . who have not paid their poll tax and will therefore be disenfranchised. As a general thing the colored people have taken a greater interest in the matter of qualifying themselves than the white people, but there will be a large number of both who will not be able to vote in the Fall elections."

Historians agree that the purpose of the new poll tax laws of Alabama, Louisiana, and Mississippi was to disenfranchise the Black population. In Alabama, an annual poll tax of $1.50 was cumulative from the time a person was eligible to vote until age forty-five. If a forty-year-old man wanted to register for the first time, he would have to pay the impossible sum of $28.50. The tax disenfranchised an estimated 98 percent of voting-age Blacks, compared to 17 to 23 percent of the white population.[8] Literacy tests were whatever town officials decided they were. A Black person seeking to register to vote could be asked to guess the correct the number of beans contained in a jar.

In Mississippi in the 1960s, national media began to give news coverage to problems around voter registration in the South. A county clerk in Mississippi might ask a Black person seeking to register to interpret the meaning of an article of the state constitution. Even if the prospective registrant could read the article, it was the clerk who decided whether the interpretation was correct. The poll tax and literacy test achieved their intended purpose. In Mississippi in 1868—a year after the federal Reconstruction Act of 1867—an estimated 96.7 percent of the male Black voting-age population was registered. In 1892, the number of registered Black voters was an estimated 5.9 percent. The number for the male white population was estimated to be 80.9 percent and 57.7 percent.[9]

AS POMP AND WASHINGTON APPROACHED HOUSTON IN THEIR WAGON, one of the first things they would see was the tower on top of the courthouse. Courthouse Square remains the center of commerce. Among the businesses bordering the square today are stores, a bank, an apothecary, law offices, and a coffee shop. In 1910, the square brought farmers and sharecroppers from the surrounding area to the marketplace, where they would sell their produce—watermelons, squash, tomatoes, corn—and use the money to buy dry goods and other household necessities.

When it was new, the red-brick bank building might have been impressive for a small town in northeast Mississippi, but the massive courthouse dominated the square. The courthouse opened for the county's business in 1909, when Washington was a little boy. The building had stood there all his young life, so was a familiar sight when he returned to Houston in 1976 for only the second time in many years as a guest of honor during the town's celebration of the United States Bicentennial.

In the same year, 1976, I sat next to Booker White in a hospital room in Beverly, Massachusetts, from which he would be discharged the next morning to return to Memphis. Not sure how to begin a conversation with a Mississippi blues musician, I asked about his hometown. He responded:

> Houston's not too large. It's just an old town. I 'spect Houston's about a thousand years old. . . . Only thing I can remember in Houston is the courthouse. That's where I used to sit and eat peanuts. Me and my grandfather would bring our wagonload of stove wood [on the] bottom bed [of the wagon], and he'd sell it for a dollar—just get a dollar for it—and all I ever wanted, a nickel pack of peanuts, parched peanuts. And I'd sit there in front of the courthouse on the street, and I'd eat them until he got around—take that dollar, get flour, sugar, and whatever like that . . . coffee . . . We headed [to town] for what everybody . . . want around there.[10]

One can imagine that as the boy in short pants broke open the shells to eat the peanuts, he watched with considerable curiosity as white men went in and out of the courthouse and often congregated on the courthouse steps. His parents, grandparents, and others on the farm had instilled in him that the courthouse was not his place. Neither were the wooden sidewalks in town; those were for white folks. His grandfather and other Black men doing business in town walked in the street until they got where they were going. Then they went into the store, made their purchases, and left, holding their hats in their hands if a white person was coming their way. To a boy growing up on a country farm, the magnificent building in the middle of Courthouse Square must have looked as if it had been there forever. Its architecture was imposing, topped by the domed cupola supported by pillars. In 1910, the courthouse stood for the power of the law and the way things were in Chickasaw County.

Chapter Two

EARLY YEARS

BORN ISSAC WILEY HARRINGTON ON OCTOBER 1, 1855, WILLIE HARrington became a well-respected man in Chickasaw County. He was eighty when he died of an apparent heart attack on January 28, 1936. The Houston *Times-Post* treated his death as important news: "Houston and vicinity was shocked . . . All of his life had been spent in this county where he had been engaged in farming. There had been no indication of his illness, as he walked in from the Weaver place in the afternoon, coming to spend the night in town."[1] He died in the home of his daughter.

Willie Harrington's farm was about twelve miles from Houston near Little Cane Creek and Sparta. At its peak, Sparta had two churches and a school. From 1850 to 1905, the community had its own post office. Today, Sparta has a population of 150 and is the home of the Sparta Opry—a country music and bluegrass venue in a small brown building off County Road 389. When I visited in July 2017, it was closed, perhaps for the summer.

Harrington had farmed in the vicinity of Little Cane Creek as far back as 1880, when he was twenty-five and his wife Kittie was twenty-one.[2] Most farmers in the Sparta precinct were in their twenties. It would be interesting to know how Sparta grew over the next ten years, but there is a gap in the census records. Fire damaged the 1890 population schedules while they were in storage in Washington. They were moved to another location, but when a second fire struck on January 10, 1921, Congress ordered the Department of the Interior to destroy the records that remained.[3] After a twenty-year gap, a new census was conducted in Sparta on June 6, 1900. By then, Willie Harrington and his second wife, Alta, had six children living with them—four daughters and two sons. Their ages ranged from one to sixteen.

The 1900 census was the first to record that members of the White-Davidson family lived on Willie Harrington's farm. John and Lula White lived with their young daughter, Estelle. John was twenty-five, and Lula was seventeen. When John and Lula were married in Chickasaw County on January 20, 1898, they had a church wedding.[4] Reverend A. Haughton officiated. Estelle was born in December 1898, and was eighteen months old when the census was taken.

Pomp Davidson was listed as thirty-eight, and Jane as forty. Their household included eight children, who ranged in age from three to seventeen. Listed in 1880 as a farm laborer, Pomp now was identified as a farmer, suggesting that he was no longer a sharecropper. The four oldest children were farm laborers. The birthplaces of Pomp and Jane's fathers were listed as "unknown." While the census listed the birthplace of Pomp's mother as Mississippi, the birthplace of Jane's mother was "unknown," suggesting that her parents might have been enslaved.

Pomp and Jane were together for many years in a society where such relationships often were transitory. Frequent marriages—both church weddings and domestic partnerships—reflected an economic reality in Mississippi. White landowners were reluctant to take on single Black men as sharecroppers or renters. They believed that couples and families were more stable and posed less of an economic risk. Single men would be hired for seasonal labor. Single women were less likely to be hired as farm workers.

On April 30, 1910, Chickasaw County census enumerator William B. Freeman listed Estelle White as ten and her younger brother Washington as five.[5] Estelle and Washington now lived with their grandparents. Pomp's age was listed as forty and Jane's as forty-eight. The census also recorded four Davidson children in the household. They were sons Garfield, fourteen, and Burkitt, twelve, and daughters Mattie, twelve, and Benula B. The total number of six children is close to the number that Booker gave in an interview. In their 1981 biography "Bukka White," University of Memphis professors F. Jack Hurley and David Evans wrote, "Lula [White] was a God-fearing woman who produced five healthy children."[6]

Among tenant farmers around Sparta, Pompey Davidson was a man to be reckoned with. For one thing, he was a preacher. As a young boy, Washington held Pompey in awe and more than a touch of fear. His grandfather was temperamental and could become angry at a young boy. This was a side of Pompey that Booker did not mention in interviews, perhaps because it became more apparent as his grandfather grew older. Instead, Booker gave interviewers an exaggerated picture of what an important man his grandfather was—that he owned 400 acres of land and was a bishop in charge of four different churches.[7]

The reality appears to have been that Pompey was a tenant farmer who preached in several different churches.

Booker's exaggerated recollection of his grandfather suggests that in the world of his boyhood, Pomp Davidson was larger than life—perhaps as influential as his father. In an undated interview with journalist and novelist Bruce Cook in *Listen to the Blues*, Booker described his father this way: "My father, John White, was a railroad man from New York. He come down to work as a fireman. Oh, he was a huge man. He musta weighed about 286 pounds, and he worked all his life on the railroad—first for the M & O, and then he went to Frisco. I got the trains from him, and I got the music from him, too."[8]

By working for a railroad line, John White was able to lift himself above sharecropping. He was hired for the position of fireman—one of the most important positions available to Black men on the railroad. They also could be porters. In *Brotherhoods of Color: Black Railroad Workers and the Struggle for Equality*, historian Eric Arnesen writes that Black men were "excluded from the most highly skilled and better-paid positions as engineers and conductors," and they "could work as locomotive firemen and brakemen only in the South."[9] According to Arnesen, it was common for Black workers to hold fireman and brakeman jobs in the nineteenth century, but racial prejudice changed that. "By the early twentieth century, their hold on even those positions grew tenuous," Arnesen writes. The all-white brotherhoods of railroad workers increasingly resented having to work with Blacks and made a concerted effort to exclude them.[10]

The job of fireman required both size and strength. John White had both. He was responsible for shoveling wood or coal into the steam furnaces that powered the engines. In the years John and Lula had young children, John worked for the Mobile & Ohio Railroad, whose tracks extended from Mobile, Alabama, to Cairo, Illinois. The Mobile & Ohio had come to Houston in 1905. John's job took him away from home much of the time, but provided a regular paycheck above what a farm worker could make. The work of raising his children became the responsibility of the Davidson family—Lula when she lived on the farm, and grandparents Pomp and Jane after she left.

Music was a constant in the Davidson-White family. "The mother sang hymns as she did the work around the house," Hurley and Evans wrote. "Bukka and the other children heard these and sometimes joined in. They also went to his grandfather's church and joined in the music there. Bukka's uncle Jesse Davis was a good blues guitarist."[11] The authors cited John White as his son's most important musical influence. "John was a natural musician who could play almost anything." Booker remembered his father "as being primarily a fiddler, but he also played mandolin, guitar, piano, drums, and later, saxophone."[12] John White's friend Luke Smith played guitar and harmonica. They played together in the Houston area at dance parties called frolics.

Booker became animated when recalling the events. "Frolics! We're going to have a frolic tonight! Who's playin'? Luke Smith and John White! And, brothers, I'm going to tell you the truth, you could hear they feet way across the field to them old log houses."[13] As a young boy, Booker was impressed by how much musicians were respected in his community. "There were not many avenues open to a young Black man in Mississippi who wanted to have some status," wrote Hurley and Evans. "Music was one of the few, and Bukka learned to appreciate that early." He told interviewers that his father gave him a Stella guitar for his ninth birthday, tuned the strings, and told him he was on his own.[14]

Booker developed quickly as a musician. According to Hurley and Evans, "It wasn't long before Bukka was entertaining his friends with the blues songs he had learned. Inspired by an elderly local guitarist named Sam Peterson, he soon picked up the technique of playing sliding tones and was advised by his father's friend Luke to switch from a pocketknife held in his left hand to a short piece of bottleneck worn over the little finger."[15]

Booker would go on to become an important figure in the history of slide guitarists who played blues. In a cover story for *Guitar Player* magazine, "Blues with a Feeling: The Great Slidemen," author and musician Jas Obrecht wrote, "With his raspy voice, hypnotic guitar-body percussion, and slashing slide, Bukka White recorded fabulous music suitable for the country ball and juke joint."[16] When I interviewed Booker, he discussed the evolution of his choice of sliders.

> The way I started off, my father was a musician and my father's friend, he's a musician. . . . And they used to use a pocketknife for a slide, which is mainly young people don't know nothing about that 'cause I hadn't seen nobody play with a pocketknife since I don't know when. So they left a pocketknife and went to a bottle neck, and they got away from a bottle neck to a steel bar . . . 'cause sometime you'd be stuck on the street corner or on the hard concrete floor or something and go after your bottle neck and drop it and it's broke. And so they left from that. I think I

> was about the first one that they ever seen [using] a steel slide on the thing, and everybody wanted to know why I leave the bottle neck and go to the steel, and they hadn't thought about the steel won't break and the bottle neck would.[17]

Booker's maternal grandmother was another musician in the family. Booker recalled that a local man playing guitar in the slide style would move Jane Davidson to tears. "And so many nights, my grandmother was a church going woman, he would play church songs, you know, blues and things, and she sit up [and] cried," he said.[18]

In the fall of 1976, Booker told guitarist John Battaglia about his grandmother's influence on him. On his way to Florida for a real estate deal, Battaglia made a side trip to Memphis, where Booker's partner Leola Morris invited him into their apartment at 867 Mosby Avenue. Battaglia asked Booker to show him how to play "Aberdeen Mississippi Blues." Sitting on a chair in his undershirt, Booker explained to Battaglia that he was weak from being in the hospital, but would try to oblige—except he no longer owned a guitar. He had sold his second National steel guitar, bought as a replacement for the 1930s National Duolian that he nicknamed "Hard Rock," to a Canadian buyer because he needed the money. Battaglia went back to his car, and returned with his wooden cutaway guitar. Booker played "Aberdeen Blues" slower than he once did, and without the rhythmic slapping on the body of the guitar that made the number a showstopper. As he watched Booker play, Battaglia noticed that because of the size of his hands, Booker could hold down two strings with a single finger. "He told me he learned that lick from his grandmother," Battaglia recalled.[19]

Chapter Three

A BOY IN GRENADA

IN THEIR BIOGRAPHY, HURLEY AND EVANS COMMENTED ON BOOKER'S struggle in his early years between the routines of farm life and bouts of restlessness. They wrote, "From all indications, Bukka's early family life should have been close and stable, but it was not. Bukka didn't seem to be able to identify those elements that were wrong, but whatever they were, he began to drift out of the family circle at a very early age."[1]

One factor contributing to Booker's restlessness might have been that when he was growing up he lived with two different families—the first on the farm near Houston in Chickasaw County, and the second fifty miles west of Houston and only thirty miles from the Mississippi Delta. Booker told Hurley that during his early school years, he lived on his uncle Alec Johnson's farm in Grenada, Mississippi. The farm was "as good a land as a bird ever flew over."[2] Living with his uncle's family helped develop his musical talents. He learned to play the pump organ—a keyboard instrument—that his uncle had bought for one of his sons.[3] The attraction of the music being played on the Delta in Clarksdale and Greenville would have been irresistible to a young man with a keen interest in the blues.

"Basically, Grenada was a very rural area [in those days]," recalled Lewis Johnson, who has served on the Grenada City Council for thirty-six years. Councilman Johnson has studied the history of the city and its Black community. "At that time, transportation and infrastructure would have been somewhat primitive, but Grenada was very much a center. It was a hub of commerce. There was banking, and one thing Grenada had was a railroad. One of the main lines of the railroad [contributed to] a lot of commerce development." The line serving Grenada was part of the Illinois Central Railroad system.[4]

"Grenada had a striving Black community at that particular time," he said. "There were a lot of Black business people. There was a section of downtown that was a well-developed section of Black business owners."[5]

"My mother was an educator, and my father was a hard worker," Johnson said. "I had six other siblings. Growing up, I had a happy life. It was a poor life, but happy. I lived on a street where the only people who lived there were teachers and preachers. It was good." Johnson learned from his family that education was the key to a better life.

Relatives on Chicago's South Side made it possible for him to finish high school in the city. He went to college at what is now Jackson State University in Jackson, Mississippi. After college, he "traveled all over the place" as a musician, playing guitar, keyboards, and saxophone. "I sing and play," he said. "I spent a lot of years backing up other musicians and playing with bands. I played wherever they paid me." Johnson appeared with big names. He was in the original Sam & Dave group and shared a stage with B. B. King.

Before I interviewed Councilman Johnson, I thought that the reason for Booker's being sent to Grenada was that he was becoming too difficult for his grandparents to raise. He told Jack Hurley that when he was nine, he ran away from his grandfather's farm to work at a sawmill in Houston. Now I believe that his family wanted him to attend school. In a 1964 conversation with blues musician Alan Wilson, Booker said that he promised his mother that he would stay in school until he learned to read.[6] Living in Grenada would have made that possible.

"Grenada was very fortunate to have people who were very astute about education," Lewis Johnson said. "It was one of the few communities that actually had a high school for Black kids. In other areas, school stopped in the sixth grade." Black families in Grenada also took in school-age children so that they could get an education. "People who resided outside city limits would send kids into Grenada, and they would stay with relatives," he said. "A lot of people made money that way, running boarding houses for students."

With a population of five thousand, "Grenada was a striving, productive place to be during that particular time," Johnson said. "It was a place of commerce and rail systems and quite a few jobs." Johnson's description of Grenada in the early twentieth century explains why Booker's family in rural Chickasaw County would decide to send their boy to live where there was education and opportunity. To find out more about Booker's second family, I drove the fifty miles from Houston to Grenada in July 2017.

LIKE HOUSTON, GRENADA IS A COUNTY SEAT (OF GRENADA COUNTY), but the county courthouse is quite different from the historic Chickasaw

County Courthouse. Courtrooms and offices are housed in a modern three-story structure on the city square. Memorials commemorating two quite different histories share the green space at the center of the square. One is a tall stone monument to the city's Confederate war dead, which has been covered by tarps since August 2020 after the City Council voted to relocate it. The other is a blue plaque with silver lettering mounted on a silver pole. The plaque is one of more than two hundred markers put up by the Mississippi Blues Trail Commission to identify the birthplaces of musicians and locations that are important to the history of blues.

As I had seen in 2017, standing on top of the Confederate war memorial is the figure of a young soldier carrying a rifle and canteen. The inscription reads, "To the noble men who marched neath the flag of the stars and bars, and were faithful to the end. . . . Glorious in life, in death sublime." Chiseled in the base is the date June 3, 1910, when the dedication of the monument made the city's historical connection to the Confederate cause apparent.

Property transactions in Grenada County are kept in a room across the hall from the chancery clerk's offices. Picking an appropriate time period, I took down a bound volume dated from 1890 to 1900. I was not able to find a transaction involving Alec Johnson, but came across two transactions involving a person with the last name Johnson whose first name began with A.[7] Both transactions were recorded on May 12, 1889, when M. J. Cheatham sold land for $200 to A. A. Johnson, and A. J. Peacock transferred land to Augustus A. Johnson for $300.[8] Like the name Pompey, Augustus was a name taken from the Roman classics that could have been given to a slave before Emancipation. Finding the two transfers encouraged me. A helpful assistant in the clerk's office made photocopies of the documents, and suggested that I might find additional information in the history section of Grenada's library. Picturing dusty volumes in a quaint town building, I hesitated, but the Elizabeth Jones Library turned out to be modern and spacious.

The library had Grenada census data, including the 1910 census, on microfilm. With the help of reference librarian Sandra McCaulla, I soon was scrolling through the faded reels of microfilm in search of an Augustus or A. A. Johnson. I focused my search on the last name Johnson and the demographic information of sex (male), color (Black), and age (40–60). I was looking for a head of household about the same age as Pompey Davidson. I came upon a couple who matched my parameters. They were Andrew Johnson, 55, and his wife Mariah, 45. The name Andrew was close enough to A. A. or Augustus to be a possibility. The census listed two stepsons, twenty and seventeen, four daughters seven to sixteen, and a son, nine. The family was a possible match to the family with five children that Booker had described in an interview with Hurley.

I decided to keep looking. As I scrolled through the remaining data from Grenada in the 1910 census, a familiar name flashed by. I carefully backed up the reel. The name was Booker T. He was a four-year-old boy who lived in the household of Edward and Georgia Johnson. Edward was fifty-three, and Georgia was forty. Their eleven children ranged in age from seven months to eighteen years—four daughters and seven sons. Based on the similarity of the boys' ages and the fact that Booker T. Johnson had the same last name as the uncle Booker recalled in later years, I thought it was possible that the two boys were the same person.

In 2023, I brought this information to Lewis Johnson, and asked for his opinion. "People took on different names," he said. "In that particular time, people changed their names on their own without going through the legal process. They might take on a different family's name if they stayed with them. If they lived with them, it was associated with them. That was not uncommon at all throughout the Black community. People were often raised by relatives and called by that name."[9]

At last I had a possible answer to a question that had bothered me since I began researching this biography. How did a child born Washington White come to be called Booker T. Washington White? If the two boys were the same person, it explained why Washington might have chosen to call himself Booker as he grew older. A compelling reason for the adult to use Booker instead of Washington was that when he was convicted of murder and sentenced to life in prison in 1937, a court document identified him as Washington White. Moving out of Mississippi—possibly because authorities told him to—he would want to leave his old identity behind.

Another indication that Washington and Booker might have been the same boy was that when his wife Emma gave birth to a son, she and Booker named the boy Edward, perhaps after the head of the Johnson household in Grenada.

Booker shared additional details of his early years with Julius Lester, the only Black writer to publish an interview with him. At the time of the interview, Lester served on the board of directors of the Newport Folk Festival. He interviewed Booker in 1966 as he traveled in the South to visit the blues musicians who had come north to perform at the festival. Booker told Lester:

> My father was an engineer on the M & O railroad and he played music, too. That's why I taken it up and started playing. I wanted to be just like him. He played guitar, mandolin, saxophone, piano and violin. I could've been an engineer if I'd wanted to, but I didn't want any part of it. But I appreciate him starting me with the music. He bought me a guitar and tuned it up one time and he said, "I done bought it and I done tuned it. Now if you don't play it, it's nobody's fault but yours." And that's where I started from.

In the interview, Booker identified an early influence on guitar and described a fight he had over his guitar playing with a cousin in Grenada:

> There was a lotta guitar players around there when I was coming up. B. B. King's grandfather, Cap Pullian [or Pulliam], played with a pocket knife and to this day I pick the guitar or play the piano. So one night my brother jumps out of bed, grabs the guitar out of my hand and breaks it across a chest. I was kin' o' glad he broke the guitar and not me. So I sneaked on in and went to bed. But the next day my aunt went and bought me another guitar. She said, "I'm not gon' let this boy go without no music and Jesse shouldn't have broke the guitar." He said, "Well, it was two o'clock in the morning and I told him to put the guitar down." And that was the truth. He sho' told me to put it up. What they didn't know was that I was trying to get good enough so that I could play at the roadside houses and at the plantation balls. That's what I had my eye set on.

When Booker was an aspiring musician, his role model was Mississippi Delta guitarist and songwriter Charley Patton. "Yeah, he [was] the man that I really wanted to take talent after," he would recall. "Charley Patton records then were selling just as fast as anything I ever knowed that was selling. They were selling fast as food. . . . Within my heart I said I'm gonna take in behind of Charley Patton at that time."[10]

Though Booker said he wanted to follow in Patton's footsteps, he was not imitative of Patton's guitar style. His influences were closer to home and more diverse. In answer to my question about Booker's guitar style, blues scholar and country blues guitarist David Evans responded:

> I'm sure Booker came out of a local tradition, though he was highly original and creative. He also seems to have gone on the road early in life and probably picked up influences from here and there. And then he tried somewhat to keep up with commercial trends probably at least through the end of the 1940s. So I'm not sure how well the concept of a *local* tradition applies to him. The main problem though is that we really don't have anyone else from his local area to compare him with. So you can posit a local tradition, but our knowledge of it begins and ends with Booker. In a larger regional sense, he fits in well with a "Deep South" style of blues.[11]

Booker's guitar style may have been shaped in Houston, Grenada, and Clarksdale, but he went on to develop a style that was unique to him. In the early twentieth century, however, there were more serious problems facing a young Black musician than perfecting his guitar technique.

Chapter Four

BETWEEN TWO WORLDS

LIKE OTHER BLACK CHILDREN BORN IN MISSISSIPPI IN THE EARLY 1900s, Washington White entered an oppressive, sometimes dangerous world. Black girls were born into a world where the violence often was sexual. According to historian Neil R. McMillen, the thirty years from 1889 to 1919 were among the hardest on the Black population in the state's history.[1] A faculty member at the University of Southern Mississippi, McMillen wrote in *Dark Journey: Black Mississippians in the Age of Jim Crow*:

> By nearly any measure—the frequency and sadism of lynching and other forms of white vigilantism, the extension and formal codification of black disenfranchisement, segregation and exclusion; the prejudicial character of the criminal justice system; the prevalence of peonage and the adoption and selective application of stringent vagrancy and contract laws—the current of white fear and repression ran wide and deep during these years.

Throughout his second career, which began in 1963, Booker had little to say on the subject of race in interviews—with one notable exception. Writer, professor, and musician Julius Lester, who was Black, interviewed Booker in the summer of 1966—two years after the so-called Freedom Summer of 1964 during which activists from the North traveled to Mississippi to register Black people to vote. The majority of white Mississippians resented their presence. A voter registration drive was bound to be contentious in the state. Freedom Summer activists were predominantly white and young. Many were college students. Some were ministers. Planning for the registration drive, the Black leaders of the Student Nonviolent Coordinating Committee (SNCC) became concerned that most white volunteers lacked the field experience necessary to understand the assumptions behind race relations in the South.

During the summer, volunteers would be left to navigate among white Southerners while living in Black homes and encouraging Blacks to challenge the existing voter registration system, which—in the view of white residents—was the law.

Though conducted in the summer of 1966, Julius Lester's interview did not appear until the October–November 1968 issue of *Sing Out! The Folk Song Magazine*. As he had done in an interview with blues musician Son House, Lester edited out his questions, so the published interview takes the form of a continuous narrative. Since the contents of the interview are so different from others, Lester's questions almost certainly influenced the direction of the conversation.

Booker described oppressive circumstances in his own life that matched the pattern of repression Professor McMillen identified in *Dark Journey*:

> Like I said . . . things used to get rough in them days. Not that they don't these days [1966], but back then, they wouldn't think no more about killing a Negro than they would about a chicken. I became more acquainted with lynchings than I was with hanging up my socks. I can show you places now where they hung Negroes from. There was one place 'round there that if somebody started through there, he never did get through. He just start. The only way he got through there was that he had the same thing that they had and could shoot just as good as they could. There was some rough dark people, just like there was some white back there. Now, everybody can't stand up and fire a shot. They run. And that's what the folks be looking for. Now, they didn't mess with my family, 'cause we'd be shooting just as good as they could. They couldn't push us around. They don't push me around today. I love Booker better than I do you, if it comes down to where you gon' do me wrong.[2]

Growing up on the farm, Booker learned to be deferential to Willie Harrington, his family, and any other white people he encountered. When Pomp took young Washington with him to Courthouse Square, he told his grandson how a Black should behave in the white community. From Booker's account of those times, he learned about the wider world as he stayed close to the wagon and ate peanuts. He had opportunities to observe how his grandfather and other Black men interacted with white people when selling crops and buying household necessities.

As an older boy, he learned about the power of white people from his own experience. At age nine, he left the farm to work at a sawmill in Houston. As the grandson of a tenant farmer, he learned that sharecropping was an unfair system. He explained how the system worked to Julius Lester in colorful detail:

> On the plantations at that time, some of the plantation owners treated their people all right. And some of 'em only give them food and clothes and when the end of the year come they would tell you, "You did nice. You like to come out of debt. If you'd taken that other little cut across the ditch like I told you, you would've cleared some money. But you didn't do that and you owe me three hundred dollars. But next year if you take five more acres, I believe you'll come out of debt. Now, how much money you want to borrow for Christmas?" So John would say, "Three hundred." And the man would give him the amount of money he was supposed to give him in the first place. But he loan him that, which means that John was then six hundred dollars in debt. And he'd be there trying to pay that off as long as them peach trees and apple trees be sitting in his back yard. He'll never come out of debt. And he still just a boy. He never be grown. Just a boy. Working for fatback, Karo molasses and oatmeal. Long about every three months, the man give John a ham, 'cause his meat be done run out. John would keep that ham there and mix it with that fatback and John was so strong and could hit a mule so hard until the man would tell him, "Now, look-a-here. I don't want my mules coming in with no whip on 'em, 'cause I'm feeding my mules good and I'm feeding y'all good. Let him take his time." That was a nice man in them days. On a lotta of them plantations, the man had a heart in his body, a good heart. He'd say, "I'm gon' let Sam clear some money this year. He ain't cleared nothing in three years. He made thirty-five bales of cotton. He cleared $235. What you want for Christmas, Sam?" "Well, I cleared $235, I'll spend all that on my family. I want $500." The man knew he was gon' borrow that money. He'd held that money back that Sam had already made. So the next year the man'll say that Sam owe a thousand and that's the way it go on. The reason that kind of situation exist was because the folks didn't know no better. They didn't know nothing else to do and no place else to go. How can you fly an airplane if you ain't never been in

> one? The folks didn't know nothing else but how to plow and pick cotton and do farm work.[3]

As this excerpt demonstrates, storytelling was an important aspect of Booker's personality. Canadian music agent Roberta Richards commented on this when she and fellow Canadian Bo Basiuk visited him in Memphis in the summer of 1975. She wrote, "Bukka is a natural-born storyteller. When he begins one of his famous tales, he finds himself with a captivated audience. The tale, usually unbelievably long, is told with such style, suspense and balance that it slowly becomes a Bukka White classic. However, Bukka is the first one to admit, as he does frequently, 'I lie some of the time, but not all of the time.'"[4]

Booker's compulsion to exaggerate is responsible for many of the apparent contradictions in his personal narratives. To Roberta Richards, his tales were entertaining. "Often, as I sit and speak with Bukka and listen to his stories, I understand how much he truly loves life and people closest to him," Richards wrote.[5] "Bukka never cries the blues; he just sings them. A gentle, kind man (but stubborn as a mule at times), he is a beautiful person. Bukka never forgets the experiences which still leave scars—what was done to him many years ago, unjustly—and uses these experiences to lyrically express his theories."

To those researching the details of his life, the accounts seemed at first to be inconsistent and unreliable. From 1963 onward, he showed a variety of faces to those who met him. To young white blues zealots like John Fahey and Alan Wilson, Booker's convoluted stories were part of his charisma. Fahey both appreciated such stories and wrote them himself. A collection of his writings—a blend of memoir and fiction—was published in 2000 as *How Bluegrass Music Destroyed My Life*. Fahey's tall tale "Fish" is entertaining, but also unsettling. Beginning as the account of a time (probably imaginary) he and Booker fished together near Memphis, the story progresses from catching a giant catfish to a description of Fahey being abused by his father.[6]

To Chris Strachwitz, who recorded two albums of Booker's "sky songs" (by which Booker meant lyrics he plucked from the sky), the musician was no less than "brilliant." To his manager of two years Dick Waterman, Booker was the most "disloyal" blues musician Waterman ever represented. When I asked Chris Strachwitz what he thought of Waterman's harsh judgment, he said that Booker might pose a problem for "certain inflexible personalities."

When I interviewed Booker, he told me things that I would read years later in other interviews—and recalled some subjects and details that I have not seen anywhere else. In hindsight, I think that the seriousness of his stroke and a month spent in the intensive care and rehabilitation units of a hospital gave him time and a good reason to reflect on his life. One such recollection was the story he told to interviewers about how he accidentally caught a train that took him all the way to St. Louis.

Chapter Five

THE ST. LOUIS STORY

IN 1966, BLUES SCHOLAR DAVID EVANS, THEN A GRADUATE STUDENT in folklore at UCLA, published an article on Booker in *Blues Unlimited* that contained an incisive comment about the musician: "If any blues singer can be considered 'legendary,' it is Booker White, since his autobiography is told in a series of legends in which he is the protagonist, the center of his wit and imagination."[1] It is worth exploring what Evans meant by taking a closer look at how Booker told and retold the story of his unintended train trip to St. Louis in separate interviews.

There are elements that appear in all versions, and details that are present in only one or two. Because Booker presented the St. Louis story as an important part of a formative time in his life, one would like to think that the basic elements of the story were true, but in 2009, blues expert Bob Eagle emailed other members of the Mississippi Blues Research and Writing Team that he may have found the model for Booker's St. Louis mentor Old Man Ben. Ben turned up closer to Houston, Mississippi, than to St. Louis.

In 1967, University of Memphis professor F. Jack Hurley took part in an oral history project whose purpose was to document the history of jazz and blues in the Memphis area. One of the people he chose to interview was Booker White. On December 5, Hurley visited Booker in his apartment on the first floor of 867 Mosby Avenue, a brown stucco building with several units that is no longer there. On the tape, Hurley made the purpose of his visit clear. "Mister White, we are going to talk a little about how you got involved in music," he said, "and you are going to play us a little on a very unusual guitar."[2] He asked Booker if he remembered when he first earned money by playing the guitar. Booker did. In 1926, a second cousin paid him two and a half dollars to play all night. That sparked a memory:

> Well, that $2.50 made me want to go from then on. I just had that faith that I could make more. Then I left and went to St. Louis, you see, some boys tole' me on the freight train I couldn't get off until I got to St. Louis. I was nine then. I was down there playing my guitar and they said, "We're going to St Louis," and here I was with my ole' piece of guitar and the train started picking up fast, and I got scared and just went on to St. Louis. I wasn't going to get off and kill myself.
>
> So after I got up there, the ole' man met me, I was going across the Missouri Bridge on the Missouri side (that's on the west side) and this old colored fellow, he saw me sittin' on the step on that side of the Mississippi River, and he said, "You're strange, I can look at you and tell you are strange." I told him . . . I told him the truth. He said, "Well, you've got to believe you can—[have] confidence in yourself, you're going to be a musician. I'll take you in and call your people to let them know where you are and you can stay on here with me. There's nobody here but me—I run a roadhouse."[3]

Booker's 1967 response to Jack Hurley appears to be the first time he told an interviewer the story of the St. Louis trip.

Hopping a freight train was dangerous. It required running next to the engine, putting one foot on the step of the tender (a coal or fuel car) behind the engine, grabbing the handle on the tender, and swinging onto the narrow space between the tender and the first baggage car.[4] Sneaking aboard a stopped train was much easier—simply a matter of not getting caught.

In their biography of Booker in *Tennessee Traditional Singers*, Hurley and Evans approached the story of his train adventure with mild skepticism:

> If his memories are at all to be trusted, he moved around a great deal, had his own friends, and spent long periods of time away from home. In two separate interviews years apart, Bukka recounted going to St. Louis by himself at the age of nine. Even though Bukka's concept of years was often hazy and internal evidence in the story seems to indicate that he was twelve or thirteen, the story gives a general indication of the sort of life young Bukka led.[5]

Booker recalled that he did not intend to go to St. Louis, but was with his brother and two other boys "playing with a freight train."[6] The boys were tired of plowing behind a mule, "and there was a wire fence between there and the railroad . . . so we jumped on a freight train that was stopped along there." When the train began to move, the other boys jumped off. "I want to get off," Booker said, "but the train was going faster than I thought it was going." His friend Henry ran along with the train and tossed his guitar to him. "So I got to St. Louis next morning about eight o'clock, soda cap on, knee pants and barefooted. And every time I be in St. Louis to this day I look at that old railroad bridge and think how I felt that morning. Nobody knew what be on my mind but the good Lord."

In the summer of 1968, Booker performed at the Mariposa Folk Festival, held on an island near Toronto. Writer Dick Flohil first had met him in 1966 when he was one of the musicians taking part in the Canadian Broadcasting Corporation's "massive blues television show."[7] Performers included Sonny Terry and Brownie McGhee and Muddy Waters. "Bukka impressed everyone he met—he is a large man, but a very friendly one who is rarely fazed by strange people or strange surroundings," Flohil wrote. "In this way, he has adjusted to the limited measure of fame he has achieved in recent years—and has done so better than some of his contemporaries, who still feel ill at ease among the young, enthusiastic, over-curious white people who are anxious to talk with them."[8] Booker returned to Toronto in 1968 to play a poorly attended week at George's Kibitzeria. During one of those visits, Flohil interviewed him for the cover article in *Coda: Canada's Jazz Magazine* in advance of his performance January 11, 1969, at Guelph University. In the article, Booker once again told the story of his accidental train ride to St. Louis.

> When I was about nine I went on a freight train, I went to St. Louis. I was on the train and it went to going, and there was no way I could get off. So when I got there, these people got in contact with my mother, who was called [Lula], and she told that they'd all been might near crazy. And she said "Hey Bukka, do you want to send out to get you, because I don't want you to hobo back." She says: "Do you like it there?" and I told her "Yes, ma'am I do." I said I wanted to stay up here until I'm ready to come back. I said I've never seen such a place before. And my Uncle Ben, who I was with, well he was in his seventies, and he learned me to play the piano. Give me two years, and I'll be back home, then I'll go back to St. Louis, and then I'll be on my own . . . And when I did go back, I was playing in those road houses. Oh, the other singers I

> was hearin,' there was Son Jackson and Charley Patton and others., they was all playing them road houses. . . .[9]

IN MAY 1972, FRED J. HAY AND BILL LYNDS WERE IN THEIR SECOND semester at Southwestern at Memphis College (now Rhodes College). In the fall, Hay had taken a class with eminent folklorist John Quincy Wolf, who taught the class in his living room.[10] In the spring, Hay and Lynds enrolled in a "directed inquiry" class with Professor Richard C. Wood. Wood introduced them to blues promoter Steve LaVere, who gave the students a list of names and addresses of blues musicians. Following LaVere's advice, Hay and Lynds were prepared to offer twenty dollars to each musician for an interview. Hay wrote, ". . . we volunteered to bring beer but were often asked for whiskey instead."[11]

Booker was waiting for the students at his outdoor "office"—several old chairs backed up to a wall on a street corner near his home. Responding to their first question, he told the students that he was born in Houston, Mississippi, "and left there and went to the Mississippi Delta . . . I went to Mississippi Delta in Clarksdale . . . that's where the blues were really ringing around there like birds then."[12] He talked about his slide guitar style and Charley Patton. "They was playing some [slide] but not too many with a bottleneck, and a lot of guys come along with Charlie Patton."[13] When the students suggested a connection between Booker's style and Patton's, Booker heard them making a request. "Well, you want to hear a little Charlie Patton? Now, I can't play [like] him, and I seen Charlie Patton wasn't using no pick. But I can play it, but I can't slap it with these picks on." He said no one influenced his playing. ". . . I tells everybody, white and Black, if you playing music you got to learn something yourself. Don't sit around these record players and learn all the other fellow's stuff."[14] He used his experience with record producer Lester Melrose as an example. When Booker went to Chicago in 1940 to record, he brought a list of songs he intended to play. Melrose showed him that most had been recorded, and said to take a couple of days to write his own songs.

The students knew enough about Booker to ask music-related questions, but little about his life. So, as he did with me years later, Booker took over. He played his song "Give Me an Old, Old Lady" with a pick, ending with the spoken aside "She's going there with Charlie Patton." Then he told the story of his train ride to St. Louis:

> Well, I stayed in the Delta until I was growed up, around twelve or thirteen years old, and I slipped off from my uncle. And I got tired, you know, looking at them mules every morning. And I caught the freight train on the Dog. And I came, went to St. Louis. I stay with an old man up there named Old Man Ben. And he really the one who put me on track. Old Man Ben then was about sixty-four or -five, and he didn't have any kids. He had a big nightclub there. He had a baby grand piano, so he told me he'd send me to school and all I had to do was stay around there and, uh, what I knowed, and still I would know more. And he said he would call my peoples and let them know where I was. So he did; he called them up and let me talk to them. Asked me did I want to come home. I told them no, I wouldn't be home in about five or six years.[15]

A SECOND TEAM OF INTERVIEWERS APPROACHED BOOKER IN 1972. Memphis journalists Margaret McKee and Fred Chisenhall were researching a book about the city's famous Beale Street. McKee had been a reporter on the staff of the *Memphis Press-Scimitar*, where Chisenhall was the assistant managing editor.

Booker told them that he received a guitar from his father "and by age nine . . . was playing at country frolics and suppers for fifteen cents, two apples, and a box of sardines a night. . . ."[16] He grew frustrated with farm work. "My grandfather had me hauling fodder for the mules," he said. "Them mules was slow. I'm just steady whupping them with a bullwhip, and they got slower. I say, 'When I get you to the barn, old buddy, you won't be bothering Booker no more.' The mules ain't seen me from that day to this. That just wasn't my talent to fool with nothing like that."[17]

He told his interviewers that he ran away from the farm and walked barefoot to Houston, where he found work in a sawmill and a store. Contacting the Chickasaw County Historical Society, I was told it was possible that a nine-year-old Black boy who looked older could have found work in a sawmill. "There would have been several sawmills in and around Chickasaw County at the time," Larry Davis wrote. "Most likely they would have been owned by white people who would need Black labor to work in them. In speculation, depending on how big Bukka would have been at the age of nine, he may have passed himself off as someone older and looked like he could physically do certain types of jobs."[18] Davis added that a Black boy finding work in a store was unlikely. In this account, Booker did not mention a train, but spoke of a long trip. He told McKee and Chisenhall that he worked "long enough to get himself shoes and a knee-pants suit and then hitchhiked a hundred miles across the state to the Mississippi Delta. . . ."

In August 1975, Canadian journalist Bo Basiuk traveled to the American South. As editor of *Blues Magazine*, Basiuk said, "I wanted to develop contacts with some of the bluesmen and possibly interview them."[19] Accompanying him on the trip was Toronto music agent Roberta Richards. They arranged a meeting with Booker in Memphis. An accomplished blues guitar player himself, Basiuk spent much of the interview asking Booker about tunings he used for various songs and how he developed his style of playing.

Booker talked about how he learned to play slide guitar. He said that an older man, who he claimed was his second cousin, B. B. King's grandfather, taught him how to play guitar by sliding a closed pocketknife along the strings.[20] Hurley and Evans later identified the man who introduced Booker to playing slide style as "an elderly local guitarist named Sam Peterson." Booker told Basiuk that he was a young boy when Peterson's slide guitar sound captivated him, and he was determined to play in that style:

> [Peterson] just had a pocket knife. It wouldn't be open. It would be closed up. And so many nights, my grandmother was a church going woman, he would play church songs, you know, blues and things, and she just sit up and cried. I said, "If I ever lived to get over seven or eight years old, I'm gonna try that." But I never could get no music out of the pocket knife good this way.[21]

As Booker and Basiuk talked about guitar tunings and technique, Roberta Richards took notes for her article on "The Legendary Booker White."[22] In yet another version of the train ride to St. Louis, Booker was fifteen when "he was playing quite well and made up his mind to leave the Delta for good":[23]

> One morning, with guitar in hand and a few personal possessions, Bukka hopped aboard a freight train headed for St. Louis, Missouri. Upon his arrival, Bukka was fortunate enough to find odd jobs to pay for his keep but certainly nothing that even

> remotely resembled becoming a professional blues musician. During the next few years, Bukka had many different jobs. On occasion, he got the rare opportunity to play his guitar and sing at dances and very small clubs. Composing blues songs filled most of Bukka's free time and helped bring back memories of his home and family and even the Delta which he missed so terribly. One of his most famous blues, "Po' Boy" . . . was inspired at this time.[24]

In this telling, Booker was older and more prepared to take on the challenges of moving from rural Mississippi to a big city. Richards wrote, "St. Louis, Baltimore, Memphis and Chicago were to become Bukka's new homes. Moving to Chicago in 1930 was, hopefully, a big step toward becoming a recognized artist."[25] When Booker was in Chicago, she continued, "A friend of Bukka's, the great Big Bill Broonzy, suggested to Bukka that he try to tone his voice down to ease some of the harshness. No matter how much he admired Big Bill, Bukka was quite satisfied with his powerful voice, which he felt matched the full sound of his guitar."[26]

Richards's reporting of the St. Louis story includes two details that are absent in other versions. The first was that Booker left Mississippi for St. Louis in his mid-teens, rather than as a nine-year-old. The second was that he traveled to Chicago sometime after recording in Memphis in 1930. However, blues scholar David Evans believes that Booker "probably was in Chicago only in the late 1930s and 1940, perhaps only for recording sessions."[27]

In 1976, Booker told the story of the train ride for perhaps the last time. Recalling that he had mentioned leaving Houston at age nine, I returned to the subject:

> DAVID JOHNSON: So you left Houston when you were about nine, you said?
>
> BOOKER WHITE: Yeah, I was nine. I wasn't intending to leave. We was playing next to a railroad track, and my father just had bought me a Stella guitar, and we were playing getting on the train and getting off, and so I didn't know nothing about no hoboing—they didn't either—and the train was going faster than I thought it was. I wasn't paying the other boy no attention, and he commenced to jumping off. I was figuring on him jumping back on. Well, the train got too fast for him to jump back on, and I stayed on. I ended up in St. Louis. I was cry-

ing every step of the way, ever from where I caught it after I couldn't get off, then I got to St. Louis the next morning at eight o'clock. I had on a soda cap and knee pants.

JOHNSON: What did you do?

WHITE: Well, I went across the bridge. An old man was sitting out across a bridge down there fishing—had something on the hook there, and he called me—told me—asked me what's the matter, and I told him, and he said, "Well, you don't have to worry about that. I got some friend. I know an old man; he will take you in and be nice to you. He don't even have no relatives here." He say he be a millionaire. He say, "How would you like to stay with a millionaire?" I didn't know what a millionaire meant. I didn't know. I didn't act dumb about it. I say anyplace would beat a freight train staying on it—that's what I say to him. That's what I'm talkin' about. So he carried me down there to Old Man Ben, and Old Man Ben showed me around his place, and he had a big baby grand piano, you know, and I was just full of music. That's what I was wanting to do. So I went to playing the piano, and he said I'll write you parents and tell them all about you—you're doing fine. And he said now if you want to go back home, you won't have to ride no freight train back—I'll put you on a passenger train. I said no, I want to stay here awhile.

The credibility of a literal version of Booker's story rests on the unlikely proposition that a nine-year-old boy could hop a train in Mississippi, ride behind the tender and first boxcar to Memphis, and stay there unnoticed until the train reached St. Louis—a distance of 415 miles. However, Booker told folklore students Fred J. Hay and Bill Lynds this in 1972: "Well, I stayed in the Delta until I was growed up, around twelve or thirteen years old, and slipped away from my uncle. And I got tired . . . looking at them mules every morning. And I caught a freight train on the Dog. And I came, went to St. Louis. I stay with an old man up there named Old Man Ben."[28] But what if the boy was older than nine, or the destination was closer than St. Louis? Either circumstance would make the trip more credible.

In 2009, Australian blues researcher Bob Eagle was investigating a report that Booker had lived with an Uncle Ben in 1918–19 between the community of Brazil and the town of Webb in Tallahatchie County, Mississippi. Eagle had found five men named Ben in that area in the 1920 census.[29] Going back to the 1910 census to check a name, Eagle came across Ben W. White living in the Brazil-Webb area on MS (Mississippi State Road) 321 along the Cassidy Bayou—a stream running southeast through Tallahatchie County parallel to the Tallahatchie River.

Locating Ben White's draft registration card, Eagle learned that Ben was from Charleston in the hills further east in Tallahatchie County. Ben moved back to Charleston in 1917. Sorting through questions raised by Ben and Booker being relatively close in age, Eagle wrote, "I favor Ben White as his uncle—it seems too obvious to be mere coincidence, and it is clear from the draft card that he was the main farmer in the family at that time . . . so the recollection would be of Ben, not Ben's parents. There may have been some hero worship of a cousin who was 8 or 9 years older than Bukka."

Eagle concluded that if Uncle Ben was indeed Ben White, he would have been the brother of John White—Booker's father. Ben was born in the hills around Charleston, so John White was likely to have been born in the same location—rather than in Texas or New York, as Booker claimed. The distance between Houston in Chickasaw County and the section of Cassidy Bayou that is in Tallahatchie County is less than a hundred miles.

THE ST. LOUIS STORY MIGHT REMAIN UNVERIFIED, BUT IN MY research into Booker's life, I found there often was an element of truth even in seemingly exaggerated recollections. As Booker said to Bo Basiuk and Roberta Richards in 1975, "I lie some of the time, but not all of the time."[30] This led me to give further consideration to the St. Louis story.

First, I looked into the bridges connecting East St. Louis in Illinois to the city of St. Louis in Missouri. In his interview with Jack Hurley, Booker recalled Old Man Ben speaking to him as he sat on a step to a bridge. Upon reading the Hurley interview, I pictured a small country bridge, but the bridge would have had to cross the Mississippi River. In the 1920s, trains used such bridges, but did the bridges accommodate people on foot? Adele Heagney in the St. Louis Room of the public library responded that at least two bridges did, and they were in the right spot in relation to the rail system:

> There were five bridges spanning the Mississippi at St. Louis in the 1920s: The Merchants, McKinley, Eads, Municipal (Free Bridge), and Alton, plus a car ferry for the Missouri Pacific. The

> Municipal Free Bridge and the Eads definitely carried pedestrian traffic. They are also the farthest south, and were more likely to handle trains from Memphis. It's hard to say on which side of the river [Booker] might've stopped. Good arguments for both.[31]

Booker could have been sitting on the step of a bridge over the Mississippi when Old Man Ben realized that he was a stranger.

Yet how likely was it that a boy as young as nine could have hoboed a train in rural Mississippi and traveled all the way to St. Louis? Railroad researcher Adam Burns thought it was possible:

> Booker could have made it by train to St. Louis from either Grenada or Houston. Grenada was served by the Illinois Central, while Houston was on the Mobile & Ohio. Both of their main lines ran right through those towns and reached St. Louis. I would say that it would have been relatively easy during that time for a boy that age to hop a ride by train.[32]

As a newspaper reporter who had listened to Booker tell his St. Louis story and thought that he must be exaggerating, I now think there is a certain amount of truth to it—and that the truth might not matter. When I described Booker's story to Yale psychologist Zorana Ivcevic Pringle, who researches the psychology of creativity, she told me, "Even if a story is not completely factually true, it says something about a person's identity, and the memory of it can have an influence on a person's life."[33]

In 1976, my perception had been that Booker believed his story. By telling it repeatedly in interview situations, he made clear that it was important to his identity. Since his father had been a railroad fireman, Booker may have been emphasizing the importance of his own relationship with trains. Telling and retelling the story would have made it more true to him. Acknowledging the importance of the story—and considering its meaning to the storyteller—is one way to get a look into Booker's inner sense of self.

Chapter Six

TRYING TO SETTLE

WHEN HE WAS IN HIS LATE TEENS, WASHINGTON WHITE WAS MAKing an effort to adapt to the life that his family had prepared him for: farming. The 1920 United States Census listed him as a farm worker in Clay County, just south of Chickasaw County. He and his wife Jessie B. (or Bea) were living in the same household as farmer Thomas Clay, forty-six, and his wife Lula, forty-two, and their four children. Decades later, Booker would recall that he married Jessie B. (or Bea) when he was sixteen and she was six years older.[1] On the census document their respective ages are given as nineteen and twenty. Booker recalled that during this time, he worked at several jobs as he tried to make ends meet. According to Hurley and Evans, "He sharecropped, played music all night, and apparently helped make moonshine whiskey on the side."[2]

As Booker told it, tragedy struck the young couple in the winter of 1928. He said Jessie B. became sick with appendicitis, and her appendix burst before he could take her to the hospital in Houston. He was devastated. "I always have this with me until I die," he recalled.[3] "I feel bad . . . she didn't have none of her people at the hospital. She had some nice people and they had a car, but the water was up and there wasn't a phone. The only way I could have went over there [to her people] was to ride a mule forty-five miles."[4]

Fact-checking for this book, members of the Mississippi Blues Trail Writing and Research Team could not find evidence of the death of a Jessie B. White in Chickasaw County in 1928. What they discovered was a certificate of the death of Chesa B. White, "about 28," in Chickasaw County on May 10, 1923.[5] On the certificate was the report that after Chesa White received medical attention from Dr. Charles A. Davis of neighboring Trebloc, she died from appendicitis, and was buried the following day at New Hope Cemetery in Woodland, Chickasaw County. The circumstances of her death are similar to those that Booker described as occurring in 1928. On the death certificate, the first name of Chesa's husband is illegible, but his last name was White.

For several years after his wife's death, Booker "ran with a fairly tough crowd. The manufacture and sale of moonshine whiskey was an important part of this phase of his life."[6] He tried his hand at jobs other than farming, working as a roustabout with the Silas Green from New Orleans tent show until he got tired of the job and returned to farming on the Delta in Tallahatchie County. The location was Swan Lake. At the time, the name was used to identify both a plantation and the community that had grown up at the plantation's center. Swan Lake was located about forty miles west of Grenada, where Booker had lived with his uncle.

The continuing thread in Booker's life was playing music. The lifestyle of a musician seemed to offer an outlet for his restlessness. As he became more serious about wanting to entertain people, he began to move around to find new audiences. On occasion, he may have played in establishments set up for music, dancing, and selling liquor—roadhouses, or juke joints—but more often would walk or hitch a ride from town to town to play at informal gatherings where payment came in the form of food, liquor, and tips. These weekend dances, called balls or frolics, would take place in a two-room shack where the furniture had been pushed back for dancing. On a plantation, a building sometimes was set aside for gatherings. The people who organized the event could sell food and liquor, and stood to make money if enough friends and neighbors attended.

As a musician, Booker would make a little money at frolics, but was reluctant to host one himself. "I never gave a dance at my house, 'cause I knew people wouldn't act right," he said.[7] He changed his mind one Christmas when he found himself with five dollars to spend and a partner to work with:

> . . . A fella named Sam Woodford, he always give dances, and so he got me go in with him. He asked me would I go fifty-fifty. And I thought that was a good deal—take five dollars, I had chance to bring it on up to thirty dollars. I give him my five dollars; he already had a hog. He killed the hog and barbecue him and have a big bottle to sell off.

Booker had a special appreciation for one of the women who attended. "That was a good dance for Clara Bates," he recalled. "She was a great dancer from Okolona, Mississippi. She dressed like Mae West. I liked that ol' girl, though I never did say nothin' to her. She could see it in my face and the way I would talk to her." According to census documents, Clara Bates was born at or near Okolona in 1905, and lived in the city most of her life. She died in Okolona in April 1966, apparently without having married.[8]

House parties would get rowdy. At Booker and Sam Woodford's frolic, two men entered the building carrying big firecrackers. "They lit one of them firecrackers and throwed it out there in the middle of the floor," Booker recalled. "It went off and scared me and everybody else. I thought somebody turned a shotgun loose." Seeking more information on Sam Woodford, our research turned up a Sam Woods, born 1904 or 1905 in Chickasaw County, and Sam Woodfork, born in 1898, who lived in Aberdeen in Monroe County.[9] Either one could have been the man who put on dances.

As early as 1928, Booker teamed up with harmonica player George "Bullet" Williams. Years later, Booker would call Williams "as fine a harp blower as ever drawed his mouth across the harp."[10] According to *78 Quarterly*—a magazine for record collectors and blues researchers—Booker and George began performing all around the hill country and on the Mississippi Delta.[11] Booker recalled:

> The first time I met George, that was in West Point, Mississippi. At Bapterville, a colored settlement there. I met George in '28 in January. I was real young then. George was a grown man.
>
> He was just sittin' there in a cafe there blowin' for friends, you know. He was gonna play there that night. . . . I had my guitar. And we start to workin' out there. When he put that harp up to his mouth, he make your hair start to walk on your head.
>
> I was playin' in open G. That's the first time somebody had ever played a harp with me in open G. He said, "I don't care *what* key you get in. If it's a song, whatever kinda song it is, I'll blow the song with you." He carried all kinda harps.[12]

After deciding to travel together, the duo performed in a number of cities and towns. "We went through Charleston, went through Grenada, we went through Houston," Booker told *78 Quarterly* writer Stephen Calt, "went to Hickory Flat, went to Albany, Holly Springs, and all them places like that . . . from there on down to the Delta."

For the most part, these were well-populated communities. Today, West Point is a mid-sized city and county seat of Clay County.

Charleston lies east of the Tallahatchie River and is one of two capitals of Tallahatchie County. Grenada is the county seat of Grenada County, and Houston is one of two county seats of Chickasaw County. Hickory Flat is a town in Benton County near the northern border of Mississippi, sixty-five miles southeast of Memphis. New Albany is a city in Union County and the birthplace of author William Faulkner. Located near the Tennessee border, Holly Springs is the county seat of Marshall County.

Performing with an outstanding harmonica player earned Booker a regional reputation—and sometimes good money. When the musicians met, Williams had been living in the town of Glendora. In the *78 Quarterly* article, Stephen Calt described a local roadhouse where Booker and George did very well:

> At a Delta barrelhouse in Glendora operated by a man named Eddie Smith, they each made 50 dollars for a night's performance, the most White ever earned as a blues singer. ". . . I used to play a song then about 'I was broke and hungry, ragged and dirty, too.' That was Blind Lemon's piece. . . . Me and George was playin' the devil outta that. Everybody liked to hear that; that's mostly what we had to play."

For Booker, touring with Williams gave him both valuable experience and appreciative audiences, but also had a serious drawback. Most of their performances together ended with the harmonica player "passed out on the floor in a drunken stupor."[13] As Booker told Calt, "George would go down on me 'fore day. God knows he'd be in the kitchen *under* the table drunk. . . ."[14]

In March 1964, Booker talked about George Williams to a group of interested young blues enthusiasts in Cambridge, Massachusetts, who were taping this and other interviews. One of the students, David Evans, wrote an article for the British magazine *Blues Unlimited* that contained additional details about this important time in Booker's life:[15]

> Booker's most satisfying musical partnership was with George "Bullet" Williams, a harmonica player from Alabama whom Booker met in Glendora, Mississippi, in the Delta. Before this Booker played a little holder harmonica, but he gave it up because it took too much wind. Bullet was a great harp player. "He'd make his harp sing." Anyone who listened to his recordings should be well aware of this fact. He outclassed all others. "He

was the best. Everybody, when they see him coming, would hide. They would get back." Bullet, however, was a desperate alcoholic in these prohibition days and was reduced to drinking shoe polish and rubbing alcohol. He would often get sick when they were playing together. They would go on making music until the Bullet passed out.[16]

AT ONE OF THE FROLICS WHERE BOOKER AND GEORGE PLAYED, A pretty young woman captured Booker's fancy. She was Susie Mae Simpson, the harmonica player's niece.

By 1930, Booker White, Susie Simpson, and George Williams were living in the same household in Tallahatchie County.[17]The census recorded Booker's age as twenty-two, and Susie's as seventeen. George was forty. Booker was listed as head of the household, and his occupation was farmer. George was a farm laborer. The census-taker gave Susie's occupation as none, but she would have contributed to work on the farm.

The day the census was taken in the household's section of Tallahatchie County was April 23, 1930—worth noting because only five weeks later (on May 26), Booker would travel to Memphis to make his first records, and the man who took him there was the same talent scout who had taken George Williams to Chicago two years earlier. He was a Sicilian immigrant named Ralph Lembo, who had advanced from selling fruit to owning a store.

In May 1928, Lembo brought Williams to Chicago to record four numbers for the Paramount record label. Their titles were "Touch Me Light Mama," "Frisco Leaving Birmingham," "The Escaped Convict," and "Middlin' Blues."[18] On "Frisco Leaving Birmingham" and "The Escaped Convict," Williams stretched the range of his instrument to evoke the rhythmic sounds of a train leaving the station and the howling of hounds in hot pursuit of a convict. The album notes to *The Great Blues Harp Players (1927-1936)* commented that "Frisco Leaving Birmingham" took the mouth harp to "a further stage toward personal expression."[19] Playing with Williams may have influenced Booker's first recorded train song, "The Panama Limited." The timing of their musical partnership suggests that Booker knew all about Lembo taking his partner to Chicago in May 1928. This raises the possibility that Booker might have walked through downtown Itta Bena with a guitar slung over his shoulder in order to bring himself to the talent scout's attention.

Chapter Seven

MEMPHIS 1930

ON A SPRING DAY IN 1930, BOOKER WAS WALKING TOWARD HIS DEStination when he began to feel apprehensive.[1] He had only a few miles to go before he would see his brother, but needed to pass through the downtown of Itta Bena, Mississippi, to reach the wooden bridge over Roebuck Lake. Itta Bena's name came from the Choctaw words for forest camp, or home in the woods. In 1846, white settlers from southern Mississippi had traveled up the Yazoo River in search of fertile land.[2] Finding rich soil around the lake on the Delta, they established a settlement where they could raise cotton and corn. The success of their crops attracted other farmers to the area, and Itta Bena became an important trading center among the region's plantations.

The source of Booker's wariness as he approached the downtown were rumors about Black people passing through Itta Bena who had been detained and put to work. The warnings had grown stronger after the devastating Mississippi River flood of three years before. According to historian John M. Barry, author of *Rising Tide: The Great Mississippi Flood of 1927 and How It Changed America*, events that took place during the flood forced Black residents of the Delta to give up their belief that the white planters would protect them. "The whites liked to think a flood fight represented the best of a community, all of it pulling together," Barry wrote. "Instead it simply reflected the nature of power in the community, shorn of pretense."[3]

In 1927, as the Mississippi River rose higher along levees that protected Greenville on the western side of the Delta, police and National Guardsmen "impressed every Black male they saw," forcing men to work on the levees despite the danger posed by rising flood waters.[4] When Lieutenant E. C. Sanders summoned plantation workers to repair a low place in the levee caused by automobile traffic, he reported, "The negroes ran to the break also . . . but as they arrived, they soon became demoralized and ran away. It then became necessary for the civilian foreman and my detachment to force the negroes to the break at the point of guns."[5]

Hundreds of Black men died when the levees broke and they were swept into the river. Prior to the flood, influential planter and politician LeRoy Percy put forward the notion that landowners cared enough about Black field workers to be mindful of their safety. Percy lived in Greenville, but was of no help to the Black population when the flood came. After the flood, the Greenville camps for displaced Blacks became the most notorious in the region for their shabby treatment of the population they were supposed to protect.

In one instance, a dozen ships that were sent to carry the Greenville refugees to safety stopped at the city, but left without taking Black passengers. Behind this inhumane refusal to rescue was the fact that Greenville's planters had a strong economic reason to keep the Black population in the camps and close to Greenville. Black people were the planters' workforce. The system of growing and harvesting cotton couldn't function without them.

After the disaster, a commission appointed by flood recovery director Herbert Hoover to look into conditions in Greenville and elsewhere found serious discrimination and other abuses; but before the commission submitted its report, Hoover pressured commission members to tone down the report so that the camps would look like a success. Hoover's position as director thrust him into the national conversation as a man who could solve big problems, and he was elected president in 1928. The truth about abuses that took place in Mississippi in 1927 was kept from the public for years.

ON THE APRIL DAY IN 1930 WHEN BOOKER WENT TO VISIT HIS brother, he may have crossed the Yazoo River on the steel bridge that connects downtown Greenwood (diagonally across the width of the Delta from Greenville) to the city's white neighborhood. Adjacent to the downtown is the Black neighborhood known as Baptist Town. Itta Bena is about eight miles to the southwest on the Delta side of the river. In 1976, when Booker told me about his apprehension as he approached Itta Bena, he did not elaborate, and I did not think to ask.

In July 2017, in the middle of an afternoon spent exploring Itta Bena's former downtown, I began to understand why he felt on edge. In 1930, Humphries Street had been Itta Bena's main commercial street. It ended at a body of water, Roebuck Lake. In 2017, the buildings along one side of the street were empty. On the other side of the street was a grassed park with a gazebo. As I stood near the gazebo, I could see workmen going in and out of a building. When I asked, one workman told me they were repainting the interior for a restaurant that would be occupying the vacant space. Across Roebuck Lake lay a vast sea of green leaves. A wooden bridge at the end of Humphreys Street crossed the narrow lake to the dirt road that led to the buildings of an agricultural compound. On that side of the river, a broad stand of trees began at the bank of the lake and continued inland toward the fields, which were blanketed by the green leaves of soy plants—the crop that replaced cotton as the staple.

I asked one of the workers to help me understand what I was seeing from the Humphreys Street side of Roebuck Lake. I took notes on what he told me:

> I am standing in front of the vacant store that once was entrepreneur Ralph Lembo's place of business. There is work going on in a building on the side of the downtown where Lembo's storefront still stands. Painter Bo Smart tells me the store may be torn down. In the meantime, a motorcycle club rents the space for meetings. From the outside, all I can see inside are several tables set up. The store has been a beauty parlor. I ask Bo where the bridge over the river leads. "To the plantation," he says. There are expansive fields of cotton or soy across the river. I ask Bo about the gravel road along the river. "Country," he says. "People live there." He means Black people [live there].

No wonder that Booker was worried that day about being accosted by white men. To visit his brother on the other side of the river, he needed to pass near a plantation.

IN 2017, THELMA COLLINS WAS ELECTED ITTA BENA'S FIRST BLACK mayor; her victory made national and state news. Having grown up in the city, Mayor Collins told me that at the time Booker would have passed through Itta Bena, the city was divided into two sections. "One was called the white section, the other section was called Balance Due," she said. "If you analyze that phrase, it meant that this part was due the same amenities as the white section, but did not have the amenities. It was an appropriate name. . . . The white section had sidewalks, paved streets, and no ditches. The Black side had gravel streets, no pavement, and the houses were dilapidated."[6]

In downtown Itta Bena in 1930, Booker would have been conspicuous. "It seems right that if a strange person was just walking through with a guitar on his back at that particular time, he would be stopped to inquire what he was doing in Itta Bena," Mayor Collins said. "It just happened that he walked by Ralph Lembo's store, and that would inspire [Lembo] to get more information."

Raffaele Lembo was the son of Sicilian immigrants. His father Francesco emigrated to New Orleans in 1904. After finding his way to Itta Bena and starting a fruit and vegetable business, Francesco sent for his wife and son in Sicily to join him. Young Ralph worked hard in his new home. His grandson Bo Prestidge (born Ralph Lembo Prestidge) grew up hearing stories about his grandfather. "He always would tell people he went around with a wheelbarrow of apples and oranges," Prestidge said, "and if he sold all those apples and oranges, he could sleep in the wheelbarrow."[7]

During World War I, Ralph Lembo served in General John J. Pershing's expeditionary force. Returning from the war, he took over the family business and opened a general store that sold furniture, including the console-sized appliances that played 78 rpm records. Lembo and other furniture store proprietors also stocked the 78s. As others in the furniture business had done, Lembo became a talent scout for a record company whose records he stocked. "He was a man with a vision," Bo Prestidge said. "He was way ahead of his time . . . to be a talent scout for blues music when people didn't think that was important."

Described by the *Greenwood Commonwealth* as a "clever and prosperous . . . merchant," Ralph Lembo opened a second store in Morgan City, Mississippi, and invested in commercial real estate in Greenwood. In 1924, he purchased the Dixie Theatre in Itta Bena, combining his real estate investments with entertainment and sports.[8] Three years later, he embarked on a new enterprise. In February 1927, the *Commonwealth* reported that Lembo managed a "troupe" of Black artists who would make records for Columbia. In April, Lembo traveled to New Orleans with two preachers, Reverend C. T. Thornton and Reverend Frank Cotton.

As owner and manager of a theater, Lembo kept up with developments in recorded music. His trip to New Orleans responded to one trend among record labels specializing in race records in the southern market: the popularity of sermons and religious music in the Christian South. A second trend was the emerging market for blues about downhome themes sung by men with guitars whose lyrics often included sexual double entendres. This was country blues.

The performer whose music popularized the style was Blind Lemon Jefferson from Dallas, Texas. He learned his craft playing for tips on street corners, and began his brief but prolific recording career in December 1925–January 1926 by recording songs with titles like "That Black Snake Moan." When his early recordings sold better than expected, record company talent scouts looked for as many similar musicians as possible, hoping to find individuals who could match Jefferson's success. Central to the search for marketable artists were the talent scouts.

The best known of the first generation of talent scouts, Ralph S. Peer, began to learn about audio technology and other aspects of the music business while helping his father Abram Peer at his store in Independence, Missouri. Peer Supply Company sold only sewing machines until Abram began to sell talking machines. Mechanically, sewing and talking machines were similar, "built on revolving wheels, cranks, and replacement needles."[9] The model that Abram sold was called the Graphophone, manufactured by the Columbia Phonograph Company. The company's regional warehouse and regional headquarters were located in downtown Kansas City. Young Ralph Peer's stockroom responsibilities took him to warehouses and offices to pick up records and repair parts. Ralph's regular visits acquainted him with the Columbia staff. "Just that simply, his work in the music business had begun, at age eleven," Barry Mazor wrote in his biography of Ralph Peer.[10]

Other merchants became part of the record industry when their businesses sold 78s. Intrigued by Blind Lemon Jefferson's combination of risqué lyrics and smooth guitar playing, Dallas record shop owner R. T. Ashford brought Jefferson to the attention of Art Laibly, recording director of the Paramount label. Birmingham, Alabama, talent scout Harry Charles owned a piano store. Furniture and music store owner Polk C. Brockman, of Atlanta, Georgia, persuaded a record producer to record popular local musician Fiddlin' John Carson. Recording equipment had become portable and durable enough to travel, so Carson was recorded in Atlanta during one of the first field recording sessions. Music store owner Henry Speir of Jackson, Mississippi, claimed to have brought the most influential country blues musician on the Mississippi Delta, Charley Patton, to the attention of Paramount. Patton may have approached—or been approached by—Ralph Lembo first, but if so, they failed to reach an agreement.

Talent scouts could recommend talent to company executives, but did not make decisions about putting out a record. Scouts based in the South were always on the lookout for new musicians and material, but executives from the North made business decisions in a market they knew little about. Thus many songs never were "waxed." Disagreements over money between independent agents like Lembo and record company executives were another reason why a recording session might not produce a record.

Blues musician Ruben Lacy's experience was like that. When Lacy went to work as an overseer on a plantation between Greenwood and Itta Bena, Ralph Lembo persuaded him to play in his store by holding out the possibility of a recording session. On December 9, 1927, Lembo brought Lacy to Memphis to record four songs for Columbia, but the label decided not to release any of them.[11] Blues scholar David Evans, who interviewed Lacy in 1966, explained what might have happened. "I think his agent Ralph Lembo had a dispute with Columbia following the session," Evans wrote.[12] Taking a blues musician to a recording session and returning without a record deal might have been a setback, but Lembo continued searching for opportunities to make money in the music business, He was on the lookout for new talent. Three years after taking Lacy to Memphis, he discovered Booker White.

When Lembo, or the Black man Booker recalled hailing him, noticed a man with a guitar on his back passing in front of the store, Lembo acted quickly to bring the stranger inside to see how well he could play and sing. At that time, the spare sound of an acoustic guitar accompanying a male singer was in demand. At a Seattle radio station in 1967, Booker recalled his first encounter with Lembo:

> I passed by there with the guitar on my shoulder, and they had a colored fellow come out there to flag me down. I started to go to running. I didn't know nothing about no Itta Bena. . . . It was raining, wasn't nobody working, and they always told me . . . if you go through down there and you was a stranger, they would just keep you and make you work there. You couldn't get away. . . . And so the colored fellow came over to the highway. He said "Mister Ralph said come up here to the store. He wants to see you on some business." . . . Now I ain't had no business in Itta Bena 'cause I ain't never been there. . . . It looked to me like when he said that, if I didn't come they was gonna carry me up there.[13]

Lembo offered Booker a shot of distilled bourbon whiskey—much smoother than the home-made moonshine the musician was used to—to calm him down.[14] After accepting the offer, Booker began to relax, and settled down enough to listen to what the store owner had to say. Lembo asked Booker if he would like to make a record. When Booker allowed that he would, Lembo asked him to play a couple of songs so that he could hear how he sounded. Lembo liked what he heard. He told Booker that he would bring him to Memphis to make the record. He said that he would pick him up on Saturday, May 24, in Swan Lake at the intersection of the main road from Webb (seven miles to the southeast of Swan Lake) and the railroad tracks.

The next few weeks must have been nerve-wracking for Booker, but on the appointed day, Lembo drove his Studebaker to the meeting place, where he found Booker with another musician, Napoleon Hairiston, who was Booker's friend from Itta Bena.[15] Booker recalled that two young white men who played guitar were in the car when Lembo arrived at Swan Lake, but got out because they would not ride with Black people. Another passenger was a Black preacher who would record spiritual lessons. Hurley and Evans suggested that the preacher might have been Reverend M. H. Holt,[16] who also recorded that day.

In Memphis, Ralph Peer's weeklong schedule of auditions and recording sessions was about to begin in the city's new Ellis Auditorium. Completed in 1924, the auditorium was the first building in the South designed to host large conventions. The RCA Victor Company had headquarters in Camden, New Jersey, but used the multi-room auditorium for some of its field recording in the South.

Peer had made a name for himself in field recording. For two weeks in July–August 1927, he had set up portable equipment in a vacant millinery warehouse on State Street in Bristol, Tennessee, to record historic sessions that writer Nolan Porterfield called the Big Bang of country music. Discovered during the session were yodeling songwriter Jimmie Rodgers and a homespun trio, the Carter Family—artists whose music would help define the sounds that came to be called "country."

Barry Mazor's 2015 biography of Ralph Peer shed new light on what took place during that week. The Peer family gave Mazor access to the family archives, where his research revealed that of two thousand recording sessions that Peer produced, only one set of his production notes can be found. The surviving notes came from Peer's Memphis sessions that were held from May 24 to May 31, 1930. Booker White, then known as Washington, and Reverend Holt recorded on Monday, May 26.

Peer wrote the notes as a letter to Loren L. Watson, the executive in charge of the RCA Victor office in New York. Dated June 6, 1930, the letter provided a glimpse into the way the producer-as-gatekeeper process worked at that time. If Peer was not present at all of the sessions, he appears to have been kept well informed by the RCA Victor staff who were. Contrary to his image as "the stern, stiff disengaged musically uncaring man people have basically made up over the years," Peer revealed himself in his letter and notes to be a fully engaged producer with a dry sense of humor.[17]

IN COUNTRY BLUES, BOOKER IS ONE OF SEVERAL MUSICIANS WHO first recorded in 1930 or later. Two earlier musicians who influenced him were Blind Willie Johnson and Charley Patton. Johnson made his first gruff-voiced gospel recordings in Dallas on Saturday, December 3, 1927. He made his last recording in Atlanta on Sunday, April 20, 1930, and sang the final song he recorded—the hectoring spiritual "You're Gonna Need Somebody on Your Bond"—with the same conviction he brought to his first recordings. Johnson recorded thirty songs for Columbia and the records sold well. Ralph Peer or his staff at Booker's first session must have asked him to sing in the voice and style of Johnson, because the two spirituals Booker recorded in Memphis are unlike any of his later recordings.

Charley Patton recorded thirty-eight songs in 1929 alone. By the time Booker recorded, Patton's records could be heard almost everywhere the music of Black Mississippi was played. After Booker's "rediscovery" in 1963, when interviewers were keen to ask him if he had met Patton, he gave contradictory answers. When asked by John Fahey and ED Denson, who rediscovered him, Booker recorded a four-minute personal recollection of Patton that implied he had met the man. He later told Denson and Fahey that he hadn't. Regardless, as Samuel Charters wrote in *The Bluesmen*, Booker "wanted to be just like Patton, even though he absorbed little of Charley's blues style. It was Patton as a man, rather than a singer, that drew him."[18]

EARLY IN HIS CAREER, RALPH PEER REALIZED THAT MOST OF THE money to be made by recording American roots music came from ownership of the copyrights. Original songs (and songs from the folk tradition that musicians claimed to be original) were intellectual property that could be copyrighted with the United States Office of Patents and Copyrights. From the 1920s onward, Ralph Peer's business model gave some of the musicians he worked with—notably Jimmie Rodgers and the Carter Family—the opportunity to retain a percentage of the income from their songs, rather than accept a one-time payment. Peer made this option available to his most popular country musicians, who were white, but continued to pay blues musicians (and others) a fixed amount per recorded song—and only on those songs that were issued on a record.

Blues musicians received no payment for the many songs they recorded that producers and record companies chose not to release. In 1928, in three separate sessions for the Columbia race record label OKeh, Mississippi John Hurt recorded a total of twenty songs. OKeh paid Hurt twenty dollars for each of twelve sides that were issued. Hurt's biographer John Ratcliffe wrote that the sum "was a lot of money for a Mississippi farmhand at that time."[19]

In 1976, Booker's recollection of his first recording session put a much higher figure on what Ralph Lembo paid him. He told me, "Now we had a contract for eight hundred dollars for eight songs . . . eight hundred dollars . . . a hundred dollars a song. Had a contract for that, and I put all of them . . . I put six and a half of them. You can tell how much the others put out. Didn't have but eight."[20] He may have confused the amount of money he received with Ralph Lembo's total budget of eight hundred dollars to pay the performers he brought to Memphis, including Reverend Holt.

Booker said he was grateful to Lembo for stopping him on Humphreys Street and treating him well:

> I'm glad he did stop me now. That gave me a good push off from there, you know. I didn't know nothing about it. I was green—I was a green man. I didn't know. And he was so proud of me that he didn't know what to . . . And he did nice. He give me two-hundred-fifty dollars and a brand new Gibson guitar. Man, I like had a heart attack on that. That was my first, biggest money I ever made. I didn't think a guitar could make no money. I didn't know. I was young, too.[21]

THE AUTHORITATIVE *BLUES & GOSPEL RECORDINGS 1902–1942* CREDITS all fourteen numbers recorded on May 26 to Washington White.[22] In Ralph Peer's notes, he wrote about Napoleon Hairiston as well as White. He credited nine songs to Washington White and five to "Napoleon and Washington."[23] Prior to the discovery of Peer's notes, Napoleon

Hairiston was considered a background figure whose contributions to the recording session were limited to singing and playing guitar on "The New Frisco Train." The only mention of Hairiston in *Blues & Gospel Recordings* was in the listing for Washington White—"with Napoleon Hairiston, gtr/talking."[24] On "The New Frisco Train," Hairiston sang the lyrics over the rapid strumming of his guitar, while White played slide guitar figures and shouted encouragement—the "talking" to which Godrich and Dixon refer. Peer's notes clarified that "The New Frisco Train" was Hairiston's number, with White contributing.

Peer liked what he heard from the two Mississippians. Under the heading "Washington White," he wrote "The four Blues are very good corn field type and should have a big sale in the delta country."[25] Under "Napoleon & Washington," he wrote, "The four Blues selections are sung by Napoleon Hairiston with accompaniment and other assistance from Washington White."[26] His comments on White's style and Hairiston's four blues numbers change our understanding of the relationship between the two musicians. Hairiston sang five of the fourteen songs recorded, including "The New Frisco Train." Their tight performance of "Frisco Train" suggests that White and Hairiston had played the song together many times. Their guitar parts and "call and response" between Hairiston's lead vocal and White's interjections sound practiced. Their performance shows none of the tentativeness one might expect when two musicians play together for the first time.

Peer had a specific idea in mind for the two opening numbers of the session: he wanted to release a record on which both sides were train songs. He wrote, "The selection, 'The Panama Limited,' is a train piece played on the guitar and it is intended that it should be coupled with BVE-59995, 'The New Frisco Train.'"[27] Peer paired the two numbers because they were a type of guitar (and sometimes harmonica) blues that celebrated trains: the rhythm of their wheels turning on the tracks, and the ringing of train bells.[28]

On "The Panama Limited," Booker's ringing slide guitar, rapid-fire narrative, and plaintive singing are remarkable. On guitar, he reproduces the sounds of bell, whistle, and air brakes. Speaking the story and singing the refrains, he narrates the struggles of an old woman leaving by train from Chicago, and her lamentations:

> *That old soul, you know, went down to the Union Station* [in Memphis], *you know, she asked the depot man what time it was, she heard eight thirty freight blowing, but she was gonna*

> *catch that fast Panama Limited, you know, it kind of blow a little different you know.*
>
> [Booker imitates train whistles on his guitar.]
>
> *And after she heard this freight, you know, she asks the man again what time it was, he told her to go and lay her head on the railroad line, and if she heard the rail popping, the train wasn't long, old soul stooped down, and she heard the rail popping, you know, she got up and sang, you know.*
>
> I'm a motherless child.
> I'm a long ways from my home.
> Mmmmmmmmmmmmmmmmmmmmmmmmm
> Mmmmmmmmmmmm mmmmmm mmmm mmmm[29]

Peer's notes confirmed the possibility that Booker performed four sacred (or spiritual) songs at the session because the producer asked him to. Peer was confident that sacred songs would find an audience. He wrote, "Selections BVE-62505 to 62508 are sacred selections done in the Holy Roller style. We have nothing else like this and I recommend a quick release of one of these records." The songs on the resulting record V38615 were "I Am in the Heavenly Way" and "Promise True and Grand." Two unreleased sacred songs Booker recorded were "Over Yonder" and "Trusting in My Saviour."

Peer's letter corroborated that Ralph Lembo brought the blues musicians to the session along with the Reverend Holt, who was joined on one number by a "congregation" of voices as he conducted "a complete funeral service and burial for Sister Jessie McLellen."[30]

Unfortunately, the notes don't answer one enduring question: Who was the female singer responding to Washington White's vocals on the sacred numbers? Some have speculated that the powerful voice belonged to Memphis Minnie McCoy, a much better known performer at the time than "new artist" Washington White.[31] During the Memphis sessions, Memphis Minnie performed in three different settings: duets with her sister Bessie; lead vocals with the Memphis Jug Band; and duets with her husband, Kansas Joe McCoy, who also recorded as Joe Johnson.

Cross-referencing Peer's notes with *Blues & Gospel Recordings* verifies that both Minnie and sister Bessie were present at the session on the day Washington White recorded. Peer might have asked one sister or the other to sing with White in order to create the style that was a success for Blind Willie Johnson and his wife Willie B. Richardson. Peer added details to *Blues & Gospel Recordings*' listing of the Memphis Jug Band recording two numbers that Monday: "I have already written you about 'Bumble Bee Blues,' which is a big hit [for Memphis Minnie] on Vocalion. Another Jug Band selection with vocal by Memphis Minnie is 'Meningitis Blues.' As you probably know, there is a Meningitis epidemic in this part of the country." Whether Minnie wrote the song in the hospital after making a miracle recovery from meningitis may never be confirmed, but it was a story she told often.[32]

At the Ellis Auditorium in May 1930, Memphis Minnie was at the beginning of a long career. She performed and recorded throughout the 1930s and 1940s, led a small combo as late as 1953, and continued to perform through much of the 1950s.[33] She lived in Chicago until she lost her ability to perform. Returning to Memphis in 1959, she suffered a stroke, lost her husband Joe in 1961, and suffered a second stroke. Booker visited her in the Jell Nursing Home. "I see Memphis Minnie sometimes," he recalled in 1968. "She's in a nursing home now, and I went with a white boy from Washington. You know, she got fat as a butterball, that woman did, and all she do is sit in her wheelchair and cry and cry. But in her time, she was really something. She was about the best thing goin' in the woman line."[34]

Minnie's biography, *Woman with Guitar: Memphis Minnie's Blues*, has a nursing home photograph of Booker wearing a dark suit with matching tie and silk cravat.[35] He holds Minnie's fingers as her head sinks into the nursing home pillow. At the time of the photo, Minnie and Booker had known each other thirty-eight years. When they met, she was a rising star and he might have been starstruck to find himself in the company of such well-known performers as Minnie and the musicians in the Memphis Jug Band. When Memphis Minnie died on August 8, 1973, at the age of seventy-six, Booker lost a good friend.

Chapter Eight

RESTLESS AND ROAMING

OVER THE FIRST HALF OF HIS LIFE, BOOKER WAS A RESTLESS MAN. Blues researcher Samuel Charters wrote that after the 1930 recording session in Memphis, Booker wanted to remain in the city to play music, but couldn't find enough work, possibly because of the depressed economy.[1] He had little choice but to return to farming.

For *The Legacy of the Blues,* Charters interviewed Booker at the outdoor arrangement of chairs that the musician liked to call his office—". . . three or four wooden seats and an old bench [set] against a brick wall not far from his apartment in Memphis. . . ."[2] Sometimes Booker would use the office to conduct business, but most of the time he sat talking with friends. When an occasional fan or interviewer came to Memphis to see him, he would hold court at the office. Charters wrote, "The business, now, is remembering the things that have happened to him, and as he tells you something about his life in 1934, or someone he knew in 1937, some of it comes out in blues phrases—in verses from the blues he wrote about it. There's no place for him where the two are separate."

After interviewing Booker, Charters reported that during the early 1930s, he "was still singing, working with his wife's uncle, a rough singer and harmonica player from Alabama named George 'Bullet' Williams . . . They had a job at a roadhouse outside of West Point in 1934, and the next year he moved to Aberdeen. It was a rough, hard life, and he had to become hardened to survive."[3]

Hurley and Evans mentioned the possibility that after George Williams recorded in Chicago in 1928, he may have returned to Mississippi with stories of how musicians from Mississippi and Arkansas were able to make a living in Chicago. If Williams did, the stories would have fueled Booker's determination to go to Chicago, but Booker's time in St. Louis preceded his first visit to the Windy City. In 1976 he said he had met a number of musicians while living in St. Louis, then traveled with them in the direction of Chicago.

Booker may have dreamed about traveling north as a way to achieve his musical aspirations, but the Depression led him to turn to the sport of boxing as a way to make money. Hurley and Evans wrote:

> It was probably in 1935 that Bukka made his first trip to Chicago. He recalled setting out from St. Louis with another musician, the legendary Peetie Wheatstraw, and settling in for a stay on the Windy City's South Side. Bukka had been listening to stories about the great music in Chicago for years; finally he was to hear and be part of it. . . . Musically, it was an exciting town, but financially it was pretty hard. Very few of the musicians could actually make a living with their craft. Most had to find other work to make ends meet; Bukka was no exception. His answer to the problem was to go into professional boxing."[4]

With his solid body and big hands, Booker certainly was rugged enough to go into boxing, but as a man who needed his hands to play the guitar, he may not have done much fighting or fought at the professional level.

In 1964 Booker told interviewers that he fought four fights.[5] He may have participated in some of the unofficial boxing matches that were popular during the Depression. The winner might take home twenty-five or fifty dollars.

He told interviewers that he not only boxed but played professional baseball. His claim to having played at the professional level could not be verified. There is no record of a baseball team named the Birmingham Black Cats, which is the name Booker mentioned to Hurley. The team he may have been referring to—the Birmingham Black Barons—was the Black counterpart of the all-white Birmingham Barons. The Black Barons participated in the Negro leagues from 1920 to 1960.

The level of play in the Negro leagues was close to that of major league teams. Pitcher Leroy "Satchel" Paige played in the league, and outfielder Willie Mays played for the Black Barons. Paige went on to pitch for the Cleveland Indians in the American League and St. Louis Browns in the National League, and Mays had a stellar career with the San Francisco Giants in the National League. Mays was elected to the Baseball Hall of Fame. Booker may have played baseball at Parchman Farm, though he never mentioned it in his recollections of prison. Each of the fifteen prison barracks, or "camps," at Parchman fielded a team to play games with other camps.

There was, however, a team in Mississippi named the Black Cats—and a possible connection between Booker and a player in the Negro leagues. The Laurel Black Cats played in one of the independent Negro leagues.[6] The team was established in 1932 by Black businessman Dayton Hair, a local entrepreneur whose real estate and business holdings included the Black Cat Inn and Black Cat Taxi Service.

Perhaps it was a personal connection with a bona fide baseball player that led Booker to claim he played Negro league baseball. The ballplayer Napoleon Hairston might have been the same person as the friend with whom Booker recorded with in Memphis in 1930. Both the label on the Victor record and producer Ralph Peer's notes spell the last name as Hairiston, but that may have been a misspelling or a variant of the name.

The name Hairston with only one "i" was common in Mississippi. Draft registration records for 1917–18 of men residing in, or linked to, Lowndes County, Mississippi, include a young man named Napoleon Hairston, who was born in Lowndes County on September 1, 1900.[7] Lowndes County borders on Chickasaw County, where Booker White was born. The distance from Columbus, the county seat of Lowndes, to Aberdeen is only twenty-eight miles. Napoleon Hairston would have been about twenty-nine at the first recording session.

In 1932, both Booker and George Williams had aspirations to record again, so why didn't they? Hurley brought the question to Booker. "When asked if he ever recorded for Ralph Lembo again, he answered: 'No, after that I was moving too fast for him. He couldn't catch me.' In point of fact, however, Booker did not record for seven years [after 1930]. . . ."[8]

Firsthand accounts from Booker's fellow musicians active in the 1930s—the men who played dances and juke joints in Mississippi—are rare.

Ruben Lacy met Booker after moving to the Delta in 1927. Lacy spent time at Ralph Lembo's store in Itta Bena and may have been the man who recognized Bukka as he passed in front of the store in 1930. By the time blues scholar David Evans interviewed Lacy in California in 1966, he had become a Baptist preacher. "Rube Lacy said he remembered Booker White and thought he was good," Evans wrote.[9] "That's all he said, so I don't think they were too close."

Fred McDowell, the singer and slide-guitar player who was Booker's close contemporary, crossed paths with him in Cleveland, Mississippi, as early as the 1930s. McDowell was an accomplished country blues musician and singer who did not come to the attention of the record industry until after the period of peak demand for country blues artists.

In February 1972, writer Bruce Cook interviewed an ailing Fred McDowell for his book *Listen to the Blues*. Cook wrote that he was "as easy and unassuming as Skip James was haughty and cantankerous."[10] McDowell's account of meeting Booker White in Mississippi captures not only the interest blues musicians had in each other, but also the competition they felt:

> Yeah, I stayed in Rossville, Tennessee, until I was grown, just farming then—that's what I did all my life. But after my uncle passed on, I had a sister who was married here in Mississippi, and so I came down here to live around her. That was around Lamar, Mississippi, and when I got down to there, I found out there was a few guitars in the neighborhood, and I got acquainted with them. I remember I went to a dance one night, and there were two brothers playing, a violin and a guitar. I sat down and played, and I pulled the people away from them. I got their fans from them, and that's how I got to know them. That was kind of like one night in Cleveland, Mississippi, when Bukka White was playing for them, and I started playing and the crowd commenced applauding me. And Bukka, he came up to me real tough, and he said, "I don't need no goddam help from you here." He was real tough then, but I get along pretty good with him now.[11]

McDowell and Booker would have crossed paths years later at folk and blues festivals, where they each continued to play a distinctive style of country blues, but now in front of young, white audiences who sat and listened. Fred McDowell died on July 3, 1972, five months after his interview with Cook.

Chapter Nine

A WINDING ROAD

THE YEAR AFTER THE DEATH OF HIS MOTHER IN 1933 WAS ANOTHER unsettled period for Booker, but at first, his restlessness had more of a direction to it. He and his father played together at frolics. At Booker's urging, father and son hoboed a train to Memphis to see about recording together for the OKeh label.[1] Booker had heard that the OKeh talent scout would be auditioning musicians at the Houck Music Company in Memphis, but by the time the Whites got to Memphis, the scout had left for Jackson, Mississippi.

To see if there might be another way to play music for a living, Booker traveled "for a few weeks" with the Silas Green Company, a Black-run tent show that toured the South.[2] He told F. Jack Hurley: "I had to see the world, but, man, that traveling can get you down. It was hoboing, sleeping on this railroad track—off from it, you know—boiling, roasting [an] ear of corn in a bucket. . . . Man, I'm telling you, I couldn't see no other way to keep going."[3] Eventually he arrived in St. Louis, where he appears to have lived until he had an opportunity to travel in the company of a piano player who often recorded in Chicago.

Born William Bunch in Ripley, Tennessee, in 1902 or 1903, Peetie Wheatstraw had moved to St. Louis toward the end of the 1920s. He lived across the Mississippi River in East St. Louis, Illinois. Blues singer and guitarist Henry Townsend remembered Wheatstraw. "He was mostly a guitar player in those days, and his piano playing was pretty underdeveloped," Townsend recalled. "In St. Louis there were so many piano players. It was really a piano town."[4] Singer-pianist Roosevelt Sykes set the standard. Townsend was not surprised that with this competition, Wheatstraw became an accomplished piano player.

In our interview in 1976, Booker talked about leaving St. Louis and working his way toward Chicago. "Yeah, I stayed [in St. Louis] for four years," he said. "And I left there, you know, and commenced to traveling around with different boys—me and Peetie Wheatstraw—all of us would sing, you know. And another guy named St. Louis Slim [James Oden, known as St. Louis Jimmy] . . . he'd put out that song 'Please Tell My Mother, Tell Her the Shape I'm In' ['Going Down Slow']." Apparently referring to Chicago, Booker said: "after I left St. Louis, then I got with some other boys about my age around there. Decided to hit the road, too. We left there and went to Cleveland. Left Cleveland and went to Saginaw, Michigan. Left Saginaw and went to Buffalo, New York—from Buffalo back to Chicago."[5]

He recalled playing blues in Buffalo and elsewhere on the road:

BOOKER WHITE: Why, you take in Buffalo, there's a guy there they called Black Smut [or Smoke]. He was a guitar player. He was about up in his . . . forty-five or fifty. And he just had a big flat there, and we stayed there in Buffalo, oh, about three or four months . . . He was booking us out to this place, you know, and he was a lot of help to us. We made him a smart of money, too. Money wasn't near like it is now, you see, back there. Take five dollars now, back there then take five dollars and buy as much as you would now with twenty dollars.

DAVID JOHNSON: What did they pay you?

WHITE: There was four of us, you see, and he'd give us twenty dollars. Sometimes ten dollars. It'd just depend on what kind of club or what they would be able to pay, you know. Cause they was paying at the door and everybody was paying to come in, you see . . . probably fifty cents. A dollar was the highest—two dollars a couple. Sometimes there'd be four or five hundred people there and we'd be up in the money.

JOHNSON: Did you stay long in any one place?

WHITE: Aw, we didn't . . . no, we stayed long if we was making something. If we couldn't make nothing, we'd move. We wasn't looking for no home. We just looking for the highway and the railroad. We wasn't studying about that.

JOHNSON: Did you enjoy life on the road?

WHITE: Oh, I was young then, I didn't care. I enjoyed it. We always kept money to buy what we'd want, you know. We went clean. We'd stay at a place that had a clothes laundry, you know. Intelligence and respect are two of the greatest things you can have about you. Then know how to 'spond behind them two things, you know. And people liked our music, you know, and when we got to Chicago then that's where I met

Lester Melrose. You might hear talk of him. He used to record all them guys around there.

JOHNSON: Lester Melrose?

WHITE: Yeah, Lester Melrose. I believe he did more recording . . . I don't know about Bluebird and Decca, but what he recorded, Bluebird and Decca, they must have been working together because that was on the label—Bluebird and Decca—at that time there. Bluebird and Decca were about the best ones going, that company was.

As an independent producer, Melrose produced records for RCA Bluebird, Decca, and Vocalion, which were three separate labels.

After Peetie Wheatstraw made his first recordings in Chicago on Wednesday, August 13, 1930, the Vocalion label publicized him as The Devil's Son-in-Law. By the end of 1932, he had recorded four more times in Chicago, and twice in New York. He did not record in 1933.[6] When Wheatstraw reentered the studio on March 25, 1934, he recorded six songs for Vocalion in Chicago.[7] His music was in demand. He returned to Chicago five months later for the first of what became four studio sessions, recording five songs for Decca on August 18 and 24; four songs for Vocalion on Friday, September 7; and one song for Decca on Thursday, September 11. The single song on September 11 rounded out the five he recorded for Decca on August 18 to provide enough material for three records.

The sessions of August 18–24 and September 7–11 are worth noting because they were Wheatstraw's longest visits to Chicago during 1934. He made another extended visit for recording sessions on July 17 and 20, 1935, recording six numbers on each date—the first six for Decca and the second six for Vocalion. The multi-day recording trips are important to Booker's history because when Booker traveled with Wheatstraw to Chicago, he appears to have spent some time in the city. If his recollection is accurate, he must have accompanied Wheatstraw on one of these three trips.

In the early to mid-1930s, Chicago was more than a recording hub for blues musicians. It was the urban crossroads. For a country blues performer such as Booker, Chicago was the Promised Land—a place where he could hang out with musicians who made their livings playing music and knew the ropes when it came to making records. Hurley and Evans wrote, "Bukka had been listening to stories about the great music in Chicago for years; finally he was to hear and be part of it. Within a short time he had made friends with the professional musicians on the South Side."[8] Among them were Big Bill Broonzy, Washboard Sam, pianist Memphis Slim, and guitarist Tampa Red, whose apartment had become the informal headquarters for this talented group.

Broonzy came from a background very similar to Booker's. He grew up in the community of Lake Dick, Arkansas, about fourteen miles northeast of the city of Pine Bluff.[9] With rural roots and country blues in common, Broonzy may have been the musician who called Booker to the attention of Lester Melrose, who in 1937 asked him to come to Chicago to make a record for Vocalion.

On September 2, Melrose recorded two of Booker's original songs, "Pinebluff Arkansas" and "Shake 'Em On Down." With the addition of a second guitar player (possibly Bill Broonzy) to Booker's driving guitar and intense vocal, "Shake 'Em On Down" appealed to enough record buyers in a dwindling Black audience for country blues to make the record a small hit. In 1964 Booker told blues enthusiast Alan Wilson that he was surprised when "Shake 'Em On Down" became the more popular side. He said "Pinebluff Arkansas" was "my key number that I figured would sell fast."[10] Booker mentioned that "Shake 'Em On Down" sold 1,600 copies, but Wilson—a student of country blues—believed sales were more like 16,000 copies. Whatever the number, the record sold well enough to make money for the record company and talent scout, which was the industry's measure of success.

Spending time in Chicago among a group of professional musicians had a lasting influence on Booker, but so did his home state. In Memphis looking back on his years in Mississippi, he grew nostalgic about the easy living and good money that seemed to be all around him when he played music in the Delta. In 1972 he told McKee and Chisenhall:

> I couldn't get the Delta out of my mind. There was more money in the Delta than was in Chicago to me. I know it was, 'cause I could make more. And I knowed more people down in the Delta, see. I didn't have to do no work lessen I wanted to work. I was just around there with them old musicians and we'd have a ball. Pick cotton some days, some days I didn't do anything. We'd just sit around at the house and have our white whiskey and frying fishes and just have a big time. Go to a frolic at night, we were going to ball all night long. Well, I like it that way.[11]

In the summer and fall of 1937, Booker faced more challenging circumstances than fish fries and frolics. He lived in a world where rough, sometimes violent confrontations among Black men were common—the more so for musicians, who played Saturday night house parties and the occasional roadhouse where heavy drinking was the rule and fights were inevitable. Whether real or imagined, a musician might be caught flirting with another man's woman, and carrying cash that he received from an event host or from tips. That was the situation Booker found himself in one day or night in Aberdeen. Whatever the mitigating circumstances might have been, he shot and killed a man.

For years, Booker responded to interviewers who asked about the incident with selective information and deliberate omission. Running through these accounts was the common thread that several men ganged up to do him harm, and he acted in self-defense. His interview with McKee and Chisenhall follows this narrative, with one exception. He told them that the "scrape" took place near Charleston, Mississippi, "as he waited one afternoon to catch a ride on a log truck to go to a dance":[12]

> He insisted he was threatened by a gang of men resentful of the fact that he was playing guitar and courting the women while they were working in the fields. At any rate, one man lay dead after the fracas and the judge sentenced Booker to Parchman. Booker boasted that his music made prison life easier for him. "The way they'd do us good musicians, we'd go from one camp to another playing. God knows, hear me say, I couldn't be treated no better."[13]

Most of this information is consistent with Booker's other accounts of the incident. The difference is the location. Charleston lies one hundred miles from Aberdeen in Tallahatchie County, and Booker was tried and found guilty in Monroe County.

This account was typical of how Booker described the incident, and how blues writers have framed the story. Booker bragged that he was popular with women wherever he went, while playing down the serious consequences of the behavior that gave him a reputation. Sometimes he carried a .38 pistol. When he mentioned the pistol to F. Jack Hurley, he said that he shot the man in the leg or "where I wanted to shoot him."[14] Most writers left the story at that, but in *The Story of the Blues*, blues scholar Paul Oliver wrote that Booker "drew a gun in a muddled fracas and killed a man."[15] Oliver added that Booker was spared hard labor in prison because he was a musician. Oliver continued, "When his release was secured by [record producer] Lester Melrose, he could think of hardly anything else but trains, drink, prison and death, the subjects of all his blues."

Hurley and Evans disagreed with Oliver. They wrote that "as recently as 1969, the noted British blues writer . . . wrote that Bukka killed a man 'in a muddled fracas' and was sentenced to a long prison term."[16] Arguing this and Oliver's next point, they continued:

> Oliver also states that that his release was obtained after two years by his music agent, Lester Melrose. None of this fits the facts as Bukka related them. Bukka did not kill a man. He shot a man, as he said, "where I wanted to shoot him." In Mississippi in those days such a scrape between two Blacks was common enough to elicit little reaction from the courts. Bukka was, in fact, sentenced to two years. He served his time and was duly released. It is true that he was under contract to Lester Melrose of Vocalion Recording Company and Melrose does seem to have secured one favor for him—Bukka was allowed to make a short trip to Chicago to do one recording session before his prison term began.

The recording date is certain. It was September 2, 1937.[17] But what was the date when Booker entered prison? Blues writer Gayle Dean Wardlow, who had been a reporter for two Mississippi newspapers, knew that he was likely to find more information about the incident in documents housed in the Monroe County Courthouse. In one volume of court records, he confirmed that in October 1937, a Monroe County grand jury was in session, hearing evidence in cases that were serious enough to come before the court.

The way the Mississippi circuit court system worked was that one judge presided over cases in several counties, making a circuit of county courthouses. A grand jury was called into session when a judge could be present. The murder charge against Washington White—Booker's legal name—was one such case. The grand jury indicted Booker and issued a warrant for his arrest. The case went to trial. The court document recorded the charge of murder and summarized the court's actions in the sparest terms: "10-26-37—Indictment returned, filed & copies issued Oct. term 1937. Sentenced to the balance of his life in the State Penitentiary."

An alphanumeric code referred to a separate volume containing information about the case, but Wardlow and the Monroe County Circuit Court clerk were unable to find it. Wardlow believed the indictment would "give the actual place of the slaying, the name of the victim, and the date it occurred."[18] From the documents he did find, he wrote that a jury convicted Washington White of murder on November 8, but was divided on what the sentence should be: "We the jury find the defendant guilty as charged but fail to agree on punishment."[19]

If he was given the chance to speak at his trial, Booker probably would have told the jury that he acted in self-defense—a claim that he made for the rest of his life. His testimony might have been similar to what he told Hurley:

> I was going to play at a park for a cousin of mine, Mark Davisson [perhaps Davidson]. And I just went to Aberdeen to get some strings, you know. And me and Wes Quinn was headed back to Houston to hitch a ride over to Davisson's, and them boys were layin' there for me. And they set out to start something. And there was this one boy who had it for me pretty bad. Well, I had a .38 Colt in there and I let it loose. And I just shot him where I wanted to shoot him. Broke his thigh. Them others was gone around the corner.[20]

If the jury was able to hear a version of this, some members may have softened their judgment. Others would not have. Since the jury could not decide on a sentence, there may have been an element of doubt. For whatever reason, sentencing was left to Judge Thomas Johnston. He gave Booker life and ordered a deputy sheriff to take him to the Mississippi State Penitentiary—the prison on the Delta known widely as Parchman Farm.[21] According to Wardlow's timeline, the shooting incident in Prairie took place after Booker recorded in Chicago on September 2, so stories about his jumping bail or being arrested while recording were unfounded. He was indicted on October 27, and sentenced on November 8. The interval between the recording session and the indictment was almost eight weeks—plenty of time for Booker to travel to Chicago, return to the Aberdeen area, spend time with his family and friends, and get into serious trouble.

Whatever the sequence of events, the effect of Booker's imprisonment on his family was that his wife Susie was left to raise two young children on her own. Willie Arthur had been born on January 1, 1935, in Prairie, and his sister Henrietta was born on January 12, 1938. Henrietta was less than nine months old when her father was sent to prison. The abrupt separation from his wife and children would affect Booker enough that he wrote one of his best-known songs about the experience, but his role as husband and father was effectively over. According to family members, he never fully returned to the marriage upon his release.

Either while in prison, in the months after his release, or in early March 1940 when he was under pressure to come up with new material, he wrote "Parchman Farm Blues." Along with "Feel Like I'm Fixin' To Die Blues," it became one of his most widely known numbers:

Judge give me life this mornin'
Down on Parchman Farm (2x)
I wouldn't hate it so bad
But I left my wife in mourn'

Oh, goodbye wife
All you have done gone (2x)
But I hope someday
You will hear my lonesome song

Coincidentally, Booker's stay in the Mississippi State Penitentiary overlapped that of Vernon Presley, father of Elvis Presley, who was sentenced to three years in Parchman on May 27, 1938, for altering and cashing a check. In his biography of Elvis, Peter Guralnick described the effect Vernon's imprisonment had on his family. "In fact, he remained in prison for only eight months, but this was a shaping event in the young family's life," Guralnick wrote. "In later years Elvis would often say of his father, 'My daddy may seem hard, but you don't know what he's been through,' and though it was never a secret, it was always a source of shame."[22] Booker's imprisonment had a similar effect both on him and those closest to him.

Chapter Ten

ON PARCHMAN FARM

THE MAIN BUILDINGS OF THE MISSISSIPPI PENAL FARM (NOW THE Mississippi State Penitentiary) were located near the community of Parchman, population 250, and the prison operated on a system designed to pay all operating costs by raising and selling agricultural products. The prison came to be known as Parchman Farm. It was vast—15,497 acres "planted in cotton, corn, and truck [vegetables], with cotton the leading crop."[1] In 1937, the year Booker entered Parchman, the prison population was 1,989. In 1938 a federally funded guidebook, *Mississippi: The Magnolia State*, boasted about Parchman Farm:

> A brick yard, a machine shop, a [cotton] gin, and a storage plant are operated by convict labor. The prison is self-supporting and operates at a profit when the price of cotton is good. The "fifth Sunday" of months that have more than four Sabbath days is a visitors' day, and it is then that Parchman is best seen. A train called the Midnight Special brings the visitors to the farm, arriving about dawn, and leaving at dusk. The Negro prisoners have made up ballads about the train, which they sing and chant while they work, waiting for the fifth Sunday.[2]

Even a young girl growing up in Memphis was aware of the prison's reputation. "Parchman was notorious," recalled Alyce Guthrie, whose father's company employed Booker from 1946 to around 1961. "It was in the news enough for me to know that it was a bad place."[3]

In 1933, the father and son team of John and Alan Lomax had embarked on their first song-collecting trip together.[4] The Depression was at its height. Now sixty-five, John Lomax had secured his reputation in the field of American folk songs, which began with collecting words and tunes of cowboy songs and evolved into looking for people who sang old folk songs so that he could record them for music archives of the Library of Congress. Alan was eighteen when he took his first field trip with his father. He had studied for two years at the University of Texas, transferring to the undergraduate Harvard College for a year in between, but from 1933 on "made it *my* job, too, to collect folk songs."[5] The Lomaxes began their trip in Texas in June with only a dictation machine for recording, but in July received a disc cutting machine—"the best portable machine on the market"—from the Library of Congress.[6]

Their visit to the Mississippi Penal Farm took place in August. After a long day on the road, the Lomaxes got their first look at Parchman Farm. John recalled the moment:

> Night fell before our journey ended. We had come to where in the darkness ahead we could see huge bright spots of light breaking through the Blackness. Afterward we found that each patch of light marked the home of two or three hundred convicts. A ring of white arc lights surrounded each group of buildings. The light burns the night through. Over across the Mississippi and further down in Louisiana, the convicts have a song beginning: "Angola, Angola, where the lights burn all night long."[7]

Together and separately, John and Alan Lomax were granted almost fifteen years of access to the penal farm and its prisoners. On their visit in 1933, they carried a letter of introduction from the governor of Texas addressed to the governor of Mississippi, Mark Sennet Warner. Upon arriving in the state capital of Jackson, the Lomaxes learned that Warner was not in the city. They waited a day, then convinced the governor's secretary that their mission was urgent. As he had done on other occasions, the secretary forged the governor's signature on a letter to the superintendent of the Mississippi Penal Farm, asking that the superintendent "allow us to hear the Negro convicts sing, and also asking for our entertainment."[8] On the night of their arrival, Superintendent Timm made up beds for the Lomaxes in his official residence.

Visitors to the Mississippi Penal Farm faced the inevitable question of just how bad conditions were for the prisoners. In *Adventures of a Ballad Hunter*, John Lomax recalled a conversation on the subject with Superintendent Timm. The conversation made clear how cordial their relationship was. Noticing "two broad, four-foot leather straps" hanging in the hall of Camp No. 1, where that day he and Alan recorded now-classic prison songs such as "Big Leg Rosie" and "Po' Lazus [Lazarus]," John engaged the superintendent in a conversation about the whips:

> It was difficult for me to believe that this soft-voiced, quiet-spoken, kind-faced man could use a lash on a human being. He had told me how four men would hold the offender face downward flat on the ground, one man to each hand or foot, while a man applied a strap to the bare back and buttocks.
>
> "The broad strap burns but does not cut the flesh," he explained. "We don't hurt the man so that he cannot at once go back to work. We need all our field hands."[9]

As the Lomaxes listened, Superintendent Timm explained that he resorted to the whip only after less brutal methods failed to change the behavior of unruly prisoners—especially white prisoners, according to the superintendent. If necessary, the "program" of whippings progressed through three days of escalating punishment.[10] "The practice may seem cruel," Timm said, "but it cures these white boys. I don't know of anything else that will. A Negro sometimes gets punished for repeatedly breaking prison rules, but the bad boys of the Black race present no such problem as the whites. One white convict gives more trouble than three Negroes."[11]

In his memoir of song collecting in the South, *The Land Where Blues Began*, Alan Lomax recalled in detail a conversation he had with two former inmates about punishment meted out in the penal farm:

> When we first visited Parchman [in 1933], the state approved instrument of discipline was a broad strip of leather about four feet long and a quarter of an inch thick with holes punched in the last foot so that it would draw blisters from the bare flesh with each blow and break them with the next. The monstrous contrivance was called "the bat," and Joe Savage and Walter Brown remembered it from their time in Parchman.[12]
>
> JOE SAVAGE: They whupped us with big wide straps. They didn't whup no clothes. They whipped your naked butt. And they had two men to hold you.
>
> WALTER BROWN: Four!
>
> SAVAGE: As many as they need.
>
> BROWN: I walked through the hall, comin' out of the kitchen, and looked at it. They had one down and four holdin' him.
>
> ALAN LOMAX: Did they ever injure anybody that way?
>
> SAVAGE: Wooo!

BROWN: Yeah!
SAVAGE: Kill 'um! Kill 'um!
BROWN: They'd kill 'um like that.

"Indeed," Alan Lomax continued, "the state prisons of the South in many ways resembled Nazi concentration camps, both in the way they treated blacks and in their intimidating effect on the black community. . . . Conditions in these state pens perpetuated the worst aspects of plantation slavery and of the 'free penitentiaries'—the levee and forced-labor camps."[13]

In August 1933, the Lomaxes sat with Superintendent Timm outside Camp Number One. On a night years before, when it was too hot to sleep, the superintendent remembered hearing a song:

> Down below where the men were, I heard one convict singing, and for some reason I listened. A fellow gets so used to the men hollering and singing out in the fields that after a while you don't pay them any mind. . . . One of these goddam niggers can be funny when he takes a notion, and this one certainly was singing a funny song. It was something about a man getting ninety-nine years for killing his wife.[14]

Sensing an undiscovered song, the Lomaxes asked the superintendent if he would sing it. He declined, but sent a trusty with a shotgun into the Camp One dormitory to find someone who knew the song. The trusty returned pushing a prisoner with the barrel of his gun. Alan Lomax wrote, "The poor fellow, evidently afraid he was to be punished, was trembling and sweaty with fear. The guard shoved him up before our microphone." The man asked for time to remember the song. Superintendent Timm responded, "Hell, you're going to sing it right now. Turn on your machine, young fellow."

In "Worse than Slavery": Parchman Farm and the Ordeal of Jim Crow Justice, social historian David M. Oshinsky wrote:

> Black Mississippians shot, stabbed, bludgeoned, and killed one another with monotonous ease. In an average year between 1900 and 1930, close to five hundred murders were reported in the state, making Mississippi a leader in white homicides (around 9 per 100,000),[15] Black homicides (33 per 100,000), and total homicides (25 per 100,000). The real figures were probably higher; Black murders did not arouse much attention and inquests were rare.

Oshinsky's last point—that the white population paid little attention to the killings of Black people, and law enforcement and the courts gave little time or attention to investigating such murders and sentencing the accused—helps to explain the sequence of events that changed Booker's life in the fall of 1937.

The treatment of the prisoners was, as Oshinsky quotes in his book, "worse than slavery." Located on remote land, the prison farm had no fences. Prisoners could not make a run for it because at least one trusty with a rifle watched over each work group; or two trusties would stand watch, one who would fire first at an escaping prisoner with a shotgun, and a second who would shoot to kill with a rifle if a prisoner continued to flee. The prisoners returned from the cotton fields to low barracks, where they passed the monotonous nights sleeping, complaining, swapping stories, and sometimes singing and listening to music made by fellow inmates. On his first visit to Parchman, John Lomax reported that one Sunday a month, a train carrying special visitors and others would arrive at the penitentiary:[16]

> On these days, the convicts are turned loose inside the high stockades provided at each camp, where they receive visitors. Numerous one-room shacks stand around inside the prison fences, where privacy may be had by any couple. The men work more contentedly and cheerfully and are more easily controlled, I was told, when they can be with their women once a month. Texas and Louisiana have similar rules. I found no instance of such liberty being allowed to white convicts.[17]

The prisoners were allowed conjugal visits with wives, girlfriends, and prostitutes from the Parchman area. The train visitations made it possible to have female companionship while in prison, even for brief visits. Booker benefited from this policy. He told McKee and Chisenhall, "My girlfriend Pearline, she'd come to see me in Parchman, And the clothes she wore, they would shine just like the Prodigal Son."[18]

Years later, as two young blues enthusiasts were taping Booker in Cambridge, Massachusetts, one asked about his time in prison. "Bukka, do you mind if I ask you a question about Parchman? Would you tell me a little about it?"

"Not if you go too deep in," Booker replied.

"Only as deep as you want to go."

Booker told the tapers there were all kinds of people in the penal farm. "They're not as bad as people think they are. Because if [the crime] was too bad, they wouldn't get there. They'd be hanged."[19]

Despite the isolated surroundings and authoritarian routine of life on a prison farm, oral history and a notebook shed some light on Booker White's time in the Mississippi Penal Farm. The notebook contains the detailed account of two song collectors for the Library of Congress. Booker is the only source of oral history of his time at Parchman. His recollections as told later almost exclusively to white interviewers emphasize his privileged status among the inmate population. Based on interviews and the fact of Booker's release from the penal farm after serving two years of a life sentence, most blues writers conclude that Booker received better treatment than most prisoners because he was a musician. Hurley and Evans write:

> This is not to imply in any way that he enjoyed the prison experience, for he emphatically did not. On the other hand, he was not brutalized and did learn from it. When asked what he did while at Parchman, Bukka grinned and said "Well, mostly I played guitar." It seems that word of his arrival at the farm got out in advance and the inmates and guards pooled their money to buy a guitar and even formed a band. The camp director realized that Bukka's music could be used to boost morale and encouraged Bukka's playing.[20]

These rose-colored memories must be tempered by a caution that this grandson of a former slave tended to give white interviewers answers that he thought would please them. Still, he stood up to the Lomaxes in a remarkable way for an imprisoned Black man in Mississippi. Booker's determination to be treated as he thought he should be treated became a consistent theme in his life.

In 1939 John Lomax and his second wife, Ruby Terrill Lomax, made Parchman the seventeenth stop on their official Library of Congress "Southern Recording Trip." The trip began March 31 and ended June 14. John's son Alan, who helped his father with recording on the series of trips that began in 1933, had been appointed the Assistant in Charge of the Archive of Folk Song of the Library of Congress and remained in Washington. Along the way, Ruby Terrill Lomax typed out more than three hundred pages of notes on the Southern Recording Trip. She and John stayed at Parchman for May 23 and 24, visiting two of the fifteen "camps" that had been built at distances from each other to help maintain prison security. Booker White was in Camp 10. "We could not see the Superintendent when we first arrived, but his assistant gave permission for us to visit Camp #10," Ruby wrote. She noted the lack of cooperation that she and her husband encountered:

> Rain had set in and the boys could not work. We set up the machine in the wide hall of the barracks, that separates the white dormitory from the Negroes. (A high barbed wire fence surrounds the barracks.) Singers were not plentiful or enthusiastic, but we recorded a few tunes before the rain subsided enough for the boys to chop wood and do other light jobs around the barracks. In the evening we tried again with fair results. We discovered that one barrier was the idea that we were there to make money out of the boys without "divvying-up." This they were told by one of the boys who had made some commercial records. After Mr. Lomax made it clear to them the purpose of the recording and the use to which their songs would serve, they were more generous, and helpful. The next day, Sunday, after lunch we visited Camp #10.[21]

The "boy" who had made records was Washington White.

Washington recorded two songs for the Lomaxes that day. Having served time since November 1937, he had been in prison long enough to have been given a nickname, Barrel House. The entry in the Lomaxes' field notes explains why: "Po' Boy and Sick 'em dogs on [*sic*] were sung and played by Washington (Barrel House) White, with guitar. Barrel Houses were his hangout in the 'free world.' Barrel House has made some commercial records." The song "Po' Boy" was of little interest to the Lomaxes because they already were aware of it. "Po' Boy" was an old song popular among African American songsters. As Barrel House White sang it, "Sic 'Em Dogs On" was a hybrid of traditional and original blues that also was of little interest to the song collectors. They were not looking for material other than songs and hollers that would fall under the heading of folklore.

There is no indication in the notes that the Lomaxes treated the "boy who had made some commercial records" differently than other prisoners who were recorded. Booker simply refused to perform more than two songs because he was accustomed to being paid for his music. The field notes appear to be the original source of the story. No doubt John Lomax was hoping for more from an accomplished musician who knew many songs. Toward the end of Booker's recording of "Sic 'Em Dogs On," the song collector's voice can be heard off-mike instructing Booker to keep singing.

Not only did Booker stand his ground with privileged guests from Washington, he also let his fellow inmates know that white men in the outside world would pay Black singers for their songs. Coming from a musician who had made a record shortly before he entered prison, his opinion carried weight in Camp 10. By sharing what he knew to be the case in the outside world, he subverted the willingness of his fellow prisoners to meet the expectations of the visiting white collectors. In *Nobody Knows Where the Blues Comes From*, Freeland and Smith took a closer look at Booker's resistance:

> . . . for Black musicians under Jim Crow, performing to white audiences was primarily a matter of economics, with self-expression incidental. (Self-expression is not excluded, of course, as the two songs which Bukka White eventually sang for the Lomaxes confirm. However, White's initial reaction to the Lomaxes' presumed commercial motives confirms the primacy of economic aspects. In the context of Jim Crow, such an explicitly hostile and obstructive response is both unusual and an illumination of White's character and attitudes).[22]

Others who encountered Booker during his lifetime noticed that he had a self-confidence unusual among the older blues musicians who had second careers in the 1960s and 1970s. In *The Legacy of the Blues*, Samuel Charters titled his chapter on Booker "An Inner Sense of Self—Bukka White."[23] In the profile's first paragraph, Charters writes with fervor on the subject of what makes a "bluesman":

> To define it as someone who sings the blues is too narrow. It's true, but it only defines one dimension, one aspect of the blues. To define it as someone who responds to his life, to his environment, in terms of the artistic language known as the blues comes closer to it. Closer—and at the same time suggests some of the music's larger dimensions. One of the most important aspects of

> the blues is the act of self-definition, and it's this that gives the blues its validity as language—as the language of Black culture in America.[24]

The portrait of Booker that emerges in the chapter embodies the qualities that Charters defines.

Another person who commented on Booker's sense of self was Los Angeles club owner and concert producer Ed Pearl. Booker performed several times at Pearl's club, the Ash Grove. "He was a pretty straight guy," Pearl recalled.[25] "At some point he must have been popular, or in his [own] mind popular . . . because he assumed everyone knew who he was. He spoke to the audience and told them he knew they would copy him. . . . I really got a kick out of this very proud man whose spirit had not been broken."

Chapter Eleven

BOOKER IN MEMPHIS

IN 1939 BOOKER WAS RELEASED FROM THE MISSISSIPPI PENAL FARM into what soon would become an expanding economy. After ten years of the Great Depression, the economy continued to stagger, with an unemployment rate in 1940 of 14.6 percent. But on Sunday morning, December 7, 1941, Japan's surprise attack on Navy ships anchored at Pearl Harbor and Army aircraft parked on Hickam Field in Hawaii brought the United States into the war.

The magnitude of the war effort pulled the country out of the Depression, and in 1944, the unemployment rate reached an historic low of 1.2 percent, and remained under 2 percent in 1945. The economic engine of the war machine not only restored employment opportunities that disappeared during the Depression, but created thousands of new ones. For someone looking for work, 1944 and 1945 may have been the best years ever to find a job. Booker White was among the unemployed who benefited from economic growth.

Booker's name does not appear in the Memphis City Directory until 1943, but two documents from the war years establish that he was in the city before that. On October 16, 1940, a young man from Aberdeen registered in Memphis for the draft.[1] Willie Simpson was 22. He may have been a relative of Booker's wife Susie Simpson, whom Booker had left. Hurley and Evans wrote, "His marriage to Susie did not exactly end, it just 'ran out' as his travels took him farther and farther away for increasingly long periods of time."[2]

When Booker registered for the draft in Memphis on February 16, 1942, he named Willie Simpson as his contact. A search for Booker in the 1940 United States census did not turn up his name, leaving the draft cards as the only clues to his whereabouts around this time.

In 1942, Simpson lived at 2450 Spottswood Avenue. When Booker registered, he gave his address as 2603 Spottswood Avenue. The two men were neighbors in the historically Black section of Memphis named

Orange Mound. The proximity of the addresses documents that if Willie Simpson moved to Memphis from Mississippi in 1940 or earlier, Booker would have had a place to stay with a friend or relative less than 500 feet from where he would live in 1942. Booker would have been able to stay in Memphis before he moved to the city.

On the day Booker registered, he gave his age as thirty-eight, and said he was born on November 12, 1903. On November 11, 1942, Congress lowered the draft age from twenty-one to eighteen and raised the upper limit from thirty-five to thirty-seven. The birth date Booker claimed put him over the draft age by a year. This appears to be the outcome he intended. The Selective Service System and racism in the armed forces were causing serious problems for Black men who were drafted. The four service branches—Army, Navy, Marines, and Coast Guard—resisted inducting Black men, but the Selective Service's quota system required 10.6 percent of men selected to be Black. The result was that draft-eligible Black men received selection notices, but often were not inducted.

Historian George Q. Flynn explained the men's dilemma: "Many Blacks, upon receiving their selection notice, would either lose their job or quit. They would then have to sit around in limbo until the armed forces found a place for them. During the early years of this war this became a chronic problem."[3]

At the time of their registrations, Booker and Willie Simpson both worked as laborers in the construction business. Simpson was employed by the Jack Webb Construction Company at 1715 Union Avenue, Memphis. Booker worked for the Fischer Lime and Cement Company on Pontotoc Street.[4] Around 1945, Booker found a job that supported him until the early 1960s. As a man who had served time in a state prison, he must have been relieved when he was hired by an established company. There were no background checks.[5] For the first time in his life, he could provide for his future. "I quit playing," he told writers Margaret McKee and Fred Chisenhall in 1972. "I got tired of playing and got a job at a place where they made truck tanks. I wanted to work so I can get me up a lot of Social Security, you know."[6]

The 1946 city directory listed Booker's occupation as a welder's helper for the Newberry Equipment Company, located at 683 Linden Avenue in Memphis, only blocks from the Mississippi River. The company president was James M. "Jimmy" Newberry. After serving in the United States Navy during World War II, Newberry returned to Memphis to take over the company from his father, John, who founded Newberry Equipment in 1927. "In that era, you were able to pull yourself up by your bootstraps," recalled Jimmy Newberry's daughter, Alyce Guthrie. During the war, Jimmy had been a boatswain's mate aboard a PT (short for patrol torpedo) boat in the Pacific. Life aboard an eighty-foot vessel that hunted much larger ships was dangerous. In 1943, Lieutenant John F. Kennedy became a war hero after Japanese destroyer *Amagiri* crushed PT 109 in the Solomon Islands. Kennedy and his crew swam to a shore and were rescued. The future president was awarded the Navy and Marine Corps Medal and a Purple Heart.

While Kennedy was a wealthy graduate of Harvard College, Newberry was a plain-spoken enlisted man born to tenant farmers near Finch, Arkansas.[7] Both were leaders. In Newberry's obituary, Howard Upton would write: "His formal education was limited; his personal style . . . was one of restrained gruffness. In meetings, he did not rely on charm or subterfuge to get his points across. Instead, he was direct, open, forceful."[8] Newberry brought the same leadership qualities to the Petroleum Equipment Institute—the national association that he and four other businessmen established in 1951 to advocate for their industry.[9]

After the Navy, his immediate task was to keep the family business above water. When he took over, Newberry Equipment supplied pumps, hoses, and tanks to his father's regular customers in western Tennessee and eastern Arkansas. Business was steady, but the postwar economy was growing. Newberry decided to change the company from an equipment vendor to a manufacturer of underground and truck-mounted storage tanks. The underground tanks stored petroleum at gas stations, and the truck tanks transported fuel at airports and sprayed water on race tracks.

As a Navy veteran and company president, Jimmy Newberry was well-respected in Memphis. Ellen Rogers was his secretary from 1973 until 1978, when he sold the business to an Ohio company. When Mrs. Rogers worked for Newberry toward the end of his career, he was focused less on the business and "had tunnel vision for PT boats and didn't deviate from it very much," she said.[10] His dream was to establish a PT boat museum near Memphis on Mud Island, but poor health forced him to give up his dream.

Around 1951, Newberry moved the company to East City Limits in West Memphis, across the Mississippi River in Arkansas. According to Ellen Rogers and current Newberry owner Chris Long, the company averaged between thirty to forty employees.[11] They were divided into welders and welder's helpers in one department, and the workers who finished the products in the company yard.

In the late 1940s, most of the skilled employees (or tradesmen, as they were called) were welders. His helper set out the sheet metal tank parts in the correct configuration so that the individual parts were ready for a tradesman to weld them together. The company term for this work was *fit-up*, so the helper was called a fit-up man. The work was dangerous. Newberry's daughter Alyce remembered that the sheet metal parts had sharp edges. "Someone could lose a hand," she said.[12]

Booker became good at his job. With a sturdy build and fast hands, he was both strong and coordinated. He earned about $2.10 an hour. "After he stayed there a while, he probably moved up a step or two," Ellen Rogers said. Booker's cousin Riley King worked at Newberry Equipment for a few months. In his biography, B. B. King recalled that white workers belonged to a union that Black men could not join.[13] According to Leola Morris, Booker's partner for many years, he worked at Newberry Equipment for fifteen years, leaving when he was given the opportunity to play music again.[14]

Chapter Twelve

COUSIN RILEY

WHILE BOOKER WAS MAKING A NEW LIFE FOR HIMSELF IN MEMPHIS, his cousin Riley, who would become famous as B. B. King, was driving a tractor on a farm near Indianola, just as his father Albert had done. After Albert married a woman named Nora Ella, the couple became sharecroppers near Itta Bena.[1] Nora Ella gave birth to Riley on September 20, 1925. When Riley was four, Nora Ella became involved with another man and moved back to her family in the small community of Kilmichael, Mississippi, just fifty miles from the farm where Booker grew up in Chickasaw County. Nora Ella and Riley lived with her mother, Elnora Farr, who was the sister of Booker's mother, Lula Davidson White.[2]

The 1930 census recorded Elnora Farr living on a farm on the road from Sparta to Houston in Chickasaw County. At forty, she was a widow. Riley lived with her from 1931 to 1935.[3] When his mother died in the summer of 1935, Riley's father Albert came to Chickasaw County to see about his son living with him. Riley stayed with his grandmother. They led the impoverished lives of Black Mississippi laborers, yet found community and a way to express their faith in the fundamentalist teachings and emotional music of their religion.

In 1988, B. B. King recalled for *Living Blues* magazine that a sanctified preacher who was connected to the family by marriage played an important role in his development as a musician:

> The preacher's name was Archie Fair. Of course, he was the one I think that really wanted me to play in the church because he was the preacher and he played guitar. By my uncle being his brother-in-law, he used to come over to our house, or to my uncle's house, on Sunday afternoon for dinner after services. He had a habit of laying his guitar on the bed. I would hop up there and start to fool with it 'til the day he caught me. He didn't scold me. He showed me two or three chords on it that I still remember today.[4]

B. B. recalled another influence: 78 rpm records by blues musicians Blind Lemon Jefferson and Lonnie Johnson, and jazz guitarist Charlie Christian. Later influences were his cousin Booker, and records by French gypsy guitarist Django Reinhardt and singer-guitarist T-Bone Walker, who is credited with popularizing electric guitar in blues.

As a young boy, Riley got to know Booker because his older cousin would visit the family. "In fact, I used to watch Booker," B. B. recalled.[5] "I'd stand up by his knee and watch him. And he had one of those slides. Just something about the way he played then made me want to do what I'm doin' today." B. B. was drawn to his cousin's personality. "Booker was the only one of us that ever went into show business," he said. "While I was just a kid, I always did like him. He'd keep us laughing all the time. I was crazy about him."

To Booker, "one of those slides" was an essential part of his guitar style. From the mid-1930s onward, he favored a National steel guitar. He recalled acquiring his first National in St. Louis around 1934, swapping his wooden guitar for a 1933 model that sold for $32.50 when new.

In 1929 or 1930, when Nora Ella went back to her family in Kilmichael, young Riley was introduced to the same powerful figure in the Davidson family who twenty years earlier had taken his grandson Washington to the Saturday market at Courthouse Square in Houston. Pompey Davidson was Riley's maternal great-grandfather. Riley's grandmother and Bukka's mother were sisters. From Booker and B. B.'s different experiences with Pomp, it seems that the grandfather who gave his grandson a penny to buy peanuts at the market had become a volatile old man who was feared. Charles Sawyer, whose book *The Arrival of B. B. King* (1980) was the first biography of the musician, wrote this description of Pomp:

> By the time Riley was old enough to remember him, Pomp was a gruff old man who rode a mule and carried a jug of homemade liquor in one hand and a shotgun in the other. He was known to be prone to violence, a reputation that had its advantages. His landlord had the same reputation. "Mr. So-and-So [presumably Willie Harrington] and that nigger of his are just alike," people said of them. "They're both crazy. Don't mess with them 'cause you could get yourself killed." Pomp Davidson's reputation as a volatile person may have been well deserved, but it also served as a defense mechanism in a social order where there was no recourse to the law.[6]

Sawyer admits that he filtered B. B.'s memories through his own lens. He wanted to make a point: "I admit I have an ax to grind: in telling B. B.'s story, I want to celebrate the death of Jim Crow, the mythic personification of racist segregation, the cancer afflicting the American soul on both sides of the Mason-Dixon Line."[7] Whatever the author's bias, the first biography of B. B. makes clear that Pomp Davidson made a lasting impression on young Riley King just as he did on Booker White.

In 1943, when Riley was seventeen or eighteen, he moved to the community of Indianola in the Delta. Though he was married, and his job as a tractor driver on Johnson Barrett's 1,000-acre farm was a good one,[8] he was bored. "For the first time, the routine was getting to me," he wrote (or told biographer David Ritz) in his autobiography, *Blues All Around Me*.[9] He and his wife Martha rented a house in Indianola, but that did not ease Riley's restlessness. He was discovering that his most powerful ambition was to become a musician. In the Delta there were frolics and juke joints where men played music and people danced; but Indianola offered few opportunities to make a living. In addition to performing with a quartet that called itself the Saint John's Gospel Singers,[10] Riley began busking on the streets of Indianola and neighboring towns. Busking is the time-honored practice of playing music for donations on the street or places where people would pass, such as markets and train stations. The Texas singer and songwriter Blind Lemon Jefferson scraped out a living as a busker before he began to make records; the difference was that Riley had a family to support. Early in their marriage, Martha became pregnant more than once, but suffered miscarriages.[11]

Even after the upheaval of World War II, with young men going to war and women entering the work force in great numbers, not much changed in the expectations on a young couple in Mississippi. The woman was expected to bear children and work, and the man was expected to support his family. These roles put stress on Riley and Martha. Riley often was distracted, daydreaming about women and music as he was working. The day arrived when he became so careless on the job that he got off the tractor before making sure that the engine had stopped firing. The tractor jerked in its small shed and knocked off the smokestack above the engine. Replacing a smokestack was expensive, bound to bring landowner Barrett Johnson's anger down on Riley's head. Riley panicked and left town as soon as possible. Carrying his guitar and two dollars and fifty cents, he went out to Highway 49 to hitch a ride to Memphis. He believed that his father might live there.

A truck driver hauling flour to Memphis picked him up. They arrived around 3:30 a.m. The driver dropped off Riley at Union Station. "I started to look around . . . and I found where my cousin Booker White lived," B. B. recalled. "I went over to his house."

In the Delta, Riley had heard that Memphis was "the place where big-time bluesmen performed" and its famous Beale Street was the center of Black life there.[12] The city lived up to his expectations:

> That was the very first time I went to Memphis. And Memphis to me was as large as I ever saw. I was really like a kid in a candy store. I started lookin' at the big buildings and seein' how the people lived there. I saw streetcars for the first time. I had a chance to get up close to trains. Many of 'em that I had never seen like that before. We had one that came through Indianola—it was called the Southern—but we could only see maybe one engine. But when I got to Memphis I saw all of these big locomotives and boy, these were very long trains and people ridin on 'em. And all of this was new to me.[13]

The season was summer. Memphis bustled with commercial activity, and abounded in women who "seemed half-undressed in their frilly dresses and revealing blouses."[14] He wrote, "I figured if I found Beale Street, I'd find Cousin Bukka."[15]

The music led him to Handy Park, named for W. C. Handy, the composer of "St. Louis Blues." When B. B. came upon the park, it was "just an open green space where musicians congregated."[16] He stopped long enough to play guitar with the local musicians. "The cats could play rings around me," he recalled. Someone told him that his cousin lived on Mosby Avenue in the Orange Mount section of Memphis. Arriving in front of the shotgun house at 2605 Mosby Avenue, Riley stepped onto the porch and knocked. No one was home. Booker was playing music at a party and came home to find his cousin asleep on the curb.

The two men talked until dawn. Riley thought he would play blues with his cousin in the morning, but Booker needed to go to work.[17] On that first day, Booker not only gave Riley a place to live, but got him a job. He took Riley with him to Newberry Equipment, where his cousin was hired. As B. B. later told a *Living Blues* interviewer, ". . . when I found my cousin Booker White . . . then everything was really all right."

Booker's daughter Irene Kertchaval recalled that the house on Spottswood Avenue was a two-bedroom shotgun.[18] The term "shotgun house" came from the notion that if the front and back doors were open, a person could fire a shotgun through the front and the buckshot would go out the back.

B. B. recalled living in these spare surroundings for six weeks. At Newberry, some of his co-workers taught the new arrival how to weld.[19] "I liked welding and adjusted pretty quick to life in a plant," B. B. recalled.[20] "Turned out to be a good job around $60 a week." Once his cousin was employed, Booker charged him three dollars a week for bed and board.[21] Booker told McKee and Chisenhall that his cousin "was eating the very best food 'cause I likes to eat."[22] Riley took a second job at the McCallum and Roberts textile mill as a machine operator on the midnight shift, but gave it up after five or six weeks. He stayed in Memphis for eight months before taking a bus to Indianola to rejoin Martha and pay Barrett Johnson for the damage to the tractor.[23] Despite B. B.'s later statements to his daughter Shirley that he did not learn anything about guitar playing from Booker White, he spent time with his cousin and went to parties where Booker played for tips.

B. B. devotes two paragraphs of his autobiography to time spent observing his older cousin making music:

> Like a little puppy, I'd follow him to parties and watch him play his blues. He'd earn maybe $20 a night and show everyone a good time. I'd see him take that bottleneck, slip it on his fat finger, and slide that sucker over the strings, making a haunting sound. Sometimes he'd get slick and use a pipe, and sometimes when he wasn't looking I'd give it another try, but it was no use. I wasn't born to be a slide guitarist.[24]

In his autobiography, B. B. gave more credit to Booker as a musical influence than he did in interviews:

> I could see that Bukka was born to be a bluesman, and I wondered if the same was true of me. . . . I felt something beautiful inside Bukka's soul. . . . I was moved by his sincerity. He loved telling stories, simple stories, and used his blues to tell them. His blues was the book of his life. He sang about his rough times and fast times and loving times and angry times. He'd entertain

> at a party for two hundred people with the same enthusiasm as a party for twenty. Bukka gave it his all. His music had a consistency I admired. Like all the great bluesmen, he said, *I am what I am*. I wondered if I could be that steady and strong.[25]

B. B.'s recollection is one of the very few eyewitness accounts of Booker performing before his return to music in 1963. The recollection confirms that Booker's energetic style of entertaining made an impression on his younger cousin. In his autobiography, B. B. made the distinction that he did not borrow any elements from Booker's guitar style. However, in our brief interview in 1976, Booker claimed to have had a direct influence on B. B.'s guitar playing. In Booker's view, when young Riley was not able to imitate Booker's slide guitar style (as Riley said he tried to do "when [Booker] wasn't looking"), Riley found a way to create a vibrato effect on the guitar strings. The fingers of his left hand alternately stretched and relaxed the tension on the strings along the guitar's fretted neck.

While other accomplished blues guitarists such as T-Bone Walker (whom B. B. acknowledged as an influence) and Albert King (who influenced Eric Clapton) bent the strings to create the "crying" notes found in electric blues, B. B.'s guitar playing became known for this use of vibrato that was similar to the vibrato of a singer's voice. B. B. wanted to play the guitar as if the instrument were singing. A blues guitar style contains many influences, but over the course of his remarkable career, B. B. combined emotional vocals with the vibrato of his guitar to create his characteristic sound—in his mid-career hit "The Thrill Is Gone," for example.

Another example of Booker's influence on B. B. is the older cousin's commitment to putting on a good show. B. B. said that Booker put the same effort into entertaining people regardless of the size of the audience. This commitment is consistent with B. B. King's performances at a variety of venues. I first saw B. B. King at the Boston Tea Party in 1968. With his red Gibson guitar shining in the lights, B. B. jumped into "Every Day I Have the Blues"—his signature number at the time—and performed for about forty-five minutes. The show was a carefully planned set that began with a warm-up and ended with an encore. In 1998, thirty years on the road and managing his diabetes had aged B. B. After standing for his first number at Penn State's Center for the Arts to show the audience a familiar pose, he played the rest of the show seated. Much like his older cousin had done, he told his audience stories.

Chapter Thirteen

CHICAGO 1940

IN THE FIRST WEEK MARCH 1940, BOOKER TOOK A TRAIN FROM MEMphis to Chicago.[1] Lester Melrose wanted him to record again. The winter was giving way to spring in the city, but grudgingly. When First Lady Eleanor Roosevelt arrived the following week to address the Chicago Civil Liberties Committee on the threat to civil liberties posed by the prospect of war, she remarked on the weather in her daily newspaper column, "My Day." She wrote, "When we awakened in Chicago this morning, we discovered that Illinois had a sleet storm during the night. Trees and shrubs and winter grasses in the field are encased in ice. It is very beautiful to look at, but not so pleasant when you have to drive about."[2]

Upon his own arrival, Booker made his way to the city's South Side—the common destination for Black musicians who left the Deep South to escape Jim Crow laws and find work. Big Bill Broonzy and Tampa Red lived on the South Side. Their houses served as welcome centers for new arrivals. The blues were in transition. Chicago record store owner Bob Koester, founder of Delmark Records, described the city's blues scene in the 1930s and early 1940s as "an important period of amalgamation of rural blues and jazz influences into modern Chicago style. . . ."[3] Koester believed that "the blues of this middle period not only gave birth to the subsequent modern style but had a distinctive style of its own . . . [that] might not have existed outside the recording studio."[4]

Booker had a distinctive country blues style that Melrose wanted him to keep. Booker recalled, "I got there and showed Melrose all my songs I had writ out, and he got out a book and showed me who had put them out."[5] Melrose told Booker that he if he recorded those songs, he would be sued. So Melrose gave Booker money for a hotel room, a meal ticket, and told him he had two days to come up with his own songs. Booker "got down to it" and returned with twelve original songs. Melrose was delighted.[6] He recorded enough material to provide the Vocalion and OKeh labels with three 78 rpm records each. The sessions took place on Thursday and Friday, March 7 and 8, in a small studio that Melrose maintained on the city's South Side.[7] An assistant later recalled that in 1946, Melrose used a studio above a pawn shop on South State Street.[8]

Under pressure to produce original songs, Booker wrote several that blues writers consider among the finest ever recorded. One explanation for this burst of creativity is that Booker drew on the feelings of shame and powerlessness that he had experienced during his arrest, trial, and incarceration in the Mississippi Penal Farm. However, blues scholar David Evans, in his study of songwriting processes among Black folk blues singers in the South, *Big Road Blues,* cautions against a single explanation: "Much misunderstanding has arisen over the question of whether or not blues texts are 'autobiographical.' Obviously they are not . . . if one means an actual life history (or even episodes in a life history) told by the singer. . . . Yet there is much evidence that many blues are composed as the result of personal experiences and do reflect the feelings of the singer or composer about these experiences."[9] Most of Booker's 1940 lyrics appear to have arisen from his own experiences and emotions. His rough singing is well suited to expressing raw emotion. Accompanied by Booker's propulsive guitar rhythms, the lyrics express his pain ("District Attorney Blues"), and grief ("Strange Place Blues" and "High Fever Blues"). "Fixin' To Die Blues" opens with a dreamlike image of the singer witnessing his own burial—an added dimension that elevates the lyric's foreshadowing of the singer's death to poetic art.

In *The Listener's Guide to the Blues,* writer Peter Guralnick praised Booker's 1940 recordings:

> White . . . put together one of the most emotionally compelling and moving autobiographical bodies of work, in many ways similar to that of Robert Johnson in its consciously thought-out lyrics, vocal intensity, and taut interplay between voice and guitar. As with Johnson, there is a poetic sensibility at work. . . .[10]

For Booker's best music, Guralnick directed listeners to the Columbia Records compilation *Parchman Farm,* released in 1969:

> A fascinating poetic and autobiographical document, this album shares with the work of Robert Johnson (and that of few others) the distinction of aspiring to high art. Songs like "Parchman Farm Blues," "Fixin' To Die," "Strange Place," and the existential "Sleepy Man Blues" . . . are unparalleled in the history of the

> blues. Other songs add further details of White's life and incarceration in Parchman Farm, a state prison. Unquestionably, one of the pinnacles of recorded blues.[11]

Considering the songs as a single body of work, as they are presented on *Parchman Farm*, British blues writer Simon Napier wrote in the liner notes that the twelve songs constitute "a completely unique and astonishing collection of blues."

As with other forms of art, Booker's blues were created by an artist responding to his environment. Three songs related to Booker's trial and imprisonment. In "District Attorney Blues," he sang about the power of the district attorney:

District attorney sho' is hard on a man
He taken me from my woman
Cause her to love some other man . . .
He will take a woman's man and leave her cold in hand.

Booker wrote "When Can I Change My Clothes" in response to the humiliation he felt at being ordered to take off his everyday clothing and put on the striped uniform of a convict. Hurley and Evans wrote that "When Can I Change My Clothes" was one of Booker's strongest songs: "Critics have universally regarded it as one of the best of all of Bukka's blues. . . . The musical pattern was familiar; in fact, it was almost identical to Bukka's earlier hit 'Shake 'Em On Down,' but the words cut much deeper and the images were much finer":[12]

So many days when the day would be cold
You can stand and look at these convict toes
I wonder how long
Before I can change my clothes?

IN 1976, BOOKER TOLD ME THAT A GOOD SONG NEEDED TO KEEP TO its subject. In this way, Booker's 1940 songs differed from the work of many blues songwriters who wrote songs by stringing together verses that already existed in the vast sea of uncredited blues lyrics.[13] Though the music to some of Booker's songs may sound similar, and the repeated lines of his lyrics may sound repetitious, the words are original and the sound is his own.

In his recollection of leaving St. Louis to go on the road, Booker quoted lyrics from another blues singer's song that he admired, "Going Down Slow" by James Oden. Oden recorded "Going Down Slow" in Chicago on November 11, 1941. Many performers covered it, including Howlin' Wolf and the 1960s British group the Animals. Booker probably learned the song from Oden when he traveled with "St. Louis Jimmy" and Peetie Wheatstraw on their 1930s road trip in the direction of Chicago. In the second verse, Oden sings:

I have had my fun
If I don't get well no more (2x)
Whoa, my health is failin'
Oh yes, I'm goin' down slow

"That's a good song," I said. My remark prompted Booker to identify what he thought was the most important requirement for a good song: keeping to one subject. Apparently "Going Down Slow" met that requirement:

> I sing that [song] now. Don't you think that I ain't crazy about it. After I play a few numbers' I'm coming in with that. The song is so true, and it's sad, you know. And I arranged a lot of it like I wanted to, you know. I just don't go right down the line with every word he said. Some of my words be better than what he's saying—makes the people understand, you know, make them have a feeling. Yeah, that's what you got to do with songs. People can get some understanding—get the facts on it, you know. You can't say a bird dog and then turn around and go sing about a car. That don't match up. You just have to hold whatever you started with. You have to hold it on a line. Like A B C D on down. That's just the way that goes like that.[14]

Booker had a specific concept of what made a good song, and even sitting up in a hospital bed, he was able to give a clear example of what he meant. In March 1940 in Chicago, with prodding from Lester Melrose, he wrote straightforward songs that were true to his concept.

Chapter Fourteen

MISTER MELROSE

BY 1940, WHEN IT CAME TO BLUES, LESTER MELROSE HAD BECOME THE most important record man in Chicago. When he first met Booker White sometime in the mid to late 1930s, he was a successful talent scout. His persistence in gaining Booker's early release from prison was just one example of how aggressively he scouted for musicians who wrote original songs and were ready to be recorded. Since the demand for new records was constant, he was always on the lookout for new talent.

Lester Melrose was born on December 14, 1891, on a farm near Olney, Illinois. He and his older brother Walter grew up with ambitions that took them beyond farming. Walter played piano and aspired to be a songwriter. He was the first brother to move to Chicago, finding a job that brought him a step closer to songwriting. He sold sheet music at Marshall Field's department store.

Lester worked as a fireman on the Baltimore and Ohio Railroad and, in Chicago, at Rothschild's department store. In 1914 he opened his own grocery store and market on the South Side.[1] In 1918 both brothers were drafted into the army, serving until the end of World War I. In 1920, they opened a music shop at 6309 South Cottage Grove Avenue on the South Side.[2] "At that time, the music business was very slow," Lester Melrose recalled. "We carried a full stock of pop sheet music, piano rolls, small musical instruments and records. Emerson and Gennett were the only records we could purchase at that time, so the going was pretty rough."[3]

A new theater was under construction a few doors south of the music store at 6325 South Cottage Grove Avenue, and the brothers anticipated that the theater would bring in more business. When the lavishly appointed Tivoli Theatre opened its doors on February 16, 1921, they were proven right. Lester Melrose recalled, "Business boomed and word got around to the record and music publishing companies that we were doing a tremendous business." The store became too small to accommodate the growth.

Facing a rent increase from $40 to $350 a month brought on by the success of the Tivoli, the Melrose brothers decided to move. They rented a twenty-by-eighty-foot retail space across the street at 6318 South Cottage Grove Avenue, and added a recording studio. Soon the store carried a full line of Victor, Columbia, and Brunswick records, along with records on lower-priced labels Gennett, Emerson, OKeh, and Paramount. "In the meantime we were getting inquiries from various composers, including colored, about publishing their music or getting it recorded on phonograph records," Melrose recalled. "It was impossible for us to publish pop tunes, so we decided to take a whirl at the blues. The blues selections started coming in and we soon had ten or twelve selections that we thought were good material."[4]

The popularity of the music store as a meeting place for musicians put Lester Melrose in an ideal position to become a freelance talent scout, recommending musicians with strong songs and solid performance abilities to record labels hungry for new talent. The record business was built on change, and audiences wanted to listen to music that was new.

Lester's first major discovery was King Oliver's New Orleans Jazz Band—a seminal jazz ensemble with Oliver on lead cornet, young Louis Armstrong on second cornet, and Johnny Dodds on clarinet. In 1922, the band came to Chicago to play the Lincoln Gardens at the corner of South Cottage Grove Avenue and 31st Street, conveniently close to the music store. When Lester dropped by to listen, he was impressed. He arranged to have three of the band's numbers transcribed for the brothers' publishing company. He noticed that one number in particular "was making a hit [at Lincoln Gardens], so we convinced the Gennett record company they should record King Oliver."

The popular number was "Wolverine Blues," originally composed and performed as "The Wolverines" by New Orleans piano player Ferdinand "Jelly Roll" Morton. Five years earlier, in 1917, Morton had arrived in Los Angeles, where he frequented another music store owned by two brothers, Benjamin Franklin "Reb" Spikes and his brother John.

The Spikes brothers decided to add lyrics to Morton's instrumental music and copyright the composition. They published sheet music for "Wolverine Blues" that credited themselves as co-writers with Morton. When Morton learned that Reb and John Spikes had sold the publishing rights for "Wolverine Blues" to the Melrose brothers, he moved to

Chicago to defend his right to own his song. His arrival was memorable. Lester Melrose recalled, "One day a man wearing a Western-style hat with a red bandana around his neck walked into our store and announced that he was Jelly Roll Morton, the greatest stomp and blues piano player this side of New Orleans."[5]

Morton brought with him a trove of unpublished music. Recognizing a golden opportunity, the Melrose brothers entered into a publishing arrangement with Morton and made him music director of the store's recording studio. In 1925, Lester Melrose sold his share of the music store to Walter and became a full-time talent scout. Perhaps Lester—like talent scout Ralph Peer, who agreed to work for Victor without salary if he could copyright new songs he recorded—had come to understand that the real money in the music business was in the ownership of a musical composition's publishing rights.

Delmark Records founder Bob Koester credited Melrose with breaking down social barriers between white and Black, and, for the most part, paying musicians who worked with him fairly. In his tribute to Melrose, Koester wrote:

> Lester Melrose is remembered with unusual fondness by the artists he recorded. There are noticeably fewer complaints of sharp practices and frequent praise of his musical perception and social attitudes. A picture emerges of his working on the [Works Progress Administration] in the same gang as Broonzy, of patience and understanding in the recording studios, of hard-drinking socializing with his musicians, of his presence at the lively rehearsals at Tampa Red's house and of his readiness to come across with hard cash to relieve stranded, arrested, or deprived artists.[6]

Fair treatment of artists was not always present in Melrose's business dealings. A blues musician and prolific songwriter whom Melrose had discovered singing on a Chicago streetcorner described a different experience. In the documentary film *Born in the Blues*, Arthur "Big Boy" Crudup claimed that Melrose found ways to avoid paying him for his records:

> The fact [is] that he can claim that song and get the copyright on it. But now I never knew how much progress I was making because Melrose didn't tell me. I could hear my songs on the juke box all over the South. I had one disc jockey to tell me that

> Arthur, you're supposed to be in good shape. Every time I would go to make a record, I'd ask Lester how many records would a man have to make that he didn't have to work on the farm . . . and sawmills and all that. The only thing I can get out of my songs is they give me the credit of writing the songs. When it come down to the money question, there ain't no money.[7]

Crudup wrote songs that other artists would record (or "cover")—most notably "That's All Right Mama," which was one side of Elvis Presley's first record. On the distinctive yellow label of the original 45 rpm record, numbered Sun 209, Melrose's Wabash Music Company was listed as publisher of "That's All Right." Crudup received songwriter credit. Released on July 19, 1954, "That's All Right Mama" went on to earn millions in royalties. Most earnings came much later than the year the song was released. Record buyers discovered Presley's early recordings on Sun, and on his birthday and the anniversary of his death, "That's All Right" was played on radio all over the world. From radio airplay and record sales, the song could earn $150,000 in royalties in a single year.

Manager and concert producer Dick Waterman claimed that he almost succeeded in negotiating a financial settlement to recover a portion of Crudup's lost royalties. Waterman's biographer, Tammy L. Turner, explained, "Despite the large amounts of money being made by the cover artists, [Crudup] only had received occasional, small sums."[8] According to Waterman, music publisher Hill and Range pulled out of the agreement at the last minute, leaving Crudup and his family "in stunned, dismayed silence."[9]

Booker White recalled a positive relationship with Lester Melrose. Hurley and Evans wrote that even though none of the songs recorded in 1940 came close to 1937's "Shake 'Em On Down" in sales, "[t]he session was financially profitable for Bukka . . . since Melrose proved to be trustworthy in the business relationship with him. For years Melrose continued to send Booker royalty checks twice a year, or statements if no records had been sold."[10] Melrose's daughter Blanche, who inherited Wabash Music from her father, sent Booker statements and sometimes a check.

Chapter Fifteen

TIMES OF TRANSITION

BY THE TIME BOOKER MADE HIS CLASSIC RECORDINGS IN 1940, arrangements and instrumentation of blues in the studio already had become more sophisticated. Recording sessions that once involved guitarists and piano players who sang now might include a "lead" guitarist or second guitarist, bass player, and drummer. The distinctive voice and delivery that an individual blues singer brought to a session needed to fit well with additional instruments and tighter musical arrangements.

Much of this trend could be credited to Lester Melrose's influence. In 1934, he sent a letter to RCA Victor and Columbia Records "explaining that I had certain blues talent ready to record, and that I could locate any amount of . . . talent to meet their demands."[1] He claimed that between March 1934 to February 1951, he supervised the recordings of "at least 90 percent of all rhythm and blues talent" for the two companies.

Melrose's role in the recording industry had expanded beyond that of talent scout. According to music historians Brian Ward and Patrick Huber, he was the forerunner of the post–World War II record producer. In *A & R Pioneers: Architects of American Roots Music on Record*, they wrote:

> In fact, Lester Melrose was, arguably, the single most important A&R [artist and repertoire] manager and scout working in the race records field during the 1930s and 1940s. In a portent of things to come, his studio work encompassed many of the same activities that would come to define the postwar role of "record producer." He snared some spectacular talent and . . . helped fashion a distinctive urban blues sound that was dubbed the "Bluebird Beat" in reference to the Bluebird label on which much Melrose-produced material appeared. Melrose juggled the task of finding artists with the business of shaping their repertoires and determining the styles in which they recorded.[2]

J. Mayo Williams, who was Black, played a similar role at Decca at this time.

Melrose recorded individual performers such as Big Bill Broonzy and Memphis Minnie in the context of small instrumental combos. These recordings were more sophisticated than country blues. At the same time, he continued to make recordings for the country blues market, but with production touches such as a second guitar or a washboard. His influence on the sound of country blues can be detected as early as Booker's 1937 recordings of "Shake 'Em On Down" and "Pinebluff Arkansas," when Melrose brought a second guitar player into the studio. On May 5, 1938, Melrose had Big Bill Broonzy record "New Shake-Em On Down" for Vocalion.

Unlike local and regional talent scouts who stayed close to home, Melrose traveled to the Deep South on at least one occasion to recruit new talent in the country style—specifically, Mississippians Tommy McClennan and Robert Petway. Once he brought McClennan and Petway to his Chicago studio, he had them record slightly changed versions of "Shake 'Em On Down." McClennan recorded "New Shake 'Em On Down'" on November 22, 1939, and Petway recorded "Ride 'Em On Down" on March 28, 1941. As on Booker's original recording of "Shake 'Em On Down," there may be a second guitar on both McClennan and Petway's versions. According to blues scholar David Evans, "If there is, it would likely be McClennan and Petway playing together. They had been partners and friends for some years in Mississippi and seem to have come to Chicago around the same time."[3] The additional guitarist also could have been one of Big Bill Broonzy and Tampa Red's circle of friends on Chicago's South Side, or Broonzy himself. Big Bill is believed to have played behind Booker in 1937, and for the 1940 sessions, he loaned Booker a better guitar.[4]

Unusual for that time, Melrose socialized with his musicians and listened to what they had to say—especially Broonzy and Tampa Red, who both scouted for Melrose. Born Hudson Whittaker, Tampa Red was an exceptional guitar player. His house on the South Side was the popular place for musicians to rehearse and socialize in the 1930s and 1940s. Piano player Blind John Davis played with Tampa Red in those decades. Davis told *Living Blues* co-founder Jim O'Neal that Tampa Red "had a big rehearsal room, and he had two rooms for the different artists that come in from out of town to record. Melrose [would] pay him for the lodging, and Mrs. Tampa would cook for 'em."[5]

Broonzy's friend Robert Brown accompanied Booker in 1940. Known professionally as Washboard Sam, Brown sang as well as played rhythm on the corrugated tin washboard. In November 1937, he had recorded a cover version of Booker's "Pinebluff Arkansas."[6] By the time he accompanied Booker in Chicago, Brown was five years into a prolific recording career. From 1935 to 1942, he recorded more than 160 songs.[7] In the 1940 sessions, his steady washboard playing reinforced Booker's powerful rhythms.

The English blues writer Paul Oliver explained why the combination of Booker's voice and Sam's washboard was so effective in 1940. He wrote, ". . . the volume of the boards when played with nails or forks made singing against them something of a competition," but added, "A rougher singer like Booker White sounded best with the boards behind him, where the textural quality of his voice was in accord with that of the boards."[8] Sam's washboard technique was sophisticated. He played with thimbles on his fingers, added two metal cowbells for individual notes, and screwed a phonograph turntable to the washboard, which he used as a cymbal. Melrose paid Washboard Sam $25 for the two days. Booker received $17.50 per song.[9]

AFTER HIS RELEASE FROM THE MISSISSIPPI PENAL FARM IN 1939, BOOKer's first destination was most likely Monroe County, Mississippi, where—according to the lyrics to "District Attorney Blues"—the judge and grand jury had separated him from his wife.

Though his family and friends were in Mississippi, at the time of his release Booker had a pressing reason to leave the state. Hanging over his head was the cloud of being convicted of murder and serving time for his crime. He was a known offender to law enforcement in a state whose white citizens often took the law into their own hands and lynched Black people. County sheriffs and deputies did little or nothing to prevent lynchings. Booker also had made enemies in the Black community around Aberdeen. The man he shot had been with friends when they confronted Booker in Prairie. The friends would want revenge. He was no longer safe in what had been familiar surroundings. He needed to find a new place to live.

The prospect of lynching was both real and personal to Booker. In 1966, he revealed to the Black writer and musician Julius Lester that "white boys" had murdered his cousin:

> I had a first cousin to get lynched. His name was Robert Lee Hatchett. He was just about 18 years old. A bunch of white boys was drinking one Saturday night and Robert was coming home and they killed him and laid his body on the railroad tracks for

> the train to run over. But the engineer stopped. The white boys went home and went to bed and nothing was ever done to them. And that was one of the things that started me to being mean. I wouldn't take no chances on nothing after that. There's things in your life can make you mean. He was killed for nothing. And the boys who killed him knew him. They was raised up together. But they hit him in the head with a piece of iron. It knocked him out and then they all just beat him to death.
>
> I never wrote songs about nothing like that, though. I didn't do it then and I won't do it now. It just get on my nerves. I can think of other things to sing about. It's so much of that kind of thing happening every day and I just don't want to make no songs out of it. Something like that boils my blood up. Something happen to a man without a cause, well, that just make me more mean.[10]

He told Lester that being sent to prison for what he claimed was self-defense contributed to his meanness: "I was in Parchman Penitentiary for a while. It was through a mistake. I got a bad deal from the judge. Now, what I call right is that you're supposed to take care of yourself. I'd rather to kill you than you kill me, if it comes down to that."[11] As he did in other interviews when the Prairie incident came up, he changed the subject from the killing to explaining and justifying the circumstances. He maintained that he was defending himself against several men, and that he shot one of the men in the leg, as he intended. The shooting caused the man's death, either from a more lethal wound than Booker admitted to, or bleeding to death. Apparently Booker had gotten too close to the victim's wife or girlfriend. "What it started from was that I was famous down in Mississippi with the women. If they could get rid of me, they could get some of the women. Without getting rid of me, they had a hard way to go. I was the stumbling block in the path and they tried to get the ol' stumbling block out of the path."[12]

In fact, the men of Prairie succeeded in getting rid of the "stumbling block." In the violent world Booker inhabited, he would have been risking his own life to return to the scene of the crime. By moving out of Mississippi in 1939, he could shed his identity as Washington White and become Booker T. Washington White of Memphis, Tennessee.

AMONG THE HOLDINGS OF THE MEMPHIS PUBLIC LIBRARY IS A COLlection of Memphis City Directories. The collection is missing a few volumes from the years Booker lived there, but complete enough to suggest that it took time for him to settle down. During his transition from Mississippi to Memphis, Booker might have stayed with relatives and friends. His name does not appear in a city directory until 1943, when he was listed as Booker W. White, laborer, living with Rebecca (no last name) at 2603 Spottswood Avenue in the Orange Mound neighborhood. Another laborer named Booker White (no middle initial) was listed in 1943 as living at 1485 Harlem Street. This may have been Booker at his previous address.

Spottswood Avenue is one of Orange Mound's main streets, and the neighborhood's northern boundary. Located near the center of Memphis, Orange Mound is considered the first Black neighborhood that was built by Black labor.[13] The land on which Orange Mound was built was the former John George Deaderick Plantation. In 1890, a white real estate developer, Elzey Eugene Meacham, purchased the five-thousand-acre plantation and began constructing a segregated subdivision for African Americans. The rectangular lots were small and narrow. When construction was completed, Orange Mound consisted of 982 houses built on a tight grid of lots in the two-room shotgun style—one room in front and a back room with a basic kitchen. According to tradition, the neighborhood's name came from mock orange trees and shrubs that grew on the site when it was a plantation.[14]

In the 1945 directory, Booker was listed as a laborer living at the rear of 1443 Kyle Street, close to Orange Mound. His 1946 listing added the name of Emma, whom he had married in 1944 in her hometown of Cotton Plant, Arkansas.[15]

A family photograph of Emma Lee White distributed at her memorial service shows a beautiful young woman.[16] Born on September 19, 1921, she was fifteen years younger than Booker. Her parents were well established in Cotton Plant and lived in a comfortable house. Emma and Booker's first child, Irene, was born there on September 14, 1944. Emma returned to her parents' home in Cotton Plant to give birth to their second child, Beulah Faye, on December 25, 1945. Faye, as she preferred to be called, described Cotton Plant as a place so rural "you might expect to see somebody fishing barefoot in the water with a straw hat on his head."[17]

After Booker and Emma were married, they lived in the two-room shotgun house on Spottswood Avenue. As small as it was, the house accommodated their children and gave other members of Booker's family a place to stay. "You would come in from the porch," Irene remembered.[18] "There was a row of chairs alongside the wall. I don't remember where my sister and myself slept. We had an older sister, Henrietta, from another marriage. B. B. slept in the kitchen on a little pallet and a gooseneck lamp. The water closet was out on the back porch. No sink, just a toilet."

Henrietta White Williams recalled visiting the house on Spottswood Avenue. "I only met Irene and did not meet Faye," Henrietta said.[19] Her younger brother Willie White, whom Henrietta described as looking "exactly like my father," remained in Mississippi. Tension developed between Booker and Emma. Faye learned later from her mother that Booker was very possessive of his pretty young wife, and swept the ground around the house before he went out of town so that he would be able to check for unfamiliar footprints. Jealousy was one issue in the marriage. Money was another. Booker's drinking was a third.

Irene recalled the family moving from Spottswood Avenue to public housing.[20] Faye was very young when Emma White finally separated from Booker, taking her daughters and young son Edward Lee to live with her parents in Cotton Plant. Life in Cotton Plant was more settled. A pleasant memory that stood out for Faye was the Sunday when she, Irene, and their family were voted best dressed at their church. "We wore yellow dresses," she recalled.

When Faye was nine, Emma White moved her family to Chicago. She worked hard cleaning and took other jobs. In 1950, she was employed as a maid by the Sidney H. Ravid family at 425 Aldine Street.[21] She was twenty-eight. When arthritis prevented Emma from working, she began to receive welfare payments, but Faye and Irene insisted that their mother never apply for food stamps. The sisters were too proud to take them to the store. Faye remembered her mother crying, and wondered why. Emma lived in Chicago until her death on December 22, 1990.[22] On more than one occasion, she told Irene that the worst day of her life was when she met Booker, and the best was when she left him.

BOOKER HELD A STEADY JOB DURING THE 1950S, BUT WAS IN TROUBLE with the law again in spring 1952. According to the Memphis *Commercial Appeal*, the Shelby County grand jury indicted Booker T. Washington White on a first degree charge of assault with intent to murder.[23] When he appeared in court two weeks later for sentencing, the charges had been reduced to assault with intent to commit voluntary manslaughter, and carrying a pistol.[24] He pleaded guilty to both, and was fined $30 for carrying and $100 for manslaughter. Sentenced to serve six months on the Shelby County Penal Farm for each charge, he was allowed to serve the two sentences concurrently. Extenuating circumstances or Booker's willingness to plead guilty might have led the court to reduce the original assault to murder charge to two lesser offenses, or Newberry Equipment Company owner Jimmy Newberry might have intervened for Booker with the sheriff's office. I asked Newberry's former secretary Mrs. Ellen Rogers if her boss would have vouched for a valuable employee. She replied without hesitation, "He certainly would. Mister Newberry knew a lot of people, and he would call in favors."[25]

University of Memphis professor F. Jack Hurley kept in contact with Booker. He made a point of telling me that Booker's position at Newberry Equipment had been a responsible one, requiring both strength and intelligence:

> He was a layout man for a boilermaker. That was pretty skilled work. . . . He couldn't make a living with his music. He was very valued [as a musician] and had some nice tours toward the end of his life. When I knew him, he had a nice, perfectly decent little house down in south Memphis. He liked to sit on his front porch and play his guitar.[26]

In stark contrast to this pleasing image was the 1952 penal farm photograph in which Booker wore an ill-fitting cloth shirt and looked into the camera with a sad, almost pleading look.[27] His identity as a husband, father, hard worker, and musician who made records had been reduced to a number: Shelby County Penal Farm prisoner number 22693.

According to attorney Barbara L. Dean, general counsel of the Memphis Housing Authority, Booker's 1952 conviction on a gun charge would have been grounds for eviction from public housing.[28] What is known is that the Housing Authority initiated a civil suit against him in the Shelby County General Sessions Court. No disposition of the case was recorded.[29]

By 1954, Booker had moved to the apartment at 702 St. Paul Avenue that he rented for almost fifteen years. Located in midtown Memphis close to the downtown, the St. Paul Avenue address was where John Fahey and ED Denson found him in September 1963. The 1966 directory noted that Booker was "retired," but he continued to rent the apartment in 1967 and 1968. He was absent from the directory in 1969, and by 1970 had moved to 867 Mosby Avenue, Apt. 17—the apartment of his partner Leola Morris.

Chapter Sixteen

AUTHENTIC BLUES

DURING THE 1950S, ONE MUSICIAN IN PARTICULAR CAME TO EMBODY the image of an authentic blues performer to audiences in the United States, Great Britain, and Europe. His remarkable life—and the end of it—added momentum to the movement that would result in Booker's opportunity to have a second career. The musician was William Lee Conley "Big Bill" Broonzy.

In a 2010 biography of Broonzy, blues scholar Roger House wrote, "Broonzy established a bridge of cultural exchange between the black American and European blues communities. . . . Through his consummate professionalism and irresistible charisma, Big Bill truly became an ambassador of the folk blues."[1] Broonzy was diagnosed with lung cancer in July 1957.[2] Blues and folk audiences held benefit concerts in Chicago and London to help with his medical bills and make up for his unemployment.[3] The cancer returned, and Broonzy died on August 15, 1958. He was sixty-five.

Beyond the loss of a musician and singer who recorded blues for Black audiences for more than three decades, and introduced white audiences in the United States and overseas to folk blues,[4] Broonzy's death heightened a perception among blues enthusiasts that they were losing their connection to the music's tradition. His death called attention to the apparent loss of other country blues musicians who had recorded before World War II.

Mississippi John Hurt's records had come from two sessions in 1928. The first was on February 14 in Memphis. The second consisted of two recording dates a week apart: December 21 and 28 in New York.[5] By 1958, Hurt had not been heard from in thirty years. Eddie "Son" House played guitar and sang on four records for Paramount recorded in 1930 in Grafton, Wisconsin. Eleven years went by before, in 1941 and 1942, he recorded for folklorist Alan Lomax in Robinsonville and Lake Cormorant, Mississippi. After that, House disappeared for another twenty years. Robert Johnson, who last recorded in 1937, was thought to be alive when Columbia producer John Hammond tried to bring Johnson to New York for a concert at Carnegie Hall. Hammond learned that Johnson had died. Many blues enthusiasts assumed Booker White was dead because there had been no news of him since he recorded "Fixin' To Die Blues" in Chicago in 1940.

The perception that a generation of performers was on the verge of disappearing was the theme for a cover story in the September 14, 1961, issue of *Down Beat*, a biweekly magazine that primarily covered jazz. Headlined "The Rise of Folk Blues," the article by critic Pete Welding linked a renewed interest in the blues to Broonzy's death:

> The last few years have seen a great resurgence of interest in the country blues, blues singing, and in traditional Afro-American music forms generally. It's almost as if the death of the superb blues artist Big Bill Broonzy in the early summer [*sic*] of 1958 has spurred every collector, musicologist, folklorist, and owner of a tape recorder to invade the rural South in an effort to preserve as much of the rough; natural; vigorous, and, it was feared, perishable music of the Southern Negro—especially the secular blues—as possible before all the older practitioners had died.[6]

Adding ". . . the archives of Negro record firms, large and small, flourishing and extinct, have been raided in a last-ditch attempt to preserve a supposed dying idiom." Welding concluded that a "full-scale blues revival is in full swing. . . ."[7]

From a contemporary perspective, the evidence is clear. In 1959 Alan Lomax made another field trip to the South, recording Mississippi Hill Country musician Fred McDowell and other blues artists. Two important books on the blues were published. Samuel Charters's *The Country Blues* came out in 1959, and British blues historian Paul Oliver's *Blues Fell This Morning: The Meaning of the Blues* followed in 1960. Though he had not yet traveled to the United States, Oliver had transcribed the lyrics of 150 blues recordings, and combined this abundance of information with whatever history and context he could glean from blues musicians visiting England and Europe. Oliver's informants included Big Bill Broonzy, drawing on "his inexhaustible fund of memories," and the guitar and harmonica duo Sonny Terry and Brownie McGhee, who recalled for Oliver "blues and blues singers of the thirties and forties."[8]

Record collectors began to ask questions about the vanished generation of blues musicians as they canvassed the South in search of hard-to-find 78 rpm records. Collectors and researchers contributed to a new British publication, *Blues Unlimited*, that published its first issue in April 1963. Researcher Gayle Dean Wardlow recalled the collecting aspect of the revival in his article, "Knocking on Doors for 78s: Buying Race Records in the South."[9] Wardlow began by collecting the early records of country musicians Roy Acuff and Bob Wills, but his interest shifted to early blues records in 1961 when he realized that Black residents in his community might have dusty stacks of old 78s at home.[10]

In his 1961 article for *Down Beat*, Welding captured a moment when the blues audience was looking backward to fill a void left by Broonzy even as President John F. Kennedy urged citizens to look forward toward a New Frontier. In addition to summarizing signs of the revival, Welding asked two underlying questions: "How did this situation come about, and is it a good thing?"[11] He noted that what was a rich environment for the blues record collector brought little or no economic benefit to the blues performer.[12] He noted that the principal audience for blues came from white jazz and folk music enthusiasts, and records in the blues genre had "extremely modest sales."[13]

Even for a blues record issued by a major label, sales of more than 1,500 were rare. By comparison, in 1962 a first album from Columbia Records by an obscure New York City folk singer exceeded that figure by 500 or more. Bob Dylan's self-titled debut included a version of "Fixin' To Die" at a time when many in the informed folk audience thought the song's writer was dead. The song's appearance on the album *The Country Blues* that Charters put together to accompany his book was Dylan's source. Even if Booker White had been known to be alive, he would have received nothing for Dylan's cover of the song. Record producer and music publisher Lester Melrose had held the copyright. The lack of economic reward to Booker for his song appearing on Columbia Records was a more concrete answer to Welding's question about benefits than the vague musing in his article: "It is still a sad commentary on the current music situation that the majority of the remaining representatives of the old playing styles cannot profit *more immediately* [my emphasis] in the renewed interest in their music."[14] One wonders what "more immediately" might have meant to Welding, let alone whether future considerations might have occurred to copyright owners and record companies.

The energy mustered by "every collector, musicologist, folklorist, and owner of a tape recorder" flocking to the rural South led not only to the interviewing of "older practitioners" of blues, but also to the rediscovery of many of those musicians who were believed to be gone. I use the word "rediscovery" advisedly, because in the context of rediscovering missing blues musicians its full meaning is rediscovery by white blues enthusiasts for the edification and entertainment of other white blues enthusiasts. From the point of view of the musicians, their families, friends, and communities where they lived, the musicians were to be found in their accustomed places the whole time, never having been lost.

The first of the most prominent country blues musicians to be located was Mississippi John Hurt. In his biography *Mississippi John Hurt: His Life, His Times, His Blues* (2011), Philip R. Ratcliffe devotes eleven pages to three different accounts—and variations of those accounts—of the search for John Hurt in early 1963.[15] Leading the search was Tom Hoskins, whom Ratcliffe describes as "a likable hippie with no permanent job, and a fondness for girls, alcohol, and drugs in no particular order."[16] A guitar player himself, Hoskins had a special interest in the voice and fingerpicking guitar style of John Hurt. He was determined to find him.

An important clue arrived when Australian record collector John Edwards sent Hoskins's friend Richard Spottswood a tape of a Hurt record that the Americans had not heard, "Avalon Blues." Hoskins and Spottswood realized that the song identified the singer's home town:

> *Avalon's my hometown, always on my mind.* (2x)
> *Pretty mamas in Avalon want me there all the time.*

On Friday, March 1, 1963, thirty-five years after Hurt's session in New York, Hoskins knocked on a front door in Avalon, Mississippi, to ask if this was the house where Mississippi John Hurt lived. "It was and he did, simple as that . . . and late Sunday evening . . . I was driving north again through the Mississippi darkness with a two-hour tape recording of a living, breathing treasure. . . ."[17]

After coming to the attention of OKeh Records, John Hurt had recorded eight songs in Memphis on February 14, 1928. The session produced "Frankie" and "Nobody's Dirty Business," and the record sold well enough for Hurt to be invited to a better studio in New York City. Hurt's progress from the February session in Memphis to two sessions in New York in December was more positive than what followed Washington

White's1930 session in Memphis. Though Victor's successful field producer Ralph S. Peer was enthusiastic about the sides White recorded in Memphis, there is no evidence of his being invited to a second session.

A similar lack of interest would follow Booker's recording session in 1940. In 1964, when Alan Wilson asked Booker why he did not make records after that session, he responded that the man he was dealing with would not come up to the figure he wanted.[18] In *Recording the Blues*, John Dixon and Robert M. W. Godrich gave a partial explanation for the decline in the popularity of blues and gospel records after 1940:

> From 1934 on the three companies [Victor, Decca, and Columbia] had played fairly equal parts in supplying black record enthusiasts. Then, in 1941, with industry sales once more topping a hundred million dollars, there was a further cut back in race releases; [Victor's race label] Bluebird still put out 100 new items, but Decca and Columbia, for the first time in five years, fell well short of that figure. . . . Early in 1942 the government restricted the use of shellac, and blues and gospel releases—at 125—were half what they had been in '41.[19] [Shellac was used in the war effort to coat airplane wings.]

Contributing to the diminished numbers was a ban on all recording activity imposed by J. C. Petrillo, president of the American Federation of Musicians, who feared that music played on jukeboxes would have a negative impact on the demand for live music. The ban began at midnight, July 31, 1942. Recording studios closed for two years.

The effect on Black music was significant. Dixon and Godrich wrote, ". . . race material that already had been recorded remained unissued by and large, and the catalogues were ruthlessly pruned. The December 1941 Victor catalogue listed 350 blues and gospel items, whereas in May 1943 there were only seventy-five items available. . . ."[20]

Thus Lester Melrose had taken a chance when he brought Booker to Chicago for the 1940 country blues sessions that produced "Fixin' To Die Blues" and "Parchman Farm Blues." Booker's records did not sell well, and his recordings disappeared from catalogs. As far as the blues record-buying public knew, the musician had vanished or even died.

Chapter Seventeen

1963's NOT 1962

THE NEWS THAT TOM HOSKINS HAD FOUND JOHN HURT REVERBERated through the blues community. "John was not only a bluesman, he was one of the most important bluesmen," ED Denson recalled. "And his ability to play, while dormant, was quickly regained."[1] Known by the combination of his first and last initials, Eugene "ED" Denson was one of several "expatriate blues freaks" from the Washington, DC, area who went west and became regulars at a popular folk music venue and coffeehouse in Berkeley, California, called the Jabberwock. In the spring of 1963, Denson and two other transplants from Washington, DC—Pat Sullivan and John Fahey—were students at the University of California at Berkeley. In the DC area, all three had been part of the same circle of friends whose common bond was acoustic music. Sullivan was a folk singer and songwriter who performed around Washington and Providence, Rhode Island, where she attended Pembroke, one of the Seven Sisters colleges. Fahey transferred from the University of Maryland to American University in Washington and fell in love with her. She enjoyed Fahey's company as a friend, but did not see him as a prospective life partner.

Instead, Sullivan married Denson, and the couple moved to Berkeley in 1962. After working at the University of Hawaii as a teaching assistant and returning to the East Coast, Fahey settled in Berkeley the following year.[2] Throughout Fahey's friendship with Sullivan and Denson's courting her, the two men maintained their own friendship. They took the bold step of starting their own record label, naming it Takoma Records after Fahey's hometown of Takoma Park, Maryland. It was an ego-boost for Fahey. His biographer Steve Lowenthal wrote, "John Fahey needed to properly document and share his music, and he had no intention of waiting for anyone else to do it for him. . . . Fahey self-released his first album, *Blind Joe Death*, in a pressing of 100 copies in 1959."[3] The cover art was minimal: JOHN FAHEY printed in capital letters on the front, and BLIND JOE DEATH in capital letters on the back. Fahey's style was rooted in blues, Christian hymns, and American folk music. He combined traditional elements with influence absorbed from modernist composers such as Harry Partch. The result was a unique personal style that the guitarist would express in performance and original compositions for the next forty years.

Fahey and Denson were as surprised as anyone to learn that Hoskins had located John Hurt. Hoskins's success triggered a similar impulse in them. If Hoskins could find a blues musician who had not been heard from (at least by white blues enthusiasts) since he made historic country blues records in 1928, perhaps Fahey and Denson could locate another authentic musician the same way, using one of the blues singer's songs as his reference point, just as Hoskins had done with John Hurt.

Denson described how the "rediscovery" unfolded:

> Fahey had heard Bukka's song about his hometown, Aberdeen, Mississippi, and sent him a postcard, general delivery, which said there was $100 in it for Bukka if he could still play. The postmaster forwarded it to Bukka in Memphis, and he contacted John. At that point I got involved, and told John we had to go record him. John had college finals (German, I think) coming up so while we drove to Memphis, periodically we would stop and he would practice his German. Scared the hell out of some kids at one stop. We had [John's] tape recorder, and lugged it up to Bukka's room, which was upstairs in a boarding house. But it was soon clear that we needed a real studio, so we rented one and recorded Bukka there.[4]

After lugging the heavy Wollensak up the stairs, Fahey and Denson set up the reel-to-reel recorder in a back room. "It didn't work," Denson remembered. "We had no real facilities for listening back to the recordings, the mikes were poor, and the recordings almost certainly no good." They needed to take Booker to a professional recording studio, even though their available budget for the trip was four hundred dollars they had borrowed from Pat Sullivan. "Bukka luckily was in good practice," Denson recalled, "and we were able to cut an LP without bankrupting us. . . ."

According to Memphis-based music writer Robert Gordon, the most likely facility was Sonic Recording Studio, run by musician Roland Janes. Sonic was not far from where Booker lived, Gordon noted, and "Fahey was hanging around midtown, and Sonic is where he'd end up."[5] David A. Less, author of *Memphis Mayhem: A Story of the Music That Shook Up the World*, wrote that because of the popularity of British bands in 1963, "American independent rock was dead. Roland [Janes] adapted and used the studio as a rental house for local musicians who needed a low-cost recording facility. . . ."[6]

A November 1963 article in the University of California student newspaper, the *Daily Californian*, reported incorrectly that Sullivan also traveled to Memphis. A staff writer wrote, "John Fahey, graduate in philosophy, ED Denson, senior in English, and his wife Pat, junior in English, went to Memphis, made some tapes and convinced White to accompany them back here to try to renew his once successful career as a blues singer."[7] After several paragraphs on Booker's early career and Fahey's unsuccessful quest to find the musician following Fahey's "conversion to the blues," the article quoted Fahey as saying, "I thought he was dead":

> Then in September 1963, a letter came from White. The three students left Berkeley and drove straight to Memphis, where they met White.
>
> He sang and played guitar and piano so like his old records that they asked him to return with them to make records for their record company, Takoma Records, and sing in local folk music houses.
>
> Lovers of the blues in Berkeley have given White an enthusiastic reception. . . . Sales of his first record for the Berkeley company will begin as soon as the jackets are printed, Mrs. Denson said.
>
> A novel side to the recording is that Fahey and the Denson's plan for White to receive all the profits from his recordings.
>
> "Those of us who love the music put up the money. We'll be lucky if we break even by next September. And we don't really care," they said.

WITH A BLACK-AND-WHITE PHOTOGRAPH OF A SMILING BOOKER sitting on a wooden chair, supporting his National steel guitar in the crook between his right hip and knee, the cover of *Mississippi Blues Vol. 1* looks stark but inviting. The album opens with a driving performance of "Aberdeen Mississippi Blues," on which Booker "uses an additional technique which is unique . . . : he alternately bangs and frets the strings with both hands."[8] His version of "Baby Please Don't

Go"—associated with Big Joe Williams, who was from the same region of Mississippi as Booker—lopes along with slinky slide guitar lines that echo the melody.

Noticeable on the first two tracks are Booker's enthusiastic shouts and comments about what he is playing. "New Orleans Streamline" is a fast train song organized around a woman named Lucille leaving Booker in 1944. He gets advice from an old man who witnessed him knocking her down after she greeted her cousin from Detroit with a kiss. Different from the original, Booker's new version of "Parchman Farm Blues" begins with a repeated guitar riff before he sings "So many days I would be walking up down the road / I would be looking up at my convict clothes / I would wonder how long before I could change my convict clothes." These lines are borrowed from his song "When Can I Change My Clothes," also recorded in 1940. The singer laments being marched out to work every day in a prison uniform. "Poor Boy Long Ways from Home" is a variation of the song Booker sang for John Lomax in 1939. His slide guitar playing is fast and uplifting, in contrast to the mournful mood of "Parchman Farm."

Side one closes with "Remembrance of Charlie Patton," a four-minute spoken piece in which Booker says, "I want to come to be a big man like Charlie Patton, but I didn't want to be killed like he did . . . Charlie Patton used to sing that song about hitch up and saddle up my old black mare, and I did that number about dogs downtown to be like that. I tried to be the second behind old, big Charlie Patton."

Side two opens with "Shake 'Em On Down," Booker's much-covered song from 1937. His voice sounds gravelly as he sings "Ahhh, must I holler, must I shake 'em on down . . . Ah, lookee, lookee baby, coming down the road. My baby done come and tell me she don't want me no more." On the next song, the religious number "I Am in the Heavenly Way," his voice seems to have retained some of the vibrato that it had in 1930. "The Atlanta Special" is another train song, slower than "New Orleans Streamline." Here Booker sings about being "a little boy catchin' that train when I was fifteen years old." He addresses a relative directly in the song, singing ". . . Well, Aunt Easter, Booker got to go." His guitar imitates train sounds, such as air brakes, and lays down a syncopated rhythm, like the rhythm of a train rocking from side to side on the tracks.

Booker also makes good use of the piano that was in the recording studio. On "Drunk Man Blues," he plays repeated staccato figures as he sings about needing forgiveness for his sins. He pleads with his woman for one more drink. As they stand at the corner of Beale and Main in

Memphis, she reminds him that he promised he wouldn't drink. He counters that she promised not to be with another man. The song has a moody barrelhouse quality.

The album closes with "Army Blues," which has a variation on the same churning riff that Booker plays on "Shake 'Em On Down" and "Parchman Farm Blues." His lyrics warn listeners that he is paying close attention to women whose men are in the military, boasting that ". . . [if] I don't get around to you in the daytime, ol' Booker'll be around before the sun go down."

As an album, *Mississippi Blues Vol. 1* starts strong on side one and winds down on side two. Booker shows off his musicianship. He plays in three guitar tunings: open E minor, open G, and standard tuning. His piano playing is basic but assured. The volume of his vocals varies as he moves closer to the microphone and away from it. With only his voice, guitar, and the piano on one number, the recording sounds dry and spare. Several songs have abrupt endings. John Fahey told Chris Strachwitz that he tapped Booker on the shoulder when he wanted him to stop playing.

The album notes gave purchasers the first look into Booker's life. ED Denson wrote what he had learned of Booker's biography, along with notes on the individual tracks on the album. Fahey focused on Booker's guitar technique and use of multiple tunings. The musician's full name appeared on a phonograph record for the first time: Booker (Bukka) T. Washington White.

Denson gave November 12, 1909, as the date Booker was born. He made a distinction between his account and what had been written previously: "There has been precious little information published on either Country Blues singers or their records, and much of what has been published is incorrect. In an attempt to obtain reasonable accuracy in these notes, I have made use only of information which Bukka volunteered and directly observable facts such as record labels."

Of particular interest was what Booker recalled of his early life. Denson wrote: "The Whites were a religious family and all of their 8 children faithfully attended the Baptist church—there Bukka learned to sing. His father, a skilled guitar and fiddle player, taught him to play the guitar. Between the ages of 10 and 15, Bukka left home, going to the nearby Mississippi Delta country." Booker's early influences were musicians from the Delta. "Men like Son House, Hambone Willie Newburn, Skip James, Henry Sims, and the greatest of the time, Charlie Patton, traveled from small town to small town playing for dances and performing in the roadhouse," Denson wrote.

In recalling Charley Patton on the album, Booker led Fahey and Denson to believe that he knew Patton. This prompted Denson to write, "Bukka soon met Patton and was very impressed—he recalls that later he was unable to fit into a crowded room in which Patton's latest record was being played." Recording his first album with two white men, Booker would have wanted to please them—and they would have asked Booker if he had met the man. Later, Denson wrote that Booker never met Patton. The disclosure came out during the many hours Booker spent with his young managers in Berkeley.

In his notes, Denson gave credence to another of Booker's stories: "Victor Smith, a white boy, played with Bukka and taught him one of the tunings which he uses still. They played together over a year and then Victor left to begin his career, advising Bukka to continue playing." As with his initial claim that he met Charley Patton, Booker's mention of Victor Smith may have been an effort to please his white discoverers by telling them something they wanted to hear.

While Fahey and Denson were in Memphis, they encouraged Booker to think about moving to California. With their connections on the West Coast, they thought they could restart his career. Booker must have believed that if two young college students would drive from California to Memphis to make an album with him, they must be serious people. They told him about the record label they were starting, which would release his album. Once they got back to Berkeley, Takoma Records would see to the manufacture of Booker's album and release it. Fahey and Denson assured their new client that they were on good terms with club managers who were in a position to hire him. As soon as Booker would commit to making the move, they would begin to set up gigs.

In his late fifties, Booker may have felt that an opportunity to play music for a living would not come around again. He was not in a serious relationship and could leave his job at the Newberry Equipment Company. But there was a problem. What would he do about his apartment on St. Paul Avenue? Fahey offered Booker a place to live in Berkeley to persuade Booker that he could keep the Memphis apartment. Whatever was on the table, Booker began to make arrangements to leave Memphis and take the long train trip to California on faith, not knowing what lay ahead or when he would return home.

Arriving in Berkeley, he discovered that life in a West Coast university town was very different from anything he had experienced in the South. For one thing, Fahey was not an easy person to have as a housemate. He was addicted to Coca-Cola. He was hyperactive. "John

Fahey was a strange fellow," record producer Chris Strachwitz recalled. "He talked strange and walked strange. Bukka was spooked by African sculpture in the house. I remember Bukka telling me that he's got some weird spirits in his house . . . almost like voodoo stuff. He was really scared." ED Denson had a slightly different recollection of Booker's relocation to Berkeley after making the album. "Not too long after that, Bukka came to the Bay area on the train to join us," Denson recalled, "and we were to attempt to restart his career. We got him a place to stay with a friend of mine, Gary and his girlfriend, and booked him into the local folk clubs. Ralph Gleason wrote a column about him for the *San Francisco Chronicle. . . .*"

Ralph J. Gleason wrote on popular music for the *Chronicle*. His syndicated column appeared in newspapers across the United States. On December 1, 1963, the lead paragraph made a leap from jazz to blues. "As jazz progresses and attracts more and more fans, as folk music spreads, and becomes popular, there is increasing traffic in digging up the early performers," he wrote. ". . . [O]ne valuable achievement is the rediscovery of the Mississippi blues musician Bukka White." Gleason attended a performance at the Cabale in Berkeley, interviewing Booker and John Fahey at the club. Fahey told Gleason about sending the postcard to Bukka White, Old Blues Singer, c/o General Delivery, Aberdeen, Mississippi, and his astonishment at receiving Booker's reply. "Two hours after we got the letter, we were off to Memphis, where we recorded him," he said. Gleason introduced Booker to his readers:

> [He is] a short, heavy man with a harsh, guttural voice that is strong in use but goes soft when he talks offstage . . . Bukka plays an old-fashioned metal guitar and uses picks on two fingers. He also used a short piece of metal pipe on the little finger of his left hand to slide up and down the strings instead of a bottle top, the traditional honky tonk guitarists' aid. 'I like the strings to tell the people what I'm playing,' he says as he makes them echo the sound and phrasing of his voice.
>
> This is White's first trip out of the South. "I never been past the Rockies before," he says. San Francisco was the first big Northern city he saw and it came as quite a surprise to Bukka. "It looks a little bit like the edge of heaven," he says.[9]

Gleason was wrong about this being Booker's first trip to a big city in the North, but right on most details, mentioning that Booker recorded for Victor and OKeh in the 1930s "but was thought to have died and at any rate dropped out of sight." Gleason alerted readers that the Takoma album was available, and they could hear the musician in person at the Cabale and soon at the Ash Grove in Los Angeles.

Gleason's column highlighted the significance of Fahey and Denson's search, and publicized Booker's return to active performing. What was not apparent to Gleason in the brief time he spent with Booker was that the musician had found himself in an uncomfortable situation. Having lived all his life in Mississippi and Memphis, he did not know how a Black man was expected to behave among a predominantly white population in northern California. "Culture shock was, if not extreme, certainly present," Denson emailed me in 2008. He gave an example. "It was difficult to persuade Bukka to eat at the table with us. He suggested instead that he play the guitar to entertain us while we ate."

Agreeing to be managed by Fahey and Denson was a decision Booker made with very little information, and turned out to be an overconfident commitment by the managers. Both sides had problems with the arrangement from the beginning. This was evident in Fahey's responses to a letter from Samuel Charters in November 1963. Charters mentioned having difficulties with certain blues musicians. Fahey responded that he was frustrated with Booker White:

> It is very difficult and touchy when such people continue to think you're screwing them no matter what you do and when you've explained to them 20 times, an apparently completely unambiguous contract, and they still don't understand it. There is a slight chance that Bukka will break my contract and go away and at this point has been so much trouble that I don't think I'd mind too much if this occurred.[10]

Charters shared how much the musicians he handled were paid. This information provoked Fahey:

> As for your getting so much money for the various singers you mentioned I am very amazed. But I believe you. Nevertheless some of them, noteably [*sic*] Pink Anderson I think were grossly overpaid. But I suppose you have to try to be benevolent when they're in such bad health and all. I find myself acting this way sometimes. The conflict arises when their musical output is not too good and on this we apparently still disagree. . . .

Charters asked Fahey why he turned down a contract offer for Booker from Elektra Records—a prestigious folk label in the 1960s and 1970s. Fahey responded:

> As for my turning down Electra [*sic*] records it was primarily because I didn't like the attitude of the man I talked to on the phone, Rothchild, and because I thought he was going to screw Bukka and thought that that it [would] be better to get Bukka a few small jobs for record companies before he signed an exclusive contract for anybody. That's what Rothchild wanted and I dint [*sic*] think he should get it. Besides that I can pay and am paying out of my own pocket more than Rothchild would have gotten him. . . . And finally at this point, having had so much goddam trouble with Bukka, I don't care anyway.

Trying to end his letter on a positive note, Fahey added:

> Nevertheless I shall continue to do the best by him I can, and this primarily because I promised him I would, even if he, and the whole rest of the world thinks I'm screwing him. This again I request be kept confidential. I'm all in favor of getting together with you when you get out here. Bukka should still be here and you can see him too.

Fahey's response to Charters is striking because of its timing. Fahey wrote that he had "so much goddam trouble with Bukka" only a month or two after Booker had uprooted himself from Memphis. What is apparent is that Denson and Fahey had no plan for Booker.

Though Denson mentioned setting up a tour for Booker, he did not recall details. "Finding venues on the West Coast was difficult," he wrote. "We had kind of a home club on the avenue [the Jabberwock], and then there were a couple of clubs down closer to the bay—Blind Lemon was one—that the prior generation of folkies established and hung out in. Once we got Booker a booking agent back east, we got some college dates." Denson thought the agent might have been Herb Gart, who managed Buffy Sainte-Marie.

Fahey's motives for turning down a contract with Elektra Records are unclear. In his reply to Charters, he chose not to mention that he and Denson already had recorded an album with Booker in the summer of 1963 that would be released in 1964 on their new Takoma record label.

After his phone conversation with Paul Rothchild, Fahey must have been concerned about Elektra's requiring an exclusive contract, which would complicate the release of *Mississippi Blues*. Significantly, Fahey gave no indication that he had told Booker about the Elektra offer.

ED Denson published "The Re-Discovery of Bukka White" in an article that appeared in the December 1976 issue of *Blues Magazine*, a small Canadian publication. Editor Bo Basiuk put a photograph of Booker on the cover, and used a sketch of him wearing a coat and tie and sunglasses, playing his National steel guitar, as the centerfold. Basiuk devoted most of the issue to Booker. It contained Denson's article, Basiuk's question-and-answer interview with Booker, three separate articles about his guitar technique, and a profile of Booker by Canadian blues promoter Roberta Richards.

In his final paragraph, Denson wrote, "Next time perhaps I'll take up where we get Bukka to move to Berkeley so we could manage and book him," and then offered additional details of the Memphis recording session:

> The engineer in the studio was excited by the playing—which we took to be a real sign that Bukka was good. And some of Bukka's skills as a storyteller began to come out. Among the pieces he recorded . . . was a touching reminiscence of Charley Patton, with John playing Patton pieces in the background. It was a masterful story of how Bukka met the great man, with little quotes . . . all invented on the spot. Bukka had not met Patton. He cut another piece about Frank Stokes, the great Memphis player. We were in heaven.[11]

If the engineer was Sonic's Roland Janes, he was a good judge of talent. Janes had recorded with Jerry Lee Lewis and worked for Sam Phillips at Sun Records. He entered the Memphis Music Hall of Fame as both a musician and producer.[12]

Chapter Eighteen

BOSTON 1964

CONTRIBUTING TO THE BLUES REVIVAL IN THE UNITED STATES WERE the activities of white record collectors, who began to canvass Black neighborhoods in the South in search of old 78 rpm recordings. Early records by Bukka White were among the titles they valued. Eventually, blues records considered to be of special significance by collectors and researchers were reissued on compilation albums, and several collectors returned to the South in search of the musicians who had made the records.

In 1959 Samuel Charters included Booker's "Fixin' To Die Blues" among the fourteen songs he chose for the RBF/Folkways compilation *The Country Blues*, which was meant to accompany his groundbreaking book of the same title. In the book, Charters wrote of meeting several musicians who made records before World War II, such as songster Furry Lewis and jug band leader Gus Cannon. Charters's successful searches alerted blues enthusiasts that other important blues players who were known only as names on record labels could be found.

The blues revival was gathering momentum in Great Britain as well. English blues scholar Paul Oliver wrote and produced a similar combination of a book and album. Philips Records released *Blues Fell This Morning (Rare Recordings of Southern Blues Singers)* in 1960 as the companion album to Oliver's study of blues lyrics, *Blues Fell This Morning: The Meaning of the Blues*. Among Oliver's fourteen selections was Booker's "Strange Place Blues."

Because Charters's picks for the Folkways album included more polished and urban-sounding recordings by musicians such as Lonnie Johnson and Leroy Carr, some critics didn't think the album was representative of authentic country blues. Pete Whelan and Bill Givens responded with the album *Really! The Country Blues*, released in 1962 on the Origin Jazz Library (OJL) label. Whelan and Givens selected recordings by rural musicians such as Son House, Skip James, and Garfield

Akers. Though the album did not include a recording by Bukka White, two of his train songs, "The Panama Limited" and "Special Streamline," were the first numbers on OJL's 1963 album *The Mississippi Blues 1927–1940*. The two books and four compilations did much to bring country blues into the folk revival.

The folk audience was introduced to Booker's music on three albums by contemporary folk singers who covered his songs. The first was Bob Dylan's energetic cover of "Fixin' To Die Blues" on his self-titled debut album in 1962. Singer-songwriter Buffy Sainte-Marie recorded "Fixin' To Die" for her second album, *Many a Mile*, which was released in 1965. Boston-based folksinger Tom Rush closed his first album for Elektra Records in 1965 with a virtuoso performance that he called "a mixture of several train songs by Bukka White."[1] Rush credited "The Panama Limited," "Special Streamline," "New Orleans Streamline," and "The Atlanta Special" as his sources. He reworked elements of these songs into a unified narrative that he titled "The Panama Limited," noting that "all of [the songs] are very similar in structure." Booker wrote the original "Panama Limited" about the train that ran between New Orleans and Chicago.

By the time Booker came to Massachusetts in April 1964 to perform at the Huntington Avenue YMCA, the folk revival had grown into an international musical movement. Chronicling the revival in the United States during the mid- to late 1960s were *New York Times* music critic Robert Shelton and freelance photographer David Gahr, who collaborated on a large-format book titled *The Face of Folk Music*. Gahr was in demand as a photographer of album covers as well as candid images of the folk revival. In 1962 Shelton's *Times* review of Bob Dylan at Gerde's Folk City elevated Dylan above other talented members of his singer-songwriter cohort such as Tom Paxton and Phil Ochs.

Shelton's notes on the back cover of Dylan's self-titled first album singled him out as the voice of a new generation of folk performers. The generation's best-known performer was Joan Baez, the pure-voiced singer of ballads such as "Mary Hamilton" and "Silver Dagger." An artist's rendering of Baez's long, dark hair and striking features appeared on the November 23, 1962, cover of *Time* magazine, with an accompanying cover story on Baez and folk music written by then contributing editor John McPhee.[2]

In early 1964, the Folk Song Society of Greater Boston announced that "legendary blues singer Bukka White" would perform for three consecutive nights at the Huntington Avenue YMCA in downtown

Boston, across the Charles River from Cambridge. Behind the creation of the Folk Society and producing the shows were concert promoter Dick Waterman and Dave Wilson, editor of *The Broadside of Boston.*[3] They published a full-page advertisement in the mid-April issue of *The Broadside*, noting that the YMCA's Bates Hall "will operate as a coffee house" on concert nights.[4]

The dates and times for the shows were Thursday through Saturday nights, April 23 through 25, from 8:30 p.m. to 12:30 a.m.—an ambitious plan to introduce Booker to Boston audiences, but the shows were sparsely attended. Author and blues enthusiast Peter Guralnick was there on opening night. He remembered that Booker wore a tuxedo for the occasion.[5]

Three straight nights performing two or more sets a night would have challenged the stamina of most of the rediscovered blues musicians—Mississippi John Hurt, Skip James, and Son House among them—but Booker was younger than they were, and full of vitality. Blues scholar David Evans, then a junior at Harvard, recalled how he and his peers responded to Booker:

> I think we were slightly disappointed that he wasn't a musical living fossil. We expected some sort of deep philosopher of the blues, someone who could tell us what suffering was all about. This was the personality his old recordings suggested to us. Of course, he was recently out of prison in 1940, and no doubt had mellowed somewhat since then. So we had to be satisfied with more boisterous recreations of his old recordings. . . . We were also a little taken aback that he wasn't an old and generous figure like Hurt and [Sleepy John] Estes. Rather than appearing grandfatherly, he was more like a raunchy uncle, still seeming to live an active life and looking forward to the next day.[6]

There were other disappointments. Unlike Mississippi John Hurt and Skip James, whose voices continued to sound like their early records, Booker's voice had changed since 1940. "What struck me most about his performance was how his voice had thickened over the years," Peter Guralnick recalled.[7] "And how his guitar, which had always served as such a strong rhythm instrument on the original records, now seemed like a rhythm instrument only, with much of the delicacy that could be heard on the early recordings lost."

What captured listeners' attention was his stage presence. David Evans recalled, "Whatever disappointment we had was mitigated by him being a very strong performer . . . and recreating enough of his old repertoire."

In the 1960s, most folk shows were produced on a shoestring budget. To reduce expenses, some promoters preferred that touring musicians stay with people in the folk community. For Booker's performances, Dave Wilson and Dick Waterman arranged with Alan Wilson (no relation to Dave) and his roommate Phil Spiro to let the musician stay with them in Cambridge. "Our apartment was a very low-rent place on Roberts Road," Spiro recalled:

> Al and I had hardly any money between us, and the apartment and its furnishing reflected that. The front room was Al's, followed towards the rear by what passed for a living room, then the kitchen, and finally in back, my room, in which I had a bed and a dresser. The bathroom was literally that, a room with a bathtub and a sink, with the toilet in a separate room off the entrance hall . . . Al's room was a disaster by anyone's standards, even mine. Al, understandably overcome by profound respect for the great bluesman who was to stay with us, brought in a trash can and a shovel, and cleaned up his room to a remarkably high standard. Bukka stayed in Al's room, and Al slept on the couch in the living room.[8]

Spiro had taken time off from his studies at the Massachusetts Institute of Technology (MIT). He found an entry-level position in the emerging high-tech industry, working as systems programmer for Itek—a defense contractor that supplied photo reconnaissance and optical systems to the military.[9] Booker's visit to Cambridge and Boston "came at a time when I was at my job in Lexington, which was about an hour away by generally unreliable public transit, so I missed all of these interviews and recording sessions," Spiro recalled. "Al worked at bricklaying for his father's company on occasion, and had a few guitar students, but apparently had no problem being available during the day while Bukka stayed with us."

Twenty-year-old Alan Wilson grew up in Arlington, which borders on Cambridge. He was taking courses at Boston University, intending to major in music, until he left college in the spring of 1964. Out of work and no longer a student, Wilson advertised in *The Broadside of Boston* that he was available as a teacher of blues guitar and harmonica.[10] "Learn Delta Blues," his ad headline read. The copy promised that Al could teach students "the bottleneck and open tuning styles" of a number of famous Mississippi bluesmen with "hitherto unparalleled accuracy." The bluesmen he mentioned were Skip James, Son House, Charley Patton, Robert Johnson, Fred McDowell, and Bukka White.

Advance publicity and alternative newspaper coverage were an indication that the Boston-Cambridge folk community considered Booker's three performances to be an important event (though perhaps not as important as Joan Baez's appearance at Symphony Hall on April 15, which was sold out). Booker shared the cover of the April 15 issue of *The Broadside of Boston* with Jesse "Lone Cat" Fuller, who was known for writing the folk revival staple "San Francisco Bay Blues."

Alan Wilson contributed an article on Booker to the issue. Under the headline "Bukka White, Master of the Blues Lyric,"[11] Wilson wrote, "Bukka White is a great bluesman, and 'great' is not a word I am inclined to use lightly. Bukka's recordings of 1940 for ARC [American Recording Company] comprise one of but six groups of recordings which I feel have earned such high praise. . . ." Wilson's article showed that he was familiar with Booker's recordings. He criticized Booker's guitar playing at slow tempos, calling it "probably the weakest aspect of his work," and praised his bottleneck playing at fast tempos. Wilson wrote, "Particularly exciting is his method of integrating melodic bottleneck configurations into a strum pattern with no loss of rhythmic momentum. . . ."[12] He reserved his highest praise for Booker's lyrics. "Bukka is, bar none, the greatest blues lyricist," he wrote. "Rejecting almost entirely the thousands of stock blues verses, he instead uses primarily his own lyrics. His finest efforts are not only supremely poetic, but for me achieve a degree of psychological insight comparable to the best stream of consciousness fiction."

Published a week before Wilson met Booker or heard him perform, the article set the table for the mentor-apprentice relationship that developed between the two men. In one short week, with Booker living in Al and Phil Spiro's apartment and hanging out at Harvard, Al and Booker played blues together, conducted an ongoing conversation that took the form of Al interviewing Booker about his music, and enjoyed each other's company a great deal. Socially awkward, Wilson "lost his reserve when dealing with people on a musical basis," his biographer Rebecca Davis wrote.[13] "He held legendary bluesmen like White in high esteem, but never hesitated to talk to them, learn from them, and play with them if appropriate. Most older artists recognized his genuine interest in the music, and readily taught him whatever he wanted to know. Most of his peers recall him having an uncanny ability to connect with other musicians."

John Fahey had left the philosophy program at the University of California in Berkeley and enrolled in a master's degree program in Folklore and Mythology at the University of California, Los Angeles. In spring or early summer 1965, he came east to play in coffeehouses. After meeting the musically gifted Wilson, Fahey convinced him to come back to California with him. He said he would pay Wilson to help him with his master's thesis on Charley Patton, and promised that Wilson would find more musical opportunities in California. Fahey was right. Once Wilson moved to Los Angeles, he met other blues players and formed the band Canned Heat. After a couple of false starts, a reorganized lineup of the band came to the attention of promoters. In 1967 and 1969, Canned Heat performed at the two most important festivals of 1960s rock: the Monterey Pop Festival in California and the Woodstock gathering in upstate New York. Wilson and his bandmates appear in the film *Monterey Pop* and the director's cut of *Woodstock: Three Days of Peace and Music.* The song "Goin' Up the Country," sung by Wilson, became Woodstock's unofficial anthem.

WITH ONLY THREE PERFORMANCES PLANNED, BOOKER HAD PLENTY of time to spend with a group of blues enthusiasts in Cambridge. In addition to Phil Spiro and Al Wilson, the group included Harvard junior David Evans and their friend Laurie Forti. Evans lived in the undergraduate residence hall Adams House, on Plympton Street near Harvard Square.

Wilson and David Evans had met at Briggs & Briggs, a music and record store in Harvard Square frequented by folk and blues enthusiasts. The two young men discovered that they shared a passion for blues, especially the Mississippi styles of Son House, Skip James, and John Hurt. With Wilson on harmonica and Evans playing an acoustic guitar, they performed together at open microphone nights called hoots.

The group had an informal advisor in Bruce Jackson, a Marine Corps veteran who came to Harvard from Indiana University as a junior fellow in the Society of Fellows—a highly competitive fellowship that gave its recipients the freedom to do their own research. "In a lot of ways, being a junior fellow was better than being a junior faculty member," Jackson recalled.[14] "The fellowship only lasted three years, but there was no obligation to teach, no obligation to do anything but go to Monday night dinners and follow your interests."

Jackson's interests took him to Texas, where he arrived with recording equipment that Harvard had bought for him to collect stories and songs from inmates in Texas prisons. In 1972 Harvard University Press published Jackson's *Wake Up Dead Man: Afro-American Worksongs from Texas Prisons*, and Rounder Records released an album of the original recordings in 1975, *Wake Up Dead Man: Black Convict Worksongs from Texas Prisons.*

With access to Jackson's professional-quality equipment, Wilson, Forti, and Evans were able to make tape recordings of Booker on April 24, 26, 29, and 30. Al Wilson spent the most time with him. Wilson's comfort level talking with an older Black blues musician comes through in the reel-to-reel tape recordings of him playing music with Booker and feeling free to ask him questions about his life and music.

Since Booker's recording of "Shake 'Em On Down" had become a popular country blues number in 1937, Wilson wanted to know why he didn't make another record until 1940. "The guy wouldn't come to my figures," Booker said.[15] Presumably, the "guy" was Lester Melrose. A friend of Booker's had told him that five hundred copies of the record immediately sold out. Bypassing the fact that he had gone to prison, Booker told Wilson, "I figured if it was that great, the guy would come up to my figure. So much in this kind of business that if a man don't know, he'll get his head bit off." He added that he would need a lawyer to get his percentage of the five or six thousand dollars he estimated the record had earned.

In Al Wilson, Booker had found a young man who was interested in everything about him and would pay attention to anything he had to say. On one occasion, Wilson asked him, "What do you think is the ideal place to play?"[16] Booker responded, "I like to go to different places. The answer would be where I gets the most money. Other times you feel more welcome at a place than you do others. Get yourself a smooth time. Some places I go to never have the right feeling."

On Sunday, April 26, Booker was a guest on Harvard student radio station WHRB. The program was "The Balladeer." Host Hal Edgar interviewed Booker between the songs he performed in the studio, accompanied by Al Wilson on harmonica. Booker played "World Boogie," "Baby Please Don't Go," "Aberdeen Blues," "Don't Sic 'Em Dogs on Me," and "Every Day I Have the Blues," closing with the spoken aside, "The blues follow the sun down every day."

Booker's guitar playing sounded best on "Baby Please Don't Go," as he bent notes as well as played slide style. After "Aberdeen Blues," Hal Edgar asked him how he made the rhythmic slapping sound on guitar. Booker responded that when he played baseball, he could throw the ball as fast over his shoulder as he could throw it forward. "I always like to do something different," he said. Before signing off, Edgar told listeners, "Bukka's got a very fine record out on Takoma. If you haven't bought it yet, please do so"—the first indication that *Mississippi Blues Vol. 1* had been released.

As was a standard line of questioning with older blues musicians, the Cambridge interviewers asked Booker about his date and place of birth, his parents and how they made a living, when he got his first guitar, his use of guitar tunings, learning to play piano, his marriages, places traveled, other notable musicians encountered, and even his time in prison.[17] Handwritten on lined notebook paper, notes from one interview consist of four pages of questions and brief summaries of Booker's answers.[18] Phil Spiro and Laurie Forti took the lead, with additional questions from Al Wilson.

When Forti asked Booker if his father had taught him to play music, Booker's answer was summarized as "I went my own way. He played too complicated."

What kind of music did he play? "He played in all the keys. Blues, jazz . . . on the violin." Did your father stick to blues? "No. His voice wasn't too good, like my voice isn't as good as it used to be." Did anyone else in the family play? "My sister [Estelle] played better than me. She had a better voice."

What blues musicians in Mississippi did you know? "I saw Charley Patton once. He gave me ideas. I used to slap the strings, but my fingers hurt. I switched to bottleneck." What kind of man was Patton? "He was light skinned. He was a nice guy, but would get jealous."

What does it take to be a good blues man? "Your mind, words, feeling. All your soul. And something on the outside to occupy your mind so you're not too worried, not too satisfied." What is the difference between a good musician and a good blues man? "It's a different feeling. People say, 'The devil can make you feel so good you'll jump off a bridge.' A church song player shouldn't play at a roadhouse."

Why did you go to Parchman Farm? "I got railroaded through a bad deal." How did you get out? "Some people worked for me to get out, but they kept me there to play." Were you a prison musician? "Yes. We had a band." Did they put you to work? "No." What did other inmates do? "They worked on the farm. If you treat yourself good, you'll treat others right."

Were you a boxer? "Yes." Did you make much money? "No." Where did you box? "Chicago." How many times? "Four." Did you play baseball? "I was a pitcher and played long-field. All over the place." Did you make money? "Yes. I bet on the games. I pitched cruel and cool." Did you pitch against Satchel Paige? "Yes. We won. My drop pitch was called the Hudson."

Phil Spiro asked Booker if he ever went to Texas. "Yes." Did you see many musicians? "Not much. I was playing ball." Did you see Blind Willie McTell? Lead Belly? "No. I quit music for a long time." Did you give it up for the church? "No. I wanted to rest." When was that? "It was 1940, after the records. You do the work. They make the money."

Why did you start playing again? "It was born in me." What did you do after 1940? "Job. I would feel good at the job. Play music on the weekend . . . any type music. I'm gregarious. I throw my money around."

Booker responded to every question, though the note-taker characterized a couple of his answers as "vague."

In an interview with David Evans and Al Wilson in Wilson's apartment on Roberts Road, Booker's answer to one of their questions led to the rediscovery of another important blues musician from the 1930s and 1940s. Evans recalled, "Al and I went down a list we had prepared of Mississippi artists we thought he might have known. We struck pay dirt when I asked him about Son House, and he replied that a friend had seen Son recently at a Memphis movie theater."[19] The friend was singer Lillian Glover, known in her home city as Memphis Ma Rainey. "That led to the expedition by Spiro, Waterman, and (Nick) Perls that 'rediscovered' Son House," Evans said. New Yorker J. Nicholas Perls was a record collector and founder of the reissue label Yazoo Records. Lillian Glover's report turned out to be incorrect, but after the trio of blues sleuths drove to the South looking for Eddie "Son" House, they obtained his home address by locating people who knew him and telephoning a relative of his. Learning that House was living in Rochester, New York, they drove north to meet him.

Booker was broke when he visited Boston and Cambridge. In a recorded conversation with Al Wilson, he expressed that he had gotten publicity, but no money. He said his situation was the same in Los Angeles. "Whatever you want to make of this, I been on the air. Been on the radio twice. Been on TV."[20] As someone who was accustomed to earning cash with his music, he may have felt that he was being taken advantage of.

His poverty was evident. On one occasion, several blues enthusiasts at Adams House discussed what to order from a nearby delicatessen—probably a popular deli at the corner of Holyoke and Mount Auburn Streets, Elsie's Sandwich Shop. Elsie's was a block away from Adams House. As people voiced their preferences, someone offered to buy Booker a sandwich. He told them he liked his food cooked, so a group member said they would order a hamburger for him. Booker was not part of the conversation until someone offered to pay for his food.

Booker's week in Cambridge was the collision of two worlds. The students and their friends had resources. Al Wilson may have been unemployed, but he had a roommate with a job and his family in Arlington. Booker was on his own more than a thousand miles from home. He could not count on his managers in California for support, and knew no one in Boston (though he claimed that an old girlfriend lived in the city). He kept busy by doing what his hosts expected and entertaining them.

Booker opened up to Wilson about his isolation in California, and the need to find a place where he felt comfortable. After leaving Memphis in 1963, he settled on Berkeley because that was where his new managers lived. ED Denson recalled finding a place for Booker to stay at the home of a friend and his wife. "I've forgotten Gary's last name, but not my gratitude for his taking Booker into his home," Denson wrote.[21]

In Booker's experience, Berkeley was one of those places that did not have the right feeling. He told Wilson, "It was so quiet I couldn't live long there. I used to go out on a bench and play blues all day long. Everybody is going to school. At night you go to the coffeehouses." Denson admitted that he and Fahey could have done much better by Booker. "I didn't think much about it at the time," he said, "but if we could have found Booker housing in the Black area of Oakland, he would have had much more social life."[22]

Chapter Nineteen

SKY SONGS

DURING THE TURBULENT EVENTS ON CAMPUS IN THE 1960S, ONE OF the few things that remained the same at the University of California at Berkeley was the familiar figure of the Crunchy Munchy Man. From 1952 to 1968, Polish-born Alfred Dattner stood outside Berkeley's Sather Gate selling ice cream. The UC humor magazine described Dattner as "a real friend of the Cal student, vending his wares with both a smile and a bit of counsel on anything from philosophy to physics."[1] All around him, times were changing.

The city of Berkeley and its university were among the first places to experience the political and cultural shifts that ultimately spread across the United States from the eastern shore of San Francisco Bay to Columbia University in New York City's Morningside Heights. In the fall of 1964, Berkeley students would gather outside Sproul Hall to listen to activist speakers who wanted to forge an alliance between the university's workers and its students. On December 2, graduate student Mario Savio urged students to stage a sit-in on the second floor of Sproul to force the university administration to listen to them. By the following spring, Savio and the Free Speech Movement had inspired members of Students for a Democratic Society at Harvard University in Cambridge, Massachusetts, to hand out leaflets at downtown Boston subway exits calling for a similar movement.

The emerging counterculture made Berkeley the center of a thriving music scene, especially folk music. Several of the folk scene's most active participants had come to Berkeley to attend the university. John Fahey and ED Denson had moved across the country to enter programs at UC Berkeley. California native Barry Olivier moved to the city of Berkeley as a teenager. He attended UC Berkeley for a time, became a guitar teacher, and ran the Berkeley Folk Music Festival from 1958 to 1970 in cooperation with the university.[2]

Chris Strachwitz was born into an aristocratic farming family in Gross Reichenau, Lower Silesia, then a part of Germany, but now Poland. He emigrated with his family to Reno, Nevada, in 1947, and moved to Santa Barbara, California, where he graduated from the Cate School in nearby Carpinteria. While attending Pomona College in Claremont, Strachwitz began to frequent jazz clubs in Los Angeles, taping a friend who played saxophone, then other performers. He enrolled in the University of California at Berkeley in 1952, but was drafted into the United States Army in 1954—a year after the end of the Korean War. Stationed in Austria, he was able listen to the American jazz performers who toured Europe.

After his discharge, Strachwitz reentered the university, where he found a part-time job booking jazz and rhythm and blues performers to play at the stadium during halftime at football games. He continued to pursue his interest in all forms of American vernacular music, including folk. Looking back, Strachwitz believed that the city's folk community had divided into two distinct camps that complemented each other. He recalled Barry Olivier bringing "academic folk musicians" to Berkeley while Strachwitz favored roots musicians. "That's how it was in those days," he recalled. "Academic people wanted interpreters. I was a fan of more original performers."

In 1960 Strachwitz decided to start his own record label. While continuing to study engineering and mathematics, he made a field trip to Texas. There he met up with musicologist Mack McCormick, and together they traveled to Navasota, Texas, where Strachwitz recorded Mance Lipscomb for what would become the label's first LP, *Mance Lipscomb, Texas Songster and Sharecropper*. McCormick suggested calling the label "Arhoolie" from a term that meant field holler.

In early 1964, in an effort to bring attention to their new label, Denson and Fahey took Booker into the studio to make another record. In the mid-1960s, a 45 rpm record had a much better chance of being played on radio than a track from an album. The album-oriented format for blues and rock radio was at least two years in the future. I asked Denson if he and Fahey decided to release a 45 for that reason. "Yes, some sort of air play was the hope," Denson recalled.[3] "It goes to show how much we knew about promotion and radio play."

The managers took Booker to Sierra Sound Laboratories (also called Sierra Sound Studios) at 1741 Alcatraz Avenue in Berkeley, with the idea of re-recording one of his best-known songs, "Fixin' To Die Blues." Writer Samuel B. Charters had given "Fixin' To Die" a second life during the folk revival by including it on his 1959 compilation album *The Country Blues*. After Bob Dylan covered the song on his 1962 debut album, Fahey and Denson thought that a new recording by the man who wrote the song would alert the folk and blues audiences that Booker was not only alive, but still playing his music.

Chris Strachwitz was in the studio with Denson and Fahey when Booker refused to record "Fixin' To Die Blues" a second time. What he observed that day proved helpful when he recorded Booker soon after:

> I was interested in recording Bukka for Arhoolie. One day I think Fahey wanted to make a 45-rpm record and they were at Sierra Sound Studio to record it. I dropped by and found Fahey torturing and pleading or commanding Bukka to make a new recording of this song. But Bukka was telling Fahey "I don't really feel right now that I am fixin' to die" and so he refused to redo it. They did "World Boogie" and ["Midnight Blue"] and pressed it on a Takoma 45.[4]

As Strachwitz later noted, "Bukka was gregarious and friendly except when he was pissed off."[5]

In the liner notes to the *Sky Songs* albums, Strachwitz wrote, "When I first met Bukka, I was immediately impressed by his overpowering personality—he seemed very intense and full of life—it had to come out of him and I slowly found out what Bukka was like."[6]

As Fahey and Denson found opportunities for their artist to perform in Berkeley, Booker began to add new lyrics to old songs and make up lyrics to new songs as he sang them over several of his familiar guitar accompaniments. Chris Strachwitz was quick to recognize that this new arrival in Berkeley had a gift. "I really admired Bukka for his remarkable ability as a story teller, singer, and fantastic improviser," he recalled. "For his time, he was a rapper of the first order, which apparently was a valued asset already with pre-recording days' songsters."[7]

Once Booker agreed to make a record for Arhoolie, Strachwitz used his own apartment as the studio. He recalled a routine of picking Booker up at John Fahey's house, recording him, and driving him back to Fahey's. "I liked him," he said. "In the morning he was wide awake and was ready to chat. I am not a morning person. He would get in the car and start talking. He was one of those dynamos."[8]

When Strachwitz asked Booker to talk about his life in Mississippi for the album notes, Booker surprised him. "The mike was on," Strachwitz recalled, "and after looking at it for a second, he stared out of the window at the bright sunny sky and began what turned out to be one of the most delightful folk tales I have ever heard."[9] On the record, the monologue about enticing a wide range of Mississippians to sip from a cup of moonshine and dance was titled "Mixed Water." Booker's tall tale took up an entire side of an album.

The time limit on 78 rpm records was a little over three minutes. Having learned how to make live recordings of jazz musicians in college, Strachwitz realized that the greater length of 33 rpm record albums would be ideal for capturing on vinyl the extended songs that he heard Booker making up.

Booker had a name for this kind of songwriting. He told Strachwitz, "I just reach up and pull them out of the sky—call them sky songs—they just come to me."[10] Strachwitz added, "His performances are not polished, finished Tin Pan Alley songs, but they are marvelous on the spot creations—images and recollections as they come to the artist's mind. He is no doubt a man with one of the most vivid and prolific imaginations I have ever had the pleasure of recording."[11]

In one of our conversations, Strachwitz described Booker as brilliant. I asked him what he meant:

> Bukka's mind was working all the time, especially as soon as he had somebody listening to him. He would just crank up . . . I recorded a little group in Austria once. One of the lyrics was "Your mouth went for a walk." Bukka had that ability to keep his mouth going as to what images were in his head. That's the closest thing I can come to it. There are constantly new images popping into his head. Bukka had that ability to make up these amazing tales. He probably could have recorded thousands of songs and each one would be different.[12]

A few days after recording Booker's recollections for the notes, Strachwitz went to the Cabale folk club in Berkeley to hear Booker on stage. He wanted to become familiar with Booker's repertoire so that he could decide which songs to put on the record. What Strachwitz heard confirmed what he had observed in the studio: recording Booker required a different approach. Strachwitz wrote, ". . . again I discovered that Bukka, like most spontaneous artists, would never sing the same song twice except a few selections which he had recorded long ago . . . Bukka would often play only three or four songs per set because they turned out to be long spontaneous creations which are often found in the best of folk art."[13] To satisfy members of the audience who expected to hear the songs performed as he had recorded them between 1930 and 1940, Booker often included "Fixin' To Die Blues," "Aberdeen Mississippi Blues," and the train song "Special Stream Line" in his performances.

Booker's extended monologue in Strachwitz's apartment and long-form songs at the Cabale convinced Strachwitz that his production would have to make room for the music. Booker's recordings from 1930, 1937, and 1940 were condensed samplings of how his music sounded in those years—allowing for the limitations, including running time, of available recording technology—but Booker's Arhoolie recordings represented a departure from traditional blues conventions. Strachwitz was aware that he was using a new approach. His flexible approach was deliberate. Strachwitz recalled:

> Ed Denson and John Fahey, who produced the Takoma LP by Bukka White in a more conventional manner, told me that if I wished the numbers to be within the 3 or 4 minute time limit, I ought to tap Bukka on the shoulder whenever the time was up—but I felt that I should try and capture a few of the images which he creates when left alone, and so I let him play as long as he wished, which was invariably either past the time for one reel of tape to run out at 15 inches per second—or until he happened to see me pointing at the few feet remaining on the reel.[14]

To create the long songs that Strachwitz gave him the time to perform, Booker established a rhythmic chord pattern on guitar—often taken from songs he had recorded years before—and improvised lyrics over the pattern as they came to him. The impetus to compose songs in this way came from the musician rather than a producer. When Booker spent time in the home of folklorist Bruce Jackson in Cambridge in 1964, Jackson recalled him sitting on the steps and improvising lyrics for hours. Though these improvisations might have been unusual on recordings, they were not new to blues musicians of Booker's generation. Country blues musicians often played music for dancing, so were accustomed to stretching out their material. Syndicated blues radio host Bruce Pingree of WUNH in Durham, New Hampshire, explained, "A lot of the old blues singers could do that, but they didn't record them [that way]. The idea was to keep people on the dance floor."[15]

Strachwitz's equipment at home was sufficient for recording a musician and an instrument. He recalled how he conducted the sessions:

> I was sitting next to the machine, and he was in a chair next to the window. I said okay, I punched [the record button] in, and he started playing. At 7½ [inches per second tape speed], I got half an hour. We used seven-inch reels, not ten-inch. I could record two numbers per tape. [Recording at] the Cabale was different. He liked playing the piano and could tell these stories. Once he got in that groove, he could play [a single number] for twenty minutes.[16]

By now well versed in American roots music, Strachwitz began looking for tradition-oriented musicians to make records for his new label, but it was the counterculture composition "I Feel Like I'm Fixin' To Die Rag," written and performed by Country Joe McDonald, that secured the future of Arhoolie.

Managed by ED Denson, Joe McDonald was looking for a studio where he could record his jug band. He and Denson made a deal with Strachwitz to record the band in the early Arhoolie studio in exchange for McDonald giving Strachwitz his half of the publishing rights to "I Feel Like I'm Fixin' To Die Rag." Song titles are not subject to copyright, so Country Joe incorporated one of Booker's best known songs into the title of his own song. The counterculture was quick to take elements of blues music for its own music—a cultural appropriation made easier by fact that blues songs often came from a deep reservoir of verses in a shared oral tradition, rather than from the minds and experiences of individual composers.[17] However, no one seriously questioned that Booker White had written "Fixin' To Die Blues." The song was Booker's personal response to witnessing a friend's death. The connection between the two song titles was obvious. Chris Strachwitz recorded both Booker and McDonald.

Country Joe first recorded "I Feel Like I'm Fixin' To Die Rag" with Strachwitz in 1965. In 1967, "I-Feel-Like-I'm-Fixin' To Die" became the title song of the second album by McDonald's electric band, Country Joe and the Fish, and McDonald famously played a solo version on stage at Woodstock in August 1969. Though Country Joe later maintained that his crude introduction to the song at Woodstock hurt his career, the song sold records.[18] According to Chris Strachwitz, "The [royalties from] publishing bought my building." The use of Booker's title earned the blues musician nothing.

Chapter Twenty

UNCERTAIN PROSPECTS

FROM 1963 TO 1966, THE POSSIBILITY OF BOOKER LAUNCHING A SUCcessful second career in music was uncertain. His first managers, John Fahey and ED Denson, lacked professional experience and put their fledgling Takoma record label ahead of their client's best interest, which would have involved exploring the possibility of a contract with Elektra. Two years later, Booker and his second manager, Dick Waterman, parted company amid mutual accusations and anger.

In *Pioneers of the Blues Revival,* Steve Cushing asked Waterman if—in addition to managing Son House, Skip James, and other blues musicians—he had "handled" Bukka White. "I did," Waterman responded. "And he's probably one of the few I had an unhappy and unsuccessful experience with."

In a 2004 book of his photographs and recollections of blues musicians, *Between Midnight and Day: The Last Unpublished Blues Archive,* Waterman disparaged Booker.[1] He wrote that the reason he had dismissed Booker as a client after two years was disloyalty:

> I found him to be disloyal, and through my . . . forty-five years in the music business, I'm loyal. If I have any quality at all, it's that. I'm fair and I'm loyal. You give me your loyalty, I give you mine. I shook hands with people. . . . I never had to have a piece of paper. And I put Bukka White out on tour, and it was a very good tour and a very lucrative tour. And I got no callbacks. Nothing. . . . And it turned out that he had told people that he didn't like giving Dick Waterman ten percent of his money. . . ."[2]

Waterman wrote that while Booker was on a club tour that Waterman had set up, Booker gave club owners his phone number in Memphis and told them to call him at home if they wanted him to come back. "So there was that example," Waterman wrote. "And there's another one and another one. And finally I found that I couldn't have disloyalty on my artists roster. And if you have a little bit of it, it's only going to poison the well. So I ended my relationship with Bukka and never spoke with him again."

When I visited Booker's daughter Irene Kertchaval in Tennessee in July 2017, she warned me that I would hear negative comments about her father from Waterman, and wanted to tell me the story as she had heard it from Booker himself. Kertchaval said the cause of the misunderstanding was fifty dollars that Waterman deducted from a check he received from the producers of a Canadian television program. Kertchaval said her father thought Waterman had cheated him. The show was a 1966 television special titled *The Blues*.

When I asked Waterman in 2021 about the disagreement, he told me:

> What happened with Bukka was this. A man named Manny Greenhill was booking a Canadian TV show and they really wanted him [in the show]. The money was five hundred dollars, which was good in those days. I kept making the point [to Greenhill], what if they wanted to go back to the tapes and make a second show? They should write it in the contract that if they decide to have another show, my guy gets another five hundred dollars. [Greenhill] said that's not going to happen, but I said write it in anyway. Later they decide to go into the tapes and make another show, so I got a check for five hundred dollars, which I deposited. I wrote a check for four-fifty and sent it to Bukka.[3]

Waterman and Kertchaval's accounts agreed on one point: that the two men confronted each other at the 1966 Newport Folk Festival.

"I went to the festival and had a fifty dollar bill," Waterman told me. "I spotted him across an open field and walked up to him and took the bill and folded it and put it in his front pocket. I said, 'Here's your fifty dollars and don't even speak my name or call me again.'"

Kertchaval recalled her father saying that when the two men met at Newport, they sat on a bench arguing until Waterman shoved a bill in Booker's shirt pocket and said he hoped that he wouldn't see him again until he spit on his grave.[4]

While writing this book, I was sent a copy of a letter that Booker had written on May 27, 1966, to Israel "Izzy" Young, who played a part in the folk revival as owner of the Folklore Center in Greenwich Village during the 1960s. When Young died in February 2019, the headline of his obituary in the *New York Times* proclaimed, "Izzy Young, Who Presided over the Folk Revival, Is Dead at 90."[5] Under Young's ownership, the Folklore Center had been a hub for musicians and songwriters: Bob Dylan, Peter Yarrow, Mary Travers, and Joni Mitchell, among many others. In November 4, 1961, Izzy and the Center had produced Dylan's first New York City concert, which was held at Carnegie Hall.[6]

Apparently Booker wrote to Young two months before the 1966 Newport Folk Festival, asking about a check he had expected to receive for recordings he made for the Verve/Folkways label in November 1965 at the Café Au Go Go. Booker, Son House, Skip James, and Big Joe Williams all had been recorded for an album of blues greats, and Izzy Young was the host of the sessions.[7] In his letter, Booker wrote he thought Dick Waterman had mishandled an earlier check, so he wanted to inform Izzy that Waterman no longer represented him:

> Dear Mr. Young:
>
> I was just sitting and thinking about the records we recorded at the Go Go, and I have not heard anything from them, so I decided to write you. I thought it would be time for me to be hearing some kind of information about them. What ever you do, if any money is in that recording I did, please don't let Mr. Dick Waterman get his hand on it, as I never will get it.
>
> Why I am telling you this [is] because I have been having some trouble getting some that he owe to me now. It was a check sent to me on the 14th day of March, and he cashed it on the 21st of March. He printed my name on the back and used Avalon Productions' stamp which makes him liable. . . . Mr. Waterman does not have no control to do business like that. He could be in for a lot of trouble. I would like to here [*sic*] from you right away and Mr. Waterman is no longer my booking agent.
>
> Yours very truly,
> Booker T. White[8]

Booker's partner Leola Morris probably helped him write the letter, since the handwriting appears to be the same as in Booker's later correspondence with a photographer in England that appears to have been handwritten by Morris.

IN 2009, WHEN I INTERVIEWED ED PEARL, OWNER OF THE LOS Angeles club the Ash Grove, he remembered Booker well.[9] Pearl recalled booking him into the Ash Grove in 1964 and 1965. He said he invited Booker to stay with him and his wife Kate in their house in the Hollywood Hills. On his second visit, Booker and Ed's brother Bernie were alone in the Hollywood Hills house as a riot was taking place in the city below.

"He and I stood by the windows and watched Watts burn in 1965," Bernie Pearl recalled. From a distance, Booker witnessed the infamous Watts Riots, a series of violent confrontations between Los Angeles police and residents of Watts and other predominantly Black neighborhoods in South Central Los Angeles. The riots occurred August 11 to 16, 1965.[10] Of Booker's reaction, Bernie said, "His comment was 'Lord have mercy' with probably an mmm . . . mmm . . . mmm or two."[11]

Singer-songwriter Buffy Sainte-Marie met Booker when their performance schedules brought them to the Ash Grove at the same time in early 1964.[12] Sainte-Marie was an accomplished performer who attracted attention on stage at the Newport Folk Festival, but thought of herself as a songwriter first.[13] Cover versions of her protest song "The Universal Soldier" did well for both Glen Campbell and Donovan Leitch, and her song "Up Where We Belong," co-written with Jack Nitzsche and Will Jennings for the 1982 film *An Officer and a Gentleman*, won an Oscar and Golden Globe for best original song.

Sainte-Marie was taken with the poetry she heard in Booker's lyrics, particularly in the lines "I'm looking funny in my eyes / I believe I'm fixing to die / I know I was born to die / but I hate to leave my children crying" from "Fixin' To Die Blues."[14] When she recorded her second album for Vanguard Records, she included a faithful version of "Fixin' To Die." *Many a Mile* was released in early 1965.

Following the advice of East Coast musician/folklorists such as Mike Seeger and John Cohen of the New Lost City Ramblers, Ed Pearl brought traditional blues and bluegrass performers to the Ash Grove for weeklong engagements. The performers played two shows a day for five or six days a week. Booker returned to play extended engagements in August and September 1967, and again in November 1969. Without his knowledge, portions of several performances were recorded (August 17–20 and September 8–10, 1967, and November 7, 1969) and eventually posted online.

Traditional blues and bluegrass musicians drew a crowd of younger musicians to the club, such as Ry Cooder and Taj Mahal, who would form the Rising Sons. Pearl conceived of the Ash Grove as a folk music center. He allowed performers to use the club as a place to give lessons.

"Young kids, everyone, wanted to learn from them," he recalled. Booker was in considerable demand as a teacher, Pearl said. "He had a ton of people [wanting to take lessons] because he had an important and powerful guitar style."

Ed recalled spending time with Booker, and showing him around the area. He took him to Knott's Berry Farm. "I preferred to go to that place over Disneyland because it had a very downhome section of nineteenth-century buildings," he said. On the way, Booker talked about home, and his wife and family. He was interested in the Watts Towers, which they passed as they drove. "I really got a kick out of this very proud man whose spirit had not been broken," he said. "He was not like Mance Lipscomb, who was humble." In Ed's estimation, Booker was "the holder of the torch"—a nod both to Booker's personal presence and his musicianship.

Booker made an impression on others in the music business. In his book *How Bluegrass Music Destroyed My Life*, John Fahey included a fanciful account of his friendship with Booker in a chapter called "Fish." Fahey described Booker as being larger than life, endowing him with extraordinary strength:

> Booker was as strong as an ox.
> He was a giant of a man.
> He looked like an enormous bullfrog.
> I saw him pick up an old Ford V-8 motor once out in a car junkyard where we were looking for parts.
> All by himself.[15]

Since Booker's job at the Newberry Equipment Company required handling large pieces of sheet metal, he must have been unusually strong; but Fahey's recollection of his picking up a V-8 engine in the junkyard may have been a moment of literary license, as are other elements in this tale of catching and eating an enormous catfish.

IN THE YEARS AFTER OUR INTERVIEW, I FOUND THAT SOME EVENTS Booker described that I thought might be exaggerations could be verified. Until I thought to ask Ed Pearl, I had been unable to identify the stadium concert that Booker recalled performing with other musicians in Los Angeles. Pearl immediately recognized the concert as Blues '65—a multi-performer show that he produced at the Santa Monica Civic Auditorium on February 26, 1965.[16] True to Booker's recollection, the audience was large. The Civic Auditorium seated almost three thousand people.

During our 1976 interview, as Booker recalled the big concert, my experience as a journalist told me that he was entering a reflective space that might lead to expressing his understanding of where his music came from. I knew I should follow him.

DAVID JOHNSON: Was that the biggest crowd you've played in front of?

BOOKER WHITE: That was a big crowd, man. But now you see there was more than me there playing [Chuck Berry, Skip James, Big Mama Thornton, Mississippi Fred McDowell, and the Chambers Brothers]. I'd do my thing and come off the stage for so many minutes and they'd come on and do their thing, you see. But before, after we got through playing, then that's where they'd want to know where did the roots of the blues came from, and everybody there'd want to hear that, too, 'cause I reckon a thousand people there'd want to know how that it began and what the start of the blues and how long you could remember people playing the blues and how did the blues start and all like that. Well, they couldn't get by slavery time without they go into another world. They couldn't get over that slavery time to save they life 'cause they wasn't nothing else for 'em to come back at you to get over that 'cause slavery time was the beginning of the colored peoples coming in. They'd bring them in there, you see, and so that's where it started from.

JOHNSON: Some people say that some of it goes all the way back to Africa. What do you think?

WHITE: Well, I don't know about that. You know, so many things people got their own way of believing and own way of knowing, but all I come by mine was guys actually doing that in slavery time . . . 'Cause that was the facts. That wasn't no make-up stuff 'cause peoples couldn't go nowhere unless the boss let 'em or give 'em a pass, and all of 'em would sing, and some days the boss man would have 'em sing for him. Just have days . . . I reckon you call that a holiday for 'em. Have 'em all up beating tin tubs and a wooden barrel for a drum and a guitar . . . funny old guitars and things. And they just got a big kick out of it. They'd play for 'em to dance, you know—waltz, two-step, one-step. So, that was in slavery time. . . . They'd kill hogs and cows and have 'em, give 'em something to eat, you know. And that's just where'd they have a ball. They didn't know no better. They were satisfied. They weren't worried about nothing.

JOHNSON: How did you hear about this? Was it from people you talked to?

WHITE: Well, it was . . . oh, I couldn't say one, but when I was coming on . . . see, I met people [who] was enslaved. See, I met a lady named Miss Viney. She was a hundred and . . . died at a hundred and fifteen years old. She just turned into a cat, might near, she was so old. Just dried up like a meat skin. That's the honest to God truth. You know where she sit at? In the fireplace. She had a hole in the fireplace, honest to God. That's where she'd be. . . . That's where she'd want to be. Yeah, you know, it didn't have no fire while she was sitting, but it had fire enough [sometimes]. A dirt chimney, that's where she was sitting. Back there, didn't have no bricks, you see.[17]

The image of Miss Viney shriveled up in the fireplace came alive as he told the story, and I could see him sitting on the floor—a young boy listening to the old woman's every word.

Chapter Twenty-One

RIVER CITY VENUES

WHEN BOOKER FIRST TRAVELED TO MEMPHIS IN 1930, THE CITY offered musicians a variety of places to play. Over time, the decline of Beale Street and other centers of musical activity reduced the number of performance venues. Booker had cut his first two records in Memphis as Washington White and recorded a third in 1937 in Chicago as Bukka White. "Shake 'Em On Down," paired with "Pinebluff Arkansas," was an unexpected hit in the blues market, opening the way for him to make more records, which he did in 1940. Yet it would appear that his most important priority in relocating from Mississippi to Memphis after his release from prison was to shed the baggage of his old life and make a new start. One indication was that he told people he preferred to be called Booker rather than Bukka, and left "Washington" behind. He sometimes gave his full name as Booker T. Washington White.

Another indication of a new beginning was the changes he made in his life. Within five years of arriving in Memphis, Booker married a young woman from a respectable, churchgoing family in Arkansas, rented a house in the all-Black Orange Mound neighborhood, and started a new family. He found steady work as a welder's assistant at the Newberry Equipment Company. He began to play house parties in Mississippi and West Memphis in Arkansas, but had yet to establish himself as a performing musician in Memphis. That did not happen until he was "rediscovered" in the summer of 1963.

For most of two years after Booker's return to performing, he played far away from Memphis. John Fahey and ED Denson had persuaded him to move to California while they continued their academic programs at the University of California, Berkeley. Without any previous experience managing musicians, they were able to persuade Booker to let them take over his career. Under their management in 1963, Booker played a number of club and coffeehouse dates on the West Coast, including performances at the Cabale coffeehouse in Berkeley.

Fahey and Denson recorded Booker's performances at the Cabale on the nights of November 10 and 11, 1963. The tapes were not released until 1994, when thirteen numbers were compiled on a compact disc, *1963 Isn't 1962*—its title taken from Booker's "1963 Isn't 1962 Blues." Included on the disc were three of his older songs, "Special Streamline" (called "Streamline Special"), "Fixin' To Die," and "Aberdeen Blues." The other numbers were a mix of newer material such as "Vaseline Headed Woman" and "Chi Chi Boogie," songs from the folk tradition such as "Jack of Diamonds" and "Corrina, Corrina," and a cover version of Charles Brown's "Drifting and Drifting." David Evans wrote in the notes to the CD that the material provided "a good cross section of his active performing repertoire at the time."[1] His vocals were rougher than on his original recordings, but he performed with energy and an impressive range of dynamics on his National steel guitar.

With the help of an East Coast agent (possibly Manny Greenhill of Folklore Productions), Denson and Fahey put together a tour for Booker in the spring of 1964. Venues included the Second Annual UCLA Folk Festival in March and the Huntington Avenue YMCA in Boston in April. At the festival, Booker joined Reverend Gary Davis, the Chambers Brothers, Elizabeth Cotten, and other musicians for a night of blues music on March 27. Folk music historian Ronald D. Cohen wrote, "Musical festivals multiplied like mushrooms throughout the state of California in the later 1960s, many filled with rock groups . . . but some showing folk musicians as well."[2] Booker played at the 1965 Berkeley Blues Festival along with Chuck Berry, Big Mama Thornton, Mississippi Fred McDowell, and the Chambers Brothers. In 1967 he was invited to tour Europe and England with the American Folk Blues Festival. These were exciting times for musicians and audiences alike.

Unlike other "rediscovered" blues musicians, Booker took an interest in managing his own career. After John Fahey and ED Denson managed him for less than a year following his rediscovery, Booker made a handshake agreement with Dick Waterman sometime in 1964. Their arrangement lasted two years before Waterman ended it at the Newport Folk Festival in 1966. Already having told a number of club owners to call him directly if they wanted him to come back to their clubs, Booker began to set up some of his own bookings.

When Booker took the stage at the Overton Park Shell for the third annual Memphis Country Blues Festival in 1968, he needed to get something off his chest. Before playing a note, he told the audience that Memphis, his adopted home, did not appreciate him.

> Now ladies and gentlemen, it shouldn't be, of which you don't know, I lives here and I was listening the other evening when it was on the air the guy actually said we didn't know we had nobody here like that, and I been around here ever since '39 playing, and this is my headquarters which I stay here. I live on Mosby. Well, I wanted to get to feeling here. First I have some fun here. 'Cause I just tired riding them train and bus and airplane, and last October I was way overseas and they said, "*Do you play around Memphis much*?" I couldn't say, you know. I said *occasionally*. I wouldn't say I didn't play. I said *occasionally*. That's what I told 'em.

He drew out the word *occasionally* to make sure that the audience got his drift. He wanted people to know that he had lived in Memphis for years, but, in his opinion, the city had not supported him as he would have liked.

Up until the 1960s, Memphis had been hard on its older blues musicians. The musical legacy leaned heavily on the blues, whether the compositions of bandleader W. C. Handy or the rambunctious sounds of Beale Street jug bands; yet there was no place for older blues musicians to perform other than on the street or in a public park.

In the 1920s, Beale Street was the vibrant center of Black life in Memphis. At night, the street was alive with opportunities to have a good time or get in trouble. "Beale Street was a place where a man could find a drink, a woman, gambling, some music, and a fight if he weren't careful," William Bearden wrote. "Tales abound of confidence men and hustlers. Beale was the natural progression of a boomtown populated with people on the make."[3] Individually and in groups, musicians played for tips on Beale Street or in W. C. Handy Park.

A number of blues musicians who made classic recordings in the late 1920s through 1930s gravitated to the city and its vibrant music scene. From the 1920s through the 1940s, Memphis was home to a number of jug bands. Swedish blues researchers Bengt Olsson and Peter Mählin spent time in Memphis and vicinity in the summer of 1969, collecting oral history on the Memphis Jug Band, the Beale Street Jug Band, and Cannon's Jug Stompers—groups that were more popular and sold more records than most blues musicians. Will Shade, Ben Ramey, and Will Weldon began recording as the Memphis Jug Band on February 24, 1927, and various lineups carried on the name through November 1934. Frank Stokes and Dan Sane recorded as the Beale Street Sheiks. Stokes made records under his own name in 1928 and 1929. "The jug bands were enjoyed by whites as well as blacks, and at times found their employment almost entirely at white parties," Olsson wrote.[4] "Such functions were not specially profitable, but they were the best paid jobs that could be found."

Frank Stokes "was a familiar sight on the streets of Memphis, with his strong voice and fine guitar playing."[5] At six feet tall and about 240 pounds, Stokes was an imposing man who often played in Handy Park.[6] According to fellow musician Willie Borum, "You got some good tips down there from all the country people who used to come into town on weekends."[7] After gaining a reputation as one of the most versatile performers in Memphis, Stokes was thought to have left the city in the late 1940s and turned up around Clarksdale, Mississippi. Bengt Olsson reported that Booker "claims he played with Stokes 'round Clarksdale in 1949–1951."[8]

There is evidence that he did. The 1950 United States Census recorded Booker in Memphis, working as a tank assembler at a "steel factory" (Newberry Equipment Company), but he could have played with Stokes on weekends.[9] Memphis disc jockey Captain Pete (Dee Henderson), who broadcast over community radio station WEVL, had grown up in Clarksdale. He recalled seeing Booker perform at a theater around 1950.[10] The theater appearance could have been the result of playing with the better-known Stokes. (Sadly, Dee Henderson was murdered on July 5, 2008, at a time when the city's violent crime rate was the second highest in the United States.)[11]

THE LACK OF SUPPORT FOR OLDER PERFORMERS HAD BEGUN TO change with the beginning of the folk music revival in the late 1950s and early 1960s.

In his chronicle of Memphis music during that period, *It Came from Memphis*, author Robert Gordon wrote, "The folk scene introduced the beatnik coffeehouse, which became the venue for the return of Furry Lewis, Bukka White, Joe Callicott and the other blues pioneers who had been neglected since the Depression."[12] The first of this new type of venue was the short-lived Cottage. After opening in 1960, the Cottage closed in less than a year. Next came Pastime, which opened in 1962 and lasted longer than the Cottage.

More successful than both its predecessors was Oso on North Highland Street, in part because it was located near Treadwell High School and catered to teenagers. The music was better, too. In his memoir, published posthumously in 2017, Memphis musician and record producer Jim Dickinson recalled taking his future wife to Oso to hear "a small black man with white hair and blue eyes, dressed in a dark gray suit and Sunday shoes, [who] limped to the stage on a cork leg, juggling his guitar as if he might drop it."[13] The man was Walter "Furry" Lewis, born on March 6, 1899, in Greenwood, Mississippi, who worked for the city of Memphis as a street sweeper. Singing traditional blues, songs learned from medicine shows, and church hymns, Lewis proved to be "an incredible entertainer."

The most influential coffeehouse was the Bitter Lemon, which the Memphis Music Hall of Fame Museum dubbed "the epicenter of the nascent folk and blues scene . . ."[14] The tiny brick building at the intersection of Poplar Avenue and Humes Street was ground zero for hipsters, blues aficionados, and the rising underground culture of 1960s Memphis. The blues revival was beginning and older traditional Black musicians were performing for the first time in years for appreciative audiences of mostly young white kids. In his memoir *Screening Room*, Memphis native Alan Lightman recalled Furry Lewis and banjo-playing former jug band leader Gus Cannon playing at the Bitter Lemon.[15]

According to Memphis musician Chris Wimmer, "The Bitter Lemon was the center of the universe for several years. Bands passing through town would come and see who was playing there because they might catch Furry or Booker."[16] Among the bands that played there were the Allman Joys, who changed their name to the Allman Brothers, and Memphis bands like the Box Tops.

Shortly after the Bitter Lemon opened in the summer of 1964, guitarist John Fahey gave an impromptu performance at the Bitter Lemon while visiting New York transplant Bill Barth. As the singer on stage began to lose her audience, Bitter Lemon owner John McIntire noticed that two men had been trying out the house guitar and asked if they could play. "They started playing and nobody could believe it," McIntire recalled.[17] "They played this open-tuned blues guitar, and they went into their act. John Fahey was Blind Joe Death. He wore dark glasses and Bill Barth would lead him up to the stage and they would play together. When he was done, he took his glasses off and went back into the audience."

While Booker was living in California, he kept his apartment at 702 St. Paul Avenue in Memphis. It proved to be the right decision. In 1967 his name reappeared in the Memphis City Directory, indicating that he had returned sometime before then, possibly in 1966.

Chapter Twenty-Two

FOLK FESTIVALS

FROM 1964 THROUGH 1973, BOOKER'S PERFORMANCE SCHEDULE included at least one folk festival every year. They could be local events, such as the two series of festivals held in Memphis; statewide gatherings such as the UCLA and Berkeley Folk Festivals in California; regional festivals like the Newport Folk Festival in Rhode Island and Mariposa Folk Festival near Toronto; showcases designed to appeal to national audiences such as the National Festival of Folklife in Washington, DC, and Jazz & Heritage Festival in New Orleans; and one international festival, if one includes Booker's participation in the American Folk Blues Festival ensembles that toured Europe and England in 1967, 1970, and 1972.

Soon after Booker resumed his career as a performer, the young, white blues community in Memphis decided to organize an event that would showcase the city's wealth of older blues musicians. Writer Robert Palmer, future author of *Deep Blues*, was on hand to document the birth of a blues festival, as well as to help organize it. A musician himself, Palmer had become friends with guitarist Bill Barth, who knew many of the city's older Black musicians. As Palmer described it, he was sitting one afternoon on Barth's front porch, waiting for the guitarist to arrive for a rehearsal, when "Bill came strolling up the driveway with Nancy Jeffries, the singer in our group, and a thick, heavy set, fiftyish man Bill introduced to me as Bukka White. . . . His legendary aura put me a little in awe of him at first, but Booker is an easy man to like; the legend existed in my mind, not in his idea of himself."[1]

Soon Palmer had the opportunity to hear the city's oldest bluesman, Nathan Beauregard, and again was impressed. "Hearing Nathan sing, and looking at him, I almost suspected a hidden phonograph," Palmer wrote. "He had a great technical versatility—he used bottleneck, knife, pick, and various finger-picking styles—and his voice is high, piercing, and incredibly gutsy."[2] An idea took shape. Palmer, Barth, and Jeffries met with friends to discuss the possibility of putting on a blues concert at the Overton Park Municipal Shell. The group of friends—musicians, artists, writers, and photographers—formed the Memphis Blues Society. From 1966 to 1969, the Society staged four blues festivals at the Overton Park Shell.

"Three thousand people were sitting on hard wood benches in the outdoor amphitheatre on the night of the festival," Palmer wrote in an article for the inaugural issue of the counterculture magazine *Changes*. "There were middle-aged and elderly couples, crewcut executive types, college students, teenagers and all the freaks in town."[3] Older Black musicians scheduled to appear were Furry Lewis, Reverend Robert Wilkins, Fred McDowell, and Nathan Beauregard. Booker White was absent because he was in Rhode Island at the Newport Folk Festival.

Others on the program were a group of Memphis studio musicians who called themselves Electric Blue Watermelon, acoustic blues singer Sid Selvidge, singer and keyboard player Jim Dickinson, and Bill Barth's trio. Memphis radio personality Nat D. Williams, whose program on radio station WDIA featured Black music, introduced the first performer. Seated in the middle of a clutter of amplifiers, public address speakers, connecting cables, and microphones, was the slight figure of Nathan Beauregard, rumored to be 105 but thought to be about 80. (Research established that he was born Nathan Bogard in February 1892, and died on May 25, 1970.)[4] Accompanying himself on electric guitar, Beauregard began to play a blues number as dark clouds gathered over Overton Park.

Soon skies opened. People seated at the back of the amphitheatre abandoned their seats to seek shelter under the awnings of concession stands. Those closer to the stage huddled under the shell's roofed wings on both sides of the stage. Sheltered by the shell, Beauregard kept playing. Robert Palmer recalled, "Nathan sang and played publicly for the first time since the Depression, his melodious voice and delicate fingerpicking interweaving with the drumming of the rain on the tin roof."[5] The audience showed its approval with loud applause and whistles. The downpour showed no signs of letting up. Festival organizers decided to end the show.

The following week, an advertisement appeared in the *Commercial Appeal* announcing that the festival was rescheduled for that Saturday, July 30, at 8:00 p.m.[6] The postponement allowed organizers to promise "the same great blues schedule as before, plus Bukka White and Gus

Cannon." Booker had returned from the Newport Folk Festival, where Dick Waterman had severed their relationship. Admission was a dollar. The advertisement told readers, "You can't afford not to come."

Commercial Appeal reporter Dean Pope was on hand to cover the rescheduled festival. His article carried the headline "1,000 Hear Blues Sung in Old Style":[7]

> The genuine old-fashioned blues singers were at the Overton Park Shell last night and they sang about genuine old-fashioned problems like boll weevils, dying relatives and run-away women.
>
> About 1,000 people turned out for the Memphis Blues Festival, which featured the old and the young, the Negro and the white devotees of the "old Memphis sound blues."
>
> Blues enthusiasts were a sizable minority of the audience, and most of the concert probably found what they heard quite a bit different from the "blues" they normally hear.
>
> The eldest performer was Nathan Beauregard, a small Negro who had to be helped on the stage, but whose guitar music really did shuffle rather than run.
>
> When Mr. Beauregard started singing the blues back a good many of his 76 years, he didn't have the problems of competing with the sounds of a jet airliner overhead.
>
> But even when his words were blurred, the message of frustration came through in a plaintive tone.

The photograph accompanying the article was captioned "Old Nathan Beauregard Waits His Turn."

Radio host Nat D. Williams, whose program on WDIA was the first in the city devoted to Black music, "gave some background on the blues sound of Memphis and of Beale Street. He got a cheer from the hometown folk when he declared that 'despite the claims of New Orleans and St. Louis, Memphis is the home of the blues.'"[8] In addition to Beauregard, two old-style musicians and a newcomer earned favorable mentions:

> Fresh from the Newport [Folk] Festival, Bukka White demonstrated a remarkable ability to slap music out of a guitar. Sid Selvidge, a young man from Greenville, Miss., provided a different pace with sad, slow songs about poor country people.

> And the audience had warmed up enough by the time Rev. Robert Wilkins came on to give a little hand-clapping support to his fast moving "What Do You Think About Jesus."
>
> The show started, 20 minutes late, with the Lee Baker Blues Band, which used electric guitars and an electric piano to produce its idea of the old blues.
>
> But, at least to a non-enthusiast, the result was an unfortunate near cacophony that drowned out the singing and made the rest of the show sound that much better.[9]

As could be expected at a public concert rained out after one performer and rescheduled on short notice, the audience on the second night was less than half the size of the first night's estimated attendance. The festival succeeded in attracting a diverse crowd of Memphis residents to hear older Black musicians who—with the possible exception of Furry Lewis—were not well known in their own city. Despite the lower attendance, there was enough interest to support staging a similar event the following year.

The Second Annual Memphis Blues Festival took place almost two months earlier in the summer than the first festival and attracted half the audience. The night of Saturday, June 3, 1967, was cold. This time, the *Commercial Appeal*'s reporter treated the event as a happening, focusing as much on people in attendance as the musicians. The headline was "Crowd Is Medley of Its Own at Hot, Cool Blues Festival":[10]

> A crowd of about 500 thoroughly chilled hippies, neatly-dressed collegians, and moms and dads gave hand-clapping approval to the "Real Memphis Sound"—old and new—at the second Annual Memphis Blues Festival here last night.
>
> Bearded, long-haired, bead-wearing hippies took pleasure at hearing performances by the Electric Blue Watermelon group by shouting, swaying and jumping into the pit in front of the Overton Park Shell to dance.
>
> The pipe-smoking collegians responded most enthusiastically to the strumming of such old-time 1920s-30s Beale Street performers as Furry Lewis, Bukka White, and Nathan Beauregard. . . .
>
> Though the festival program swore the music would be "Memphis Blues" and the musical children of "Memphis Blues," scenery gave the feeling of a hippie gathering.

> Scenery included a cardboard, single-seated outhouse with a half moon, a motorcycle, a plywood shamrock and leprechaun pipe, a tired plywood Buddha with a 1967 Memphis Blues sign on its chest, and a giant red-white-and-blue Uncle Sam figure.
>
> But any fears were put to rest by the sounds of Bukka White singing "Black Cat Blues," the Watermelon group with "Driving Wheel" and Miss [Nancy] Jeffries on "The Sun Is Shining But It Is Raining in My Heart."

BY THE THIRD MEMPHIS COUNTRY BLUES FESTIVAL, INTEREST IN blues and the early musicians who made records was strong on both sides of the Atlantic. On Saturday, July 20, 1968—the day of the festival—an article in the *Commercial Appeal* announced a new development. New York label Sire Records would record the performances "under the direction of Michael Vernon, British blues producer. A two-record set is contemplated. . . ."[11] In 1965, when Vernon was twenty, he made his first blues album with a fifty-year-old pianist and songwriter from Mississippi, Eddie Boyd, who wrote the blues standard "Five Long Years." Boyd and Vernon recorded the album during Boyd's tour of Europe and England with the American Folk Blues Festival. When Vernon flew into Memphis from New York on the day before the festival, he brought with him a reputation as an experienced blues producer, having recorded American piano player and singer William Thomas "Champion Jack" Dupree (1965), a second album with Eddie Boyd (1967), four albums with British blues purist John Mayall and his Bluesbreakers (1966–68), and debut albums for the blues bands Savoy Brown (1967), Ten Years After (1967), and Chicken Shack (1968).

Now twenty-three, Vernon was co-founder of the Blue Horizon record label, which partnered with Sire. That week in Memphis, he produced two albums for the label. One was of the 1968 country blues festival, and the other was a studio recording of Bukka White with a band. Sire Records executives Seymour Stein and Richard Gottehrer arranged the trip. The Memphis Country Blues Society set up the itinerary, which included a visit to Mississippi.

On Saturday, June 20, American recording engineer Margaret Tucker used a two-track Revox recorder to tape the festival performances of Nathan Beauregard, "Booker T. Washington" White, Furry Lewis, Reverend Robert Wilkins, and Joe Callicott. Vernon would select the most suitable recordings for the Sire album, which would be distributed by London Records, a larger label.

When I interviewed Mike Vernon in August 2018—fifty years after the festival—he remembered his time in Memphis. He met Furry Lewis outside the brick front of his house, which soon would be bulldozed by the Memphis Housing Authority to make way for urban renewal. "A shame," Vernon said. He spent the day after the festival in Ardent Studios in Memphis recording Lewis, Bukka White, Joe Callicott, and Nathan Beauregard. The recordings would appear later on Blue Horizon blues compilations. Members of the Country Blues Society took Vernon on a quick tour of Mississippi, on their way visiting a sharecropper's shack in Nesbit, Mississippi. "I met Joe Callicott, his wife, and a milk cow," Vernon recalled. People told him that Nathan Beauregard deserved an album, but he did not have time. At Ardent Studios, Beauregard recorded six songs.

The first generation of country blues singers was disappearing. "Country blues singers were thin on the ground," Vernon put it. He recalled meeting Booker during the Ardent sessions, before working with him on the full-length album. *Memphis Hot Shots* was recorded in three or four hours.[12] "It sounded to me like these guys had played together before," Vernon recalled, "or they had rehearsed." Several musicians came from the Memphis group Insect Trust, including an upright bass player called Anchor. Booker's friend Jimmy Crosthwait played the washboard—"Booker liked playing with washboard," Vernon recalled. Crosthwait acted as the festival's master of ceremonies at the Country Blues Festival, backing Booker during his set at the Overton Park Shell.

In 1969, civic pride intersected with blues music in Memphis—a natural match since the city claimed to be the birthplace of the blues. The Memphis Country Blues Society's vision of its fourth annual event was ambitious. The festival was no longer a one-day concert whose purpose was to showcase the city's older blues musicians. The Blues Society scheduled three afternoons and two nights of music, opening with soul act Rufus Thomas and the Bar-Kays and closing with a gospel group, The Salem Harmonizers, and Mississippi hill country blues musician Fred McDowell. In recognition of the city's 150th anniversary, organizers called this edition of their annual event the Memphis Birthday Blues Festival.

The three days of music took place at the Municipal Shell in Overton Park from Friday afternoon, June 6, through Sunday afternoon, June 8. On Sunday evening, the city put on a separate event, billed as the First

Annual W. C. Handy Memorial Blues Concert, in the Ellis Auditorium—the downtown concert and arts venue where Booker made his first recordings in 1930. According to writer Stanley Booth, who reported on the Overton Park festival for *Rolling Stone*, the evening concert drew only two hundred people.[13] A much larger audience filled Overton Park on Saturday night for the Blues Society concert, when contemporary blues-rock star Johnny Winter took the stage with a bassist, drummer, and thirteen large amplifiers. Tickets were a dollar.

Booker appeared twice on Friday. Each time on his closing number, "Aberdeen Mississippi Blues," he added crowd-pleasing effects: complex rhythmic tapping on his instrument's neck, and playing part of the song with the guitar behind his head.[14] Stanley Booth took note of the audience's response. "Bukka vigorously plays a big National Steel Standard and sings, talks, and growls magnificently incomprehensible 'sky songs' . . . ," he wrote. "[They are] part songs, part reminiscence, part tall story . . . At the Festival, Bukka received a standing ovation Friday night and every other time he played."[15] Given the reception, Booker was not ready to leave the stage. He strolled over to the piano and sat down next to Memphis Piano Red (John Williams), grinning and exhorting as Piano Red played a stride number. Red ignored him.

The Memphis Birthday Blues Festival was one of more than forty festivals that took place in 1969.[16] The year saw both the high and low points of counterculture gatherings: the peace-and-love vibrations emanating from 400,000 young people who traveled to upstate New York for the Woodstock festival, and the tension and hostility between a crowd of 300,000 fans and a cohort of Hells Angels at the Altamont Speedway in northern California. Woodstock was a ticketed festival that became free when attendees overran hastily installed fences; Altamont was a free concert put on by the Rolling Stones that turned tragic when an Angel stabbed to death a seventeen-year-old Black man, Meredith Hunter. Other major festivals included the Summer Jam at the Watkins Glen Speedway in New York on July 28 and the Harlem Cultural Festival, dubbed the "Black Woodstock" after a series of six free concerts that entertained an estimated 300,000 listeners.

In April 1970, the Memphis Blues Society announced that the fifth annual blues festival would be held at E. H. Crump Park on the Mississippi River on June 5–7,[17] but cancelled the event after learning that the cost of security personnel at the new location would be more than the projected revenue. Hiring Memphis police would cost $6,700. In its best year, the festival brought in only $5,000.[18]

Despite the cancellation in his hometown, Booker still had a festival on his calendar. He had been invited to perform at the 1970 National Festival of Folklife, presented by the Smithsonian Institution. Taking place July 1 through 5 on the National Mall in Washington, the 1970 festival was the third to focus on one of the states—in this year, Arkansas.[19] The regional accent brought a number of blues musicians to Washington. Booker performed in the daytime "Memphis Blues" showcase, and in "The Blues" segment of an evening program. Other blues performers included Mance Lipscomb and Arthur Crudup.[20]

In 1971, the first River City Blues Festival began as a benefit for the Half & Half Coffee House. Located at 2100 Union Street, the Half & Half was a church-sponsored gathering place for young people. According to coffeehouse director Reverend Jerry Lovett, fifteen hundred people attended the benefit on December 3, 1971, in the North Hall of Ellis Memorial Auditorium. Performers were Booker, Fred McDowell, Furry Lewis, Sleepy John Estes with Hammie Nixon, and the Beale Street Band. Booker had made his first recordings in the Ellis Auditorium.

"We haven't had time to count the money yet, but it was a success," Reverend Lovett reported. "All the performers were wonderful." He said the festival might become an annual event. When the money was counted, the benefit netted $1,500.[21]

The second River City Blues Festival was held on Friday, November 23, 1972. On the bill were Booker, Furry Lewis, Houston Stackhouse, and Memphis Piano Red. A number of musicians were "expected" to perform. Acting as master of ceremonies was Rufus Thomas, the Memphis radio personality and performer who had become "a major name in a much more recent chapter of black-based music."[22]

Booker was not among the musicians at the third River City Blues Festival, which took place in Memphis on November 14, 1973, but had performed earlier that year at the fourth annual Jazz & Heritage Festival in New Orleans. Bringing together a gumbo of jazz and blues musicians, JazzFest was held April 12 through 15 at the Fair Grounds Race Course, with evening concerts at the Municipal Auditorium. Booker appeared every day.

In New Orleans, a friendship began between the old bluesman and an aspiring blues musician from Bainbridge Island, Washington. TJ Wheeler had hitchhiked to New Orleans, where he introduced himself to Booker and became his roadie, carrying his guitar. This was the start of a personal relationship that would be of vital importance to Booker in 1976 when he experienced a health setback while on a plane from Memphis to Boston.

In 1973, the Jazz & Heritage Festival provided a memorable moment for Booker and the blues fans who witnessed it. On Friday, April 13, Booker's cousin B. B. King joined him on stage. Photographers captured the moment. "Since Booker is sitting stage center, I think B. B. probably came by to sit in with him that day," said festival archivist Rachel Lyons.[23] B. B.'s arrival sparked a twenty-minute jam session that included pianist Professor Longhair and other New Orleans musicians. That evening, B. B. and his band were featured performers at the Municipal Auditorium.

WHEN I INTERVIEWED BOOKER IN 1976, HE TOLD ME THAT HE HAD played with a group of musicians in pre-World War II days, but did not mention the *Memphis Hot Shots* album. Recording albums had become common for him after he returned to performing in 1963. Mike Vernon, who founded the Blue Horizon record label, made clear that Booker was not alone among older country blues musicians in making a record when any label that appeared to be solvent would ask them to:

> Bukka was always going into the studio and making an album. The problem was that he was always recording the same songs . . . "Aberdeen Blues," "Baby Please Don't Go" . . . It seemed like he was making an album a year, sometimes two albums a year. There were a lot of Bukka White records on the market. I suffered through that with [Champion] Jack Dupree. He would sign an exclusive contract to record an album, then would record an album two months later in Paris. You would tell him, "No, Jack. You can't do that," and he would say "I did." You accept that as working in the business with musicians who only were interested in getting paid at the time they were doing it, and not interested in what would happen in two months.

Talking about Dupree, Vernon mentioned a payment of five hundred dollars for an album. When I asked if Booker might have received a similar amount for *Memphis Hot Shots*, Vernon did not answer the question. Still talking about Dupree, he said that the record label would pay for the studio and additional musicians. Working with Booker White on the one album he recorded with a group, Vernon remembered, "He wasn't very talkative. The reality of it for him was that he was doing a job he was getting paid for." In retrospect, Vernon thought that *Memphis Hot Shots* "was quite an interesting record. It showed Bukka in a different light from the National Guitar-bashing, heavy-voiced singer that he appeared to be on stage. The album was one of those experiments. It was really interesting recording him with a small rhythm section. The drummer kept a good groove. And half of the tracks were of him alone."

The goal that day was modest: ". . . to get a minimum done to make sure it was long enough for an LP." His Blue Horizon label put a photograph on the cover on the record of what appears to be an African American man in a blue space suit. Again, the goal was simple: "to attract attention so that people would turn it over and see who the musician was." Vernon recalled that the album received "reasonable" reviews, though some critics could not understand why the label would record an established country blues musician with a band. Vernon countered, "This was not exactly uncommon. All the great performers of the time . . . Big Bill Broonzy, Howlin' Wolf . . . made records with a band. The guys did a very good job. It sounded like Mississippi hill music." The Booker that Mike Vernon remembers is "a powerful presence . . . absolutely awesome . . . You'd never fall asleep during a Bukka White performance. Of those singers, he was the best." He added, "I feel sorry for the guitar."[24]

Two of the musicians on *Memphis Hot Shots* were not identified by name, but credited as Harmonica Boy and Anchor. Anchor played the acoustic bass. In my research, I learned that Harmonica Boy was Linzie Collier Butler of Jackson, Tennessee, a musician whom David Evans suggested might remember Booker. Butler remembered that Booker had given him his nickname, but did not recall the recording session. He shared that he had lost many memories of that time to alcohol. We became phone friends.

During one call, I put on the *Memphis Hot Shots* album and played the first song. "That's you," I said as the harmonica wailed. "I played with all those old cats," Butler responded. In 1974 he had a regular gig accompanying Furry Lewis at the bar Peanuts on Tuesday nights.[25] Respected Memphis guitarist Lee Baker, who died in 1996, was the third member of the trio. In those years, Linzie Butler was in demand as an accompanist, sitting in with Lightnin' Hopkins and other visiting blues musicians. He also worked as a roadie for the Memphis band Moloch.[26]

Chapter Twenty-Three

THE BLUES BUS

IN 1972 TWENTY-SEVEN-YEAR-OLD ARNE BROGGER WORKED FOR Schon Productions, a small booking agency in Minneapolis. "We booked local bands in high schools and colleges," he recalled. "We did middle agent work and buy-sells. We would buy three or four days on an artist from a big agency for say $5,000 and turn around and sell it for $6,000."[1] One afternoon, he was sitting at his desk, thumbing through the *Billboard* talent directory, when he recognized the name Furry Lewis. Brogger was familiar with this blues musician from high school. "Blues music was in the air we breathed as teenagers," Brogger said. Dave Ray, later of Koerner, Ray & Glover, and Mark Naftalin, keyboardist for the Paul Butterfield Blues Band, were classmates. Barry Hansen, who later became known as the radio celebrity Dr. Demento, was disc jockey at all the high school dances. Hansen was a serious record collector. "This was just at the beginning of white blues discovery stuff in the early 1960s," Brogger remembered. "We had the hippest sock hop playlist anywhere." In 1980, Dr. Demento contributed liner notes to a reissue of Booker's 1963 album *Mississippi Blues, Vol. 1* as part of the Takoma Blues Series.

When Brogger dialed the contact number for Lewis, Steve LaVere answered. Stephen C. LaVere had learned the business side of blues music as the reissue coordinator for Imperial Records. His job was to track down master copies of recordings by older musicians such as T-Bone Walker and Champion Jack Dupree for albums repackaged as "classic blues."[2] When Brogger reached out to him, LaVere owned a store in Memphis that sold records and memorabilia—everything from old blues 78s to Nazi collectibles from World War II. After their initial conversation, LaVere followed up in a letter to Brogger confirming the prices for Furry Lewis and Reverend Robert Wilkins to appear at the Beloit College Folk and Blues Festival in Wisconsin on July 15 and 16. Wilkins would cost $300 to 400 and Lewis $500 "exclusive of expenses."

Brogger booked Lewis to perform at Beloit, adding several dates at other Minnesota colleges. To reduce expenses, Brogger invited Lewis to stay in his house in Minneapolis. "He had his own room and was treated like a king," Brogger recalled.[3] "Furry loved it. Every night we had a concert in the living room." In his original letter to Brogger, LaVere suggested other musicians for the festival such as guitarists Houston Stackhouse and Joe Willie Wilkins, who backed up Sonny Boy Williamson II (Rice Miller) , in person and on the King Biscuit radio program in the late 1940s. LaVere wrote, "They are all well-seasoned folk artists of the highest caliber and charisma. . . ."[4] LaVere named another dozen Memphis blues musicians, beginning with Bukka White, for whom he could "arrange engagements."

Brogger and LaVere were in their late twenties when they first met. "We were two young guys on the make," Brogger remembered.[5] He would later work in New York as an agent in the personal appearances department of the Agency for the Performing Arts. "It was a big deal," he said. LaVere had moved to Memphis in 1970. He worked on a reissue project for Sun Records, wrote liner notes for field recordings on Adelphi Records, and produced performances by Memphis artists. He described to author Robert Gordon his relationship with the older Black musicians who were at the center of the River City Blues Festival and Memphis Blues Caravan:

> I became acquainted with Furry Lewis, Bukka White, Piano Red, Sleepy John Estes, and all those people, and it was just mind-staggering. I couldn't believe the wealth of blues talent that was just laying there going to rot, getting one festival a year and a gig here and a gig there. I was there until May of 1975 working with the old cats.[6]

After agreeing on the initial Furry Lewis dates in Minnesota, Brogger and LaVere built a business relationship. In 1973, Brogger visited LaVere in Memphis. Throughout the visit, the two men talked about blues and the city's many older blues musicians. Their business sense led one or both of them to a marketable idea. In his notes to the CDs *Memphis Blues Caravan Vol. I* and *Vol. II*, LaVere recalled, "With the success of the River City Blues Festivals, as well as the demand I was enjoying for my artists . . . it became obvious that a traveling road show could keep the party going year 'round."[7] Brogger had a different recollection of the sequence of events: "I said let's put all these guys on the road. LaVere asked 'What shall we call it?' I said how about the Memphis Blues Caravan." He continued:

> Anyway, the concept was agreed upon. I went up to Minneapolis evangelizing on the phone and started booking dates for the caravan. I am good at selling, especially when I believe in something. The concept of the caravan was to put together a traveling blues festival. It hadn't been done before. Some of the guys had crossed paths when they were out on the road, but none of them had played together as a mobile unit. Putting everyone on the same bus was a first.[8]

Making a start toward the planned tours, LaVere took Brogger with him to recruit Booker White. Booker's partner Leola answered the door and said the musician was "at his office." As Brogger remembered it, "The office was on the shady side of the street next to the Triune Sundry Store at the corner of Leland and Mosby. He was sitting in a plastic chair and next to a wooden crate on top of which sat a glass with some whiskey in it. . . . There were two or three guys drinking out of a half pint."

Brogger recalled that "Bukka was not a guy anybody would want to fool with. He had a real aura that commanded respect. . . . When I pitched the idea of the caravan, he was very noncommittal. He said he might think about it if the money was right. I said the money is going to be right, that's a guarantee. He was the first guy I paid."[9]

Because of Brogger's background booking shows at educational institutions, the bus full of blues musicians made frequent stops at colleges and universities: Northwestern University near Chicago, the University of Missouri in St. Louis, Southern Methodist in Dallas, Illinois Valley Community College, Notre Dame University, and San Diego State, among others. The Caravan also played a number of theaters and clubs, such as the Ritz Theater in Austin, Texas.

In the mid-1970s, the music scene in Austin was thriving. The primary elements in the city's genre-busting blend of sounds were rock and country music. In a roundup of "club acts" for the week beginning Saturday, January 18, 1975, the *Austin American-Statesman* listed performances by Shiva's Headband, the Playboys of Edinburg, and the Lost Gonzo Band. Formed in 1967, Shiva's Headband played psychedelic rock. The Playboys of Edinburg scored a regional hit in 1966 with "Look

At Me Girl." Playing country rock, the Lost Gonzo Band had toured with Texas singer-songwriters Jerry Jeff Walker, who wrote "Mr. Bojangles," and Michael Martin Murphey, writer of "Geronimo's Cadillac."

Adding to this gumbo of genres was the blues. A concert poster for the Ritz Theater announced an appearance by the Memphis Blues Caravan on Sunday, January 19 at 7:00 p.m. Featured on the poster were Furry Lewis, Sam Chatmon, Piano Red, Houston Stackhouse, Joe Willie Wilkins, and Bukka White. A ticket to a full evening of blues, performed by musicians whose earliest recordings came out in 1927, was $3.50.

Brogger estimated that the Memphis Blues Caravan was active from 1973 to 1977, playing a total of sixty to seventy shows. Steve LaVere remembered a shorter time span. He wrote that the Caravan toured until he and his wife, Regina, left Memphis in the spring of 1975. He recalled, "The Caravan continued for a few performances without me, but eventually expired a calm demise later in 1975."[10]

According to Brogger, the musicians liked working in the Caravan: "The guys would ask 'When we going out again?' It was money and fun. Rolling down the highway, I'd hear 'Hey man, we got to stop at a whisky store,' and 'Hey man, we got to stop at a chicken store.' Kentucky Fried Chicken and bourbon whisky kept the wheels turning." In addition to the six original members, the two "young guys" on the tour were Joe Willie Wilkins's bass player Melvin Lee, in his early forties, and drummer Homer Jackson, in his mid-twenties.[11] Other performers on board the bus during the Caravan's four-year run included Sleepy John Estes, his musical partner Hammie Nixon, vocalist Memphis Ma Rainey (Lillie Mae Glover), and singer-guitarist Madame Van Zula Hunt. Both Rainey and Hunt had toured with several traveling shows, and Hunt fronted her own show for a time. They became popular performers on Beale Street.

The Blues Bus went on the road for three or four weeks at a time. LaVere acted as tour manager for the first year and a half, riding on the bus with the musicians, while Brogger took care of booking and promotion from Minneapolis. "I dealt with Steve, and Steve dealt with them," Brogger recalled.[12] LaVere described his Caravan responsibilities as "homebase agent, purser and on-stage [emcee], as well as its chief baby-sitter and whiskey-gitter, guitar tuner and string finder, and all-purpose gopher-boy."[13]

In July 1973, LaVere produced an excellent album with Booker, *Big Daddy*, that was recorded at Ardent Studios in Memphis, Arkansas. In the notes, LaVere writes that the album "was recorded under optimal conditions: Booker was fresh and alert, stone cold sober, well-rehearsed, playing a superb early 1930s steel-bodied National Triolian and performing everything just right—with the exception of 'Black Crepe Blues,' all are first takes."[14] The album's material is spread among Booker's familiar styles of slow blues, uptempo dance numbers, and religious songs. The first three tracks are "Black Cat Bone Blues," "1936 Trigger Toe," and "Cryin' Holy Unto the Lord."

Even as the Caravan continued to tour, Brogger and LaVere's partnership unraveled following a dispute over business practices. According to Brogger, the primary reason for the breakup was that LaVere's relationship with the musicians had deteriorated as they became convinced LaVere was taking a bigger share of the proceeds than he was entitled to. "LaVere was in there for more than ten percent, shall we say," Brogger recalled.

LaVere put forward a different account. He wrote in the notes to two Caravan-related CDs, released in 1994 on the Memphis Archives label, that he had been acting as "manager and/or agent" for some of the musicians.[15] His interpretation of these overlapping roles may have led him to deduct fees greater than an agent's customary 10 percent. After leaving the Caravan, LaVere maintained good relations with several of the musicians, continuing to book engagements for them. He died on December 27, 2015, in Greenwood, Mississippi. He was 72.

After assuming full responsibility for the Caravan, Arne Brogger became more involved in the logistics of the tour's public appearances. He hired an assistant—a college concert promoter who had impressed him—to travel with the musicians on the bus, and sometimes was on the bus himself. He said he worked hard to overcome the musicians' lingering mistrust. "I had to deal with each guy personally," he recalled. He grew to respect Booker White in the process.

> Bukka was not the warm and friendly guy that Furry [Lewis] was, but was very much his own man. He was dependable, quiet, and hugely talented. I would go so far as to venture, as far as being a major influence on a whole generation of musicians, in both material and technique, Bukka was the Caravan standout. He understood performance and connection with an audience.[16]

He recalled one performance in particular that illustrated his point. John "Memphis Piano Red" Williams opened most Caravan shows, with Booker next on the program. "John marched to his own drummer," Brogger said, "and we never knew what he was going to play."

> I always suggested to him that he open with a rockin' boogie to grab the audience. His response was always the same, "OK, li'l brother," and then he'd play whatever the hell he wanted. One night, he started with a slow blues—and stayed there for the entire set. I took Bukka aside and said we're dying out there . . . Red just took a shit on the stage. He looked at me. "I know. Don't worry about nothin'. I'll just give them a little bullshit." And he killed it. I liked the guy a lot. I think of him often.[17]

Performing at Western Illinois University, Booker was part of a blues festival that starred Willie Dixon, Muddy Waters, and Booker's second cousin, B. B. King. "I'll never forget that show," Brogger said. "I have a poster from it."

The show went on for four hours and was packed. God bless all these young white kids. B. B. called Bukka up to the stage just to acknowledge him. Bukka went straight to the microphone and began to talk to the audience. Nodding to B. B., "You remember when I gave you your first guitar . . . ?" B. B. was looking down at his shoes. ". . . and I remember you was so little sitting next to that big red Stella . . ."[18]

In 2002, when I had the opportunity to ask B. B. several questions about Booker, one was whether the story of Booker's giving him his first guitar was accurate. Without hesitating, B. B. responded, "That's not true. He helped me get a job while I was living with him—a job where he worked."[19]

Chapter Twenty-Four

BOOKER AND FURRY

IN 2019 I ASKED ARNE BROGGER ABOUT THE END OF THE MEMPHIS Blues Caravan. "When did I know it was over? It was kind of like the air going out of a balloon. I think the first guy to drop was Joe Willie [Wilkins], who was in tough shape."[1] Wilkins had toured wearing a colostomy bag. Sleepy John Estes died on June 5, 1977, leaving his friend and musical partner Hammie Nixon "alone, flailing around," according to Brogger. By that time, Brogger was in the process of winding down the project. He let SRO Productions in Minneapolis book what amounted to the final tour. "What I didn't want to have happen was they would go out and embarrass themselves," Brogger said. "Those guys who were left were frail."

Later, Brogger received what he called "death letters" from Melvin Lee, a bass player in Joe Willie Wilkins's band. Whenever a former Caravan member died, Lee sent Brogger a hand-written letter to give him the news. "Usually he would enclose the funeral program," Brogger added. In the late summer of 1981, Furry Lewis's house caught fire, injuring him. He developed pneumonia and died of heart failure on September 14. Melvin Lee reached Brogger in time for him to travel to Memphis and serve as a pallbearer at Lewis's funeral.

Over the years, Lewis had become a celebrated fixture in Memphis blues.

As a young man, he lost a leg hoboing back to Memphis on a train in Illinois. He lived the rest of his life with a prosthetic limb. Unable to support himself on his earnings as a musician, he worked several jobs for the city of Memphis—garbageman, night watchman, and street sweeper. When he resumed his musical career in 1959, recording his first LP for Samuel Charters, his sly humor and cheery demeanor attracted a new, younger, almost exclusively white audience in Memphis. The language on Furry's Mississippi Blues Trail marker in Greenwood detailed this phenomenon: "He endeared himself to a young circle of fans, writers, and musicians who visited him, chauffeured him to gigs, and took turns going to the local pawn shop to recover his guitar or wooden leg."[2]

In the 1970s, famous performers brought him to the attention of national audiences. Singer-songwriter Joni Mitchell visited him in his Memphis apartment and wrote a song about the experience, "Furry Sings the Blues." When the Rolling Stones played Memphis on July 4, 1975, they sent for Furry to play unaccompanied blues for the stadium audience after the high-powered opening acts finished their sets. The headliners wanted to wait for sundown before taking the stage.[3] Memphis writer Stanley Booth, who toured with the Rolling Stones in 1969 to research the book *Dance with the Devil* (later titled *The True Adventures of the Rolling Stones*), wrote a profile of Lewis that appeared in *Playboy.*

An experienced blues musician himself, blues expert David Evans thought white fans may have preferred Furry Lewis in the 1960s and 1970s because he was an older bluesman who played songs and told jokes, but did not make the audience uncomfortable in any way. Even though Booker wanted to win over his audiences as much (or perhaps more) than most blues musicians, he performed with an edge. Almost all of his songs were his own, and he sang about such uncomfortable topics as death ("Fixin' To Die Blues"), life in prison ("Parchman Farm Blues"), and being so popular with women that other men wanted to do him harm ("Aberdeen Mississippi Blues"). Arne Brogger made another distinction between the two men: "Bukka was the real deal when it came to blues. Furry was a songster. I'm not elevating one over the other. Furry was my pal. I loved the guy."

Going on the road for three weeks at a time on the same bus was difficult for Booker and Furry's opposite personalities. Their rivalry was bound to lead to a confrontation. Brogger remembered the blowup:

> Furry and Bukka did not get along. They lived down the street from each other on Mosby Street. I think it was professional jealousy, at least on Furry's part. Furry wanted the spotlight. There was only one other solo guitar player on the Caravan, and that was Bukka.
>
> It came to a head on the bus. Ma [Rainey] yelled "get back here right now!" Furry was coming up the aisle between the seats with his cane in one hand and knife in the other. "I'm not going to say a word with the motherfucker. I'm just going to cut his goddamn head off."
>
> Bukka said, "You ain't nothin' but a silly old man."

According to Furry, the root of the problems occurred when they were playing together somewhere in California. Furry had a wallet with a big red rubber band on it. In it he had a hundred-dollar bill, which went missing. He accused Bukka of taking it. Bukka denied it. End of story.[4]

Chapter Twenty-Five

COAST TO COAST

OVER THE WEEKEND OF MAY 3 TO 5, 1963, THE FIRST UCLA FOLK FESTIVAL did much to widen the audience for folk and blues music on the West Coast, attracting the attention of traditionalists and newcomers alike. The festival brought nationally known performers to the campus of the University of California, Los Angeles. Individual performers included banjo-playing activist Pete Seeger, original Carter Family member Maybelle Carter, old-time Kentucky banjo player and singer Roscoe Holcomb, and two Texas blues musicians with quite different styles, Lightnin' Hopkins and Mance Lipscomb. Another Texan—musician and marine biologist Sam Hinton—joined the two men. Hinton then lived in La Jolla. Groups performing included the Ashley-Watson Band with veteran entertainer Clarence "Tom" Ashley and relative newcomer Arthel "Doc" Watson; comedic bluegrass band the Dillards; Bessie Jones and the Georgia Sea Island Singers; bluegrass icon Bill Monroe; and the tradition-minded New Lost City Ramblers.

In Los Angeles, the Ash Grove was a gathering place for young guitar players who sat as close as possible to the stage to study the fretting positions and finger-picking techniques of the old-time masters of the instrument. One such listener was Barry Melton. In spring 1963, Melton was a precocious junior at Ulysses S. Grant High School in the San Fernando Valley. "I was a young, aspiring blues guitar player," Melton recalled. "My approach to learning to play was you follow in the Muddy Waters tradition. You found mentors, and I followed the oral tradition. You can't really learn to play off of records. I still have that belief."[1]

Melton brought his guitar to the Second Annual UCLA Folk Festival staged March 25 to 29, 1964, where he met Booker White. "All the young guitar players would show up with their guitars and everybody would play," he recalled. "Some part of the festival was outside the festival [itself] among the people playing at the festival and the people who came to hear them." As at similar festivals such as the Newport Folk

Festival in Rhode Island, the UCLA festival's program included workshops and musical demonstrations where performers and audience members could mingle, strike up a conversation, and join in making music. It was there, in what Melton called "the festival . . . outside the festival," that he got to know Booker White.

The high school senior from the San Fernando Valley met the fifty-eight-year-old Mississippi native less than a year after John Fahey and ED Denson had located Booker with a postcard sent care of general delivery in Aberdeen, Mississippi. Melton was enthused about meeting a mentor, and Booker was pleased to meet an enthusiastic young fan. The two of them took a break from the festival. Melton recalled:

> We went to this little lunch place not far from the festival. After we sat down, I gave him a menu and said "Bukka, get whatever you want." He picked up the menu and looked at it and turned it and said, "Well, I don't know . . ." After a minute, I must have realized what the score was. I said, "Oh, Bukka. You probably need glasses," He said, "Ah, yes. I need glasses." I took the menu and read it to him. "Okay," he said, and we ordered. . . . He was the first person I encountered who was not literate.[2]

What happened at lunch continued to bother Melton. Years later, as a public defender in San Francisco, he had clients who could not read; but he may have misunderstood the reason behind Booker's reluctance to order for himself.

From what ED Denson told me of Booker's deferential behavior in the weeks after he moved to Berkeley—that Booker wanted to entertain Denson and Fahey while they ate, rather than eat with them—Booker may have waited for Melton to order because he was not comfortable ordering before him. David Evans, who knew Booker in 1964, believes he "was partly literate, but probably not used to ordering from a menu."[3]

In 1965, years before he became a lawyer, Melton moved to Berkeley, where the folk scene in the city's coffeehouses and clubs was dynamic. There he met Denson, who would write about music for counterculture newspaper the *Berkeley Barb*. Denson introduced Melton to Joe McDonald, a singer-songwriter who was six years older than Melton, and Melton renewed his acquaintance with Booker White.

It was not hard for Melton and White to pick up the conversation where they had left off. "We knew each other from LA," Melton recalled. "He knew I was a guitar player, and to me he was a mentor. Lots of my mentors were old Black guys from the South. That was the folk tradition. I was just trying to live what I read and heard about. In the folk tradition, you learn to play by following people and you learn by the oral tradition. You didn't write anything down. You just watch their hands and ask them questions."

Melton's other mentors were Reverend Gary Davis and Skip James. "It's lost now . . . the idea of learning [from mentors] and honoring the folk tradition," he said. "Learning in the traditional way is lost in the modern age, but that was the way it was fifty years ago. It was possible to meet the people. This was before musicians played in stadiums. This was before the music went big time. The music was still accessible."

The Berkeley music scene was more than accessible. It was inviting, involving, and creative. Melton and Joe McDonald began playing together as a duo. McDonald and ED Denson sat around one day trying to come up with a name for the act. They found a phrase that caught their fancy and settled on Country Joe and the Fish. Barry Melton was The Fish.

In 1969, Booker performed at the Berkeley Folk Festival "in an eclectic lineup that included Sonny Terry and Brownie McGhee . . . Big Mama Thornton again, and the Louisiana Cajun Band."[4]

Folk music historian Ronald D. Cohen has described folk festivals as "feasts of musical celebration." The festivals directly benefited three constituencies: performers, audience, and promoters. Other stakeholders who stood to benefit from large musical gatherings that, for the most part, took place outdoors were the venues where the festivals were held and the economies around them. Some of the early promoters had learned the business by running music clubs. George Wein, who promoted the Newport Jazz and Folk Festivals, had founded Storyville, the most successful jazz club ever in the city of Boston. Ed Pearl, owner of the Ash Grove folk and blues club on Melrose Avenue in Los Angeles, produced the University of Southern California Folk Festival, booking a number of performers who had played at his club. The University of Chicago Folklore Society became hosts of the Chicago Folk Festival beginning in 1960.

The 1965 Newport Folk Festival had elements of the surreal. On Friday afternoon, folk establishment icon Alan Lomax and brash upstart manager Albert Grossman grappled on the ground over Lomax's introduction of the Paul Butterfield Blues Band, which Grossman—who managed the band—thought was condescending and offensive. On Saturday evening, Bob Dylan and members of the Butterfield Band played an electrified version of "Maggie's Farm" that surprised most members of the audience. Festival impresario George Wein recalled the scene:

> The audience, which was shocked into silence for a moment, quickly began to register its disapproval. People began booing; there were cries of "Sellout!" Others shouted about the sound quality, which was poor, since the sound system was designed for acoustic performers. The prevailing feeling among the crowd was a sense that they had been betrayed.[5]

Planning for 1966, the Folk Festival board discussed broadening its mission. Several members "urged that we consider the festival not only a showcase for folk music, but also sort of a massive, organic workshop of folk life," Wein recalled.[6] The pushback against 1965 translated into crafts activities such as cloth weaving, and primarily acoustic musicians who played in traditional styles. Booker fit the description and was extended his first invitation to perform at Newport, joining other traditional blues performers Son House and Skip James. Perhaps chastened by his public wrestling match with Albert Grossman in 1965, Alan Lomax devised an unusual format for presenting traditional blues musicians. He would have them appear together onstage and try to best the other musicians in an onstage "cutting session." Booker was in a boisterous mood. He described the contest as something that would take place on a Friday or Saturday night at a plantation. The prize would not be money, but a farm animal—a chicken or even a pig. Booker played his dynamic number "World Boogie." His large personality took over.

In 1966, two Canadian television producers—Paddy Sampson and Barry Callaghan—arranged for twenty American blues musicians to travel to Canada to tape an hour-long television special. Titled *The Blues*, the program featured the musicians' live performances, with Sampson asking the performers questions about the blues between numbers.

Performers included Muddy Waters, Sonny Terry and Brownie McGhee, Willie Dixon, Otis Spann, James Cotton, Sunnyland Slim, Mable Hillery of the Georgia Sea Island Singers, and Booker White. The taping took place over two or three days in the last week of January.

In addition to showcasing Black performers, the show's producers intended to make a statement about race relations in the United States. Years later, in a documentary about the show, Canadian music journalist Nelson George commented, "No one in American TV would put the blues on for an hour. It just wasn't gonna happen. It was music that was

Black, that was really Black. You have a show being made like this in Canada, it says, 'Look at all this great music that you have being made in America that we appreciate and you do not.'"[7]

Booker's performance was one of the longer segments. "We let Bukka White play for about nine or ten minutes," producer/host Barry Callaghan said in a CBC retrospective on the special. "Who is Bukka White? Bukka White is this guy who talks the blues."

IN 1972, BOOKER TOLD MCKEE AND CHISENHALL, "ALL THE PLAYING I ever did, I did better than I ever did in my life. I scrapped up pretty nicely."[8] He was talking about the late 1960s. Booker was in demand. When Chet Helms of Family Dog Productions wanted an authentic blues musician to open for a contemporary blues group at the Avalon Ballroom in San Francisco, Helms might choose Bukka White. His energetic repertoire was a better fit for a night of dancing in theaters and ballrooms than the music of most other rediscovered 1920s and 1930s blues singers. As far back as 1940, Booker had concluded the second day of his two-day recording session in Chicago with two numbers designed for dancing. He recorded "Bukka's Jitterbug Swing" and "Special Stream Line" on Friday, March 8, 1940. Both were issued as one side of 78 records that featured vocal and guitar blues on the other side.

Playing for hip San Francisco audiences who came to the ballrooms to dance, Booker had another advantage over his 1930s musician peers: he was younger and enjoyed better health. In the late 1960s, Mississippi John Hurt was a soft-spoken old man; Skip James was dying of cancer; and Son House was an alcoholic who needed to drink to feel comfortable performing before folk music audiences, largely young and white. Blues musician Paul Rishell understood Son's relationship to liquor. When Son's manager Dick Waterman was not able to accompany House in person, he hired young musicians to accompany House on the road. Paul Rishell toured with House as a second guitarist and custodian of pint bottles of whiskey. House needed a few swigs before he went on stage. Before one performance, House demanded that Rishell hand over the whole pint, which he drank. On stage, he began playing, then fell over. "Oh my God, I thought," Rishell recalled, "I killed Son House."[9]

Late in the summer of 1967—the Summer of Love—the name Booker White appeared twice on posters advertising concerts at the Avalon Ballroom. On a colorful orange, black, and gray poster for upcoming Avalon dance concerts from August 24 to 27, Bo Diddley and Bukka White were to play the ballroom on August 24. Headliners for August 25 to 27 were Big Brother and the Holding Company, and Ibis Alchemical Co. provided the light show. None of the performers' images appeared on the poster. Instead, the image was of novelist Fyodor Dostoevsky, who appeared to be troubled as tiny Russian soldiers marched along the bottom edge of the poster.

Ten days later, the [Steve] Miller Blues Band headlined another Family Dog production at the Avalon on September 1–3. Billed second was the band Mother Earth, whose singer Tracy Nelson possessed a powerful voice for blues, and opening was Bukka White.

IN AUGUST 1967, BOOKER TRAVELED TO SEATTLE TO PERFORM AT THE invitation of the Seattle Folklore Society. The society had organized in the mid-1960s as a non-profit corporation with the mission of bringing "legendary roots musicians" to Seattle so that they could be interviewed and preserved on tape and film performing their music. Booker played a public concert, was interviewed by folklorists on the radio, and was recorded in performance on videotape or film.[10]

Making use of community resources at its disposal, the society created permanent audio and visual documents of musicians such as Booker White and Mississippi Fred McDowell while the musicians were actively performing. Co-founding the society and shaping its mission was John Ullman, who moved to Seattle in the mid-1960s from Portland, Oregon, after coordinating folk music concerts at Reed College. Ullman reached out to the University of Washington's ethnomusicology department and Seattle public radio and television stations to record interviews with the musicians and tape or film their performances.

Booker appeared on radio station KRAB on August 30, 1967. Conducting the interview were Ullman, blues enthusiast Mike Duffy, and show host Bob West, an avid record collector who took over the station's rhythm and blues program in February 1966.[11] The program had yet to be named and was listed in the program guide as "Bob West and his giant collection of old scratchies." At his interviewers' request, Booker played an epic version of "Po' Boy" and a more conventional "Special Streamline." He mentioned on air that he was fighting a cold and needed to take his medicine.

The interview took place four months before Jack Hurley's interview with Booker in Memphis, but was not published until 2004. After an editor put the interview into chronological order, what sounded like a low-key program on air appeared in print as recollections surrounded by questions on Booker's familiarity with other blues musicians. For example, did he know "a singer by the name of William Brown, a guitar player, he played with Son House? . . ." Booker gave the interviewers an answer, whether true or not. "He's dead though, isn't he?" Booker asked. "I remember him. He's from the Delta, too . . . was a bad kid, I'm telling you. I got his records right now. That kid, he could really go. I left Monday and played it Sunday evening before I left." One interviewer asked when he first saw a National steel-bodied guitar—the instrument he became identified with in the 1960s and 1970s. "I been having them since they started makin' them," he said.

> I first see one in 1939. I met a boy in St. Louis had one and he didn't know what to do with it. My box was in bad shape and he was in bad shape, too, 'cause he didn't have a quarter. I told him "I need your box and you need mine. I'll give you a dollar, you throw in your steel box," so I just swapped mine in. It was a good box, it was a Gibson. He wasn't doing nothing but walking from corner to corner. He wasn't never gonna try and make something of hisself, so I started with them. Every time I get rid of one I get another one, step up, you know. I knew what I was doin'.[12]

On the same trip to Seattle, public television station KCTS taped (or filmed) Booker performing. Playing against a sterile studio background, he appeared comfortable and self-assured. He had on the Native American–styled poncho he wore for important engagements and showed his versatility, playing finger-picked and slide guitar numbers before moving over to upright piano.

Booker returned to the Bay area in 1969. Before playing club dates November 18 to 20 at the Freight & Salvage in Berkeley and November 30 to December 3 at the Matrix in San Francisco,[13] he performed at the Ash Grove in Los Angeles. That engagement led to meeting the Rolling Stones on November 8, 1969. The meeting took place before the second of two Rolling Stones shows at the Los Angeles Forum. Traveling with the band to write a book, author Stanley Booth facilitated the meeting. Booth knew Booker from Memphis, having seen him recently at the home of Furry Lewis.[14] At the Forum, Gram Parsons arrived with Booker and talked his way past the security personnel watching the backstage area. Parsons had decided to bring Booker to the arena after his group, the Flying Burrito Brothers, shared the bill with Booker at the Ash Grove.[15]

As the visitors arrived backstage, Booker's cousin B. B. King was on stage. B. B. was the final act before the headliners would appear.

Preceding him were British singer Terry Reid followed by Ike and Tina Turner. Even with a blood connection to the man on stage, Booker might not have gained entry into the performers' area if it were not for Booth's intercession. In *Dance with the Devil*, Booth wrote:

> We embraced, I welcomed Bukka to the Forum, and the stiff-necked guard said not a word. . . . Big jolly-looking old fat man with gold teeth in his smile, B. B.'s older cousin, murder convict freed from Parchman Farm because he sang the blues, Bukka White. . . . I introduced Keith and Mick to Bukka. Gram and Bukka were drunk. Bukka reminded me to let him know when B. B., who had just been starting his set as we came in, went offstage. "What you doing out here?" he asked me.
>
> "I'm with these guys," I said, nodding at Mick and Keith. "They play some blues. They ain't bad. For white boys."[16]

Keith brought his National steel guitar on the road with him—the same model of guitar Booker played. In the Forum dressing room, Keith began playing slide blues on his instrument, and Mick sang the lyrics to "Dust My Broom" over the ringing National sound. They followed with a slow blues, "Key to the Highway." Booth wrote:

> Bukka listened, his head cocked to one side, and said, "That's good. These boys is *good.* Has you ever made any records?"
>
> "Yes," Keith said, looking startled.
>
> "I knew good and well you had." This is a star here, Bukka announced, holding his open hand over Keith's head. "This is a Hollywood star. If I'm lyin', I'm dyin'."
>
> B. B., coming in to ask something, saw Bukka, and we had Memphis Old Home Reunion.[17]

A DRIVING FORCE BEHIND THE NEWPORT JAZZ AND FOLK FESTIVALS was George Wein. Wein grew up in the comfortable Boston suburb of Newton. At eighteen he joined the Army, serving in Europe at the end of World War II. Discharged in 1946, he enrolled in Boston University to begin a "grueling" pre-medical program out of respect for his doctor father. An accomplished piano player, he jammed with professional musicians, including trumpet player Ruby Braff. "Working with Ruby, particularly, was an education. He was by far the best trumpet player in the Boston area. . . ."[18]

After a brief flirtation with the American Communist Party in New York City, he returned to Boston, where he confounded his family by opening George Wein's Storyville, a jazz club, in September 1950. Within a few years he brought some of the most respected names in jazz to Boston: soprano saxophone player Sidney Bechet, tenor player Coleman Hawkins, vocalists Sara Vaughan and Ella Fitzgerald, alto saxophone player Charlie Parker, the Modern Jazz Quartet, and the emerging Dave Brubeck Quartet. "I was having a great time in Boston, spending every night of the week at Storyville, immersed in the music I loved," he wrote in his autobiography.[19]

He became a major figure in jazz. Boston University invited him to teach a course on jazz history.

In 1953, Boston University professor Donald Born introduced him to a wealthy Newport resident, Elaine Lorillard, who was auditing Born's English course. Mrs. Lorillard told Wein that Newport summers were boring. Since he closed the Storyville club during the summer, Wein saw an opportunity. With the support of Elaine Lorillard and her husband Louis Livingston Lorillard—heir to the Lorillard Tobacco Company fortune—Wein came up with the idea of a jazz festival, loosely based on the model of the Tanglewood Festival of classical music in Lenox, Massachusetts. Liking the idea, Louis Lorillard extended Wein a twenty-thousand-dollar line of credit and structured the nonprofit corporation Newport Jazz Festival, Inc. with himself as president and Wein as vice president. The first festival took place over two nights in August 1954 at the Newport Casino.

Five years later, Wein enlarged his idea of "a folk afternoon embedded within the 1959 Newport Jazz Festival"[20] into the first Newport Folk Festival. Because it was the first, largest, and—for a time—only folk festival, Newport assumed an outsized importance in the world of folk music, including country blues. In 1959 and the early 1960s, Newport could count on drawing a primarily white audience from New England colleges and universities. Almost all the important media covering folk music were in New York and other eastern locations. To play Newport and do well was an avenue to instant recognition and some form of success, whether in the form of media coverage or performance bookings.

The 1963 Newport Folk Festival was a high-water mark for the groundswell of the folk movement that began in the 1950s. Traditional musicians played alongside commercial acts such as Peter, Paul, and Mary and the Kingston Trio. Bob Dylan's solo performance on Friday evening was emblematic of Dylan the protest singer: he sang "With God on Our Side," "Talkin' John Birch Society Blues," and "A Hard Rain's A-Gonna Fall." Dylan was the closing act, but Peter, Paul, and Mary returned to the stage to sing his anthem "Blowin' in the Wind," which had been released a month before the festival and sold 320,000 copies in a week.[21] But for blues enthusiasts, the highlight of the festival took place the following afternoon. Rediscovered months before by Tom Hoskins, Mississippi John Hurt appeared in a blues workshop with Sonny Terry and Brownie McGee, John Lee Hooker, and John Hammond Jr.

There were other important festivals besides Newport. One was the Mariposa Folk Festival in Toronto, Canada. Michael Taft, head of the Archive of Folk Music in the Library of Congress, saw Booker at Mariposa in 1972. Booker was one of the featured artists when Taj Mahal emceed a blues concert. Others included Bonnie Raitt and Roosevelt Sykes. Taft recalled:

> Bukka White played several times during the three days of the festival, but I recall him playing at a major concert with other performers. White wore a multi-colored vest over his shirt—somewhat psychedelic, to fit the time period. He was an animated performer, interested in showmanship perhaps as much as musicianship. I remember that he was the first bluesman I ever saw who played his guitar slung behind his head, with the guitar strap dangling below his chin—I had heard about such tricks but never witnessed them before. I think White was playing a National steel guitar.
>
> After his set was over, he sat just off stage (this was an open-air stage), watching the other performers and talking to performers also awaiting their turn. Sykes began his set—also an animated performer. I remember him playing piano with one hand while gesturing with the other to emphasize the lyrics of his song. At one point, White hopped on stage and did a shuck-and-jive dance while Sykes was in the middle of a song. I don't know what Sykes thought of this, but it seemed impromptu to me, and perhaps meant to steal the limelight a bit from Sykes.[22]

If Booker played "Fixin' To Die Blues," one festival attendee would have listened with special interest because he had covered the song on his first album. Music critic Peter Goddard from the *Toronto Star* spotted

Bob Dylan "in jeans, white shirt and wearing a red bandana and rimless spectacles. He stood briefly in a crowd watching some fiddlers before moving to another area to listen to old blues pianist Roosevelt Sykes and blues guitarist Bukka White."[23]

A publicity photo from Booker White's brief time with Folklore Productions in 1964. Courtesy of Mitch Greenhill.

Booker's co-manager John Fahey in 1979 when Fahey was on Chrysalis Records. Publicity photo.

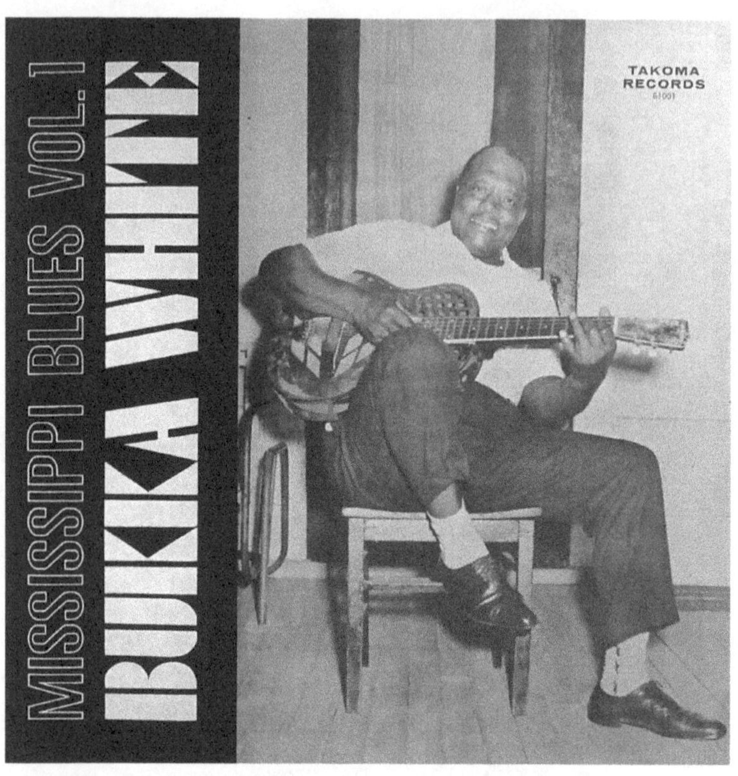

In summer 1963, John Fahey and ED Denson recorded Booker's album, released in 1964 on their new Takoma label.

THE BROADSIDE
OF BOSTON

Volume III, No. 4 Cambridge, Massachusetts April 15, 1964

Booker appeared on the cover of *The Broadside of Boston* to promote his April 1964 performances.

Booker makes his debut at the Newport Folk Festival, July 22, 1966. Photo by Dick Waterman.

Booker's friend Jack Hurley took this memorable photo of him in his "office." Courtesy of the Tennessee State Museum.

Author-activist Julius Lester gives the 1984 commencement address at Hampshire College. Photo by Nancy Palmieri. Used by permission.

Booker at Newcastle City Hall in England on his first American Folk Blues Festival tour, October 23, 1967. Photo by Keith Perry.

Booker at the Sunderland Empire Theatre in England on his second AFBF tour, November 22, 1970. Photo by Keith Perry.

On August 24, 1967, Booker opened for Big Brother and the Holding Company at the Avalon Ballroom in San Francisco. Poster by Bob Fried.

Booker plays piano at the River City Blues Festival, Ellis Auditorium, Memphis, on December 3, 1971. Photo by Amy van Singel. Courtesy of Jim O'Neal, BluEsoterica Archives.

Booker shows guitarist Lee Baker a move at the River City Blues Festival, December 3, 1971. Photo by Amy van Singel. Courtesy of Jim O'Neal, BluEsoterica Archives.

Booker at the Rainbow Theatre, North London, on his third American Folk Blues Festival tour, October 9, 1972. Photo by Sylvia Pitcher.

Booker's reunion with cousin B. B. King at the New Orleans Jazz & Heritage Festival, April 13, 1973. Roosevelt Sykes watches. Photo by John Messina, courtesy of the New Orleans Jazz & Heritage Foundation Archive.

An historic blend of jazz, funk, and blues. L to R, Professor Longhair on piano, Meters rhythm section George Porter Jr. and Ziggy Modeliste, Booker White, Roosevelt Sykes, and B. B. King. Photo by John Messina, courtesy of the New Orleans Jazz & Heritage Foundation Archive.

B. B. King plays the blues at a London club in the early 1970s. Photo by Joe Stevens.

A poster publicizing the Memphis Blues Caravan's concert at the Ritz Theater in Austin, Texas, January 19, 1974.

Booker posed for the photographer in the historic section of Bremen, Germany, March 1975. Photo by Jochen Mönch.

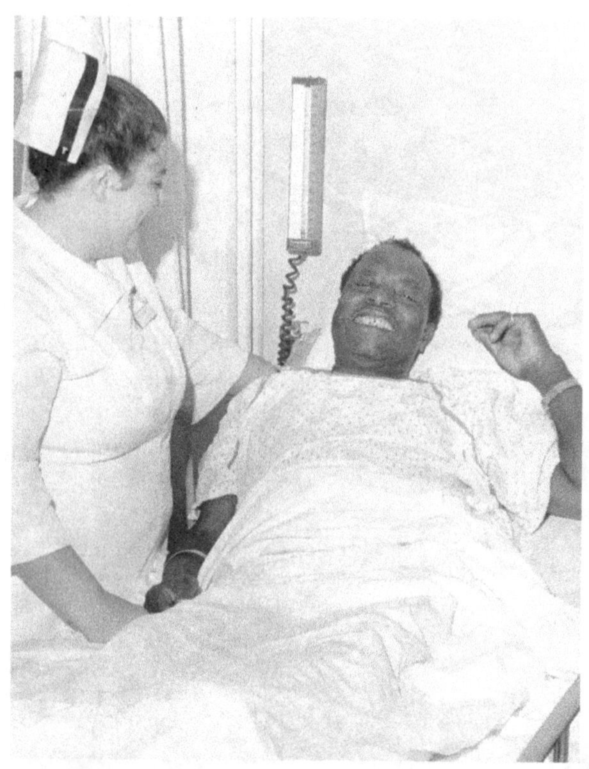

Before going home, Booker shows a smile in Beverly (Massachusetts) Hospital, July 29, 1976. Photo by Ed Wolman. Courtesy of the *Salem News*.

Booker's partner Leola Morris at home in Memphis with her granddaughter, 1982. Photo by Andrew Yale.

Booker's guitar with song list taped onto it, on the cover of 2019 auction catalogue. Courtesy of Guitar Auctions at Gardiner Houlgate.

Opened in 1909, the Chickasaw County Court House continues to dominate the downtown in Houston, Mississippi. Photo by the author.

Now covered by tarps, a memorial to Confederate soldiers could be viewed at the center of Grenada in 2017. Photo by the author.

In May 1930, talent scout Ralph Lembo summoned Washington White to his store (sign in window) in Itta Bena. Photo by the author.

The shell of the Roxy in White Station near West Point in 2017. Booker played a roadhouse around Whites. Photo by the author.

Chapter Twenty-Six

TRANSATLANTIC

FOUR YEARS AFTER BOOKER RESPONDED TO THE POSTCARD JOHN Fahey sent to him care of Postmaster, Aberdeen, Mississippi, he was invited to join a select company of Black musicians who made up the roster of the American Folk Blues Festival 1967. He had toured the United States and Canada since the fall of 1963. As club owner Ed Pearl remarked after Booker played the Ash Grove in Los Angeles, "At some point he must have been popular, or in his mind popular, because he assumed everyone knew who he was."[1]

Booker's self-confidence was on display on October 25, 1967, when the Folk Blues Festival arrived in Birmingham, England, to play at Birmingham Town Hall. Mark H. Makin was an eighteen-year-old graphic design student at the Coventry College of Art, which he entered in September 1966. He and a group of friends bought tickets to the concert, and planned to meet at the Town Hall. Not seeing any of his friends when he arrived, Mark decided to wait in one of the hallways outside the hall. As show time got closer, people began to file into the concert hall and the hallways emptied. "None of my friends had arrived," Makin recalled.[2] "There were now very few people in the passage." He was not expecting to meet all the musicians. Booker made it happen:

> While I was standing there, holding my concert program, I heard footsteps behind me. I turned round and found myself staring into the chest of Bukka White. He seemed enormous to me. He had his knitted, loud-patterned poncho cardigan on and a bootlace tie with a metal clasp with "Texas" across it. I looked up at him and he prodded me in the chest and said, "Hey, boy, have you seen my whisky?" Without waiting for an answer, he wandered off down the passage.

Mark continued to wait.

> Minutes later, [there were] footsteps behind me again, and Bukka returned. He glanced down at the program I was holding and, as we were standing just outside the small rest room that all the other performers were in, must have assumed that I was an autograph hunter waiting for the right time. Bukka grabbed the program and grabbed my arm and dragged me into the room saying, "Come on, boy, I'll get them all for you."

Booker ushered Mark into blues fan heaven.

> I found myself in this little room and as I looked round there was Little Walter standing in the corner. Bukka thrust the program under his nose and dutifully, he scribbled on it. He systematically went round the whole room, Skip James, Odie Payne, Hound Dog Taylor, Brownie McGhee and finally Sonny Terry. He was asleep in a chair. Bukka walked up to him, kicked him in the shins, picked up Sonny's limp arm, placed his rubber stamp in it and using Sonny's arm, stamped the booklet. He then put Sonny back to sleep!
>
> While all this was going on, I stood by the door to the room. Leaning against the wall next to me was a Martin D35. I idly strummed the strings and I heard this small, high pitched voice behind me say, "You be careful of that, boy. It's worth more than both of us." It was Skip James, dressed immaculately in dark blazer with silver buttons and pearl cufflinks.
>
> The concert was almost starting and some of the staff were helping Son House out to the stage. He came past me just as Bukka thrust the program under his nose. Son stopped, took the small fine point biro [ballpoint pen] and, leaning on my shoulder, started to slowly sign the program. He was so slow and labored that the impression went right through all the pages. Son was helped out of the room and, as none had bothered, I followed, carrying Son's National guitar. By now, things were starting and I went off into the hall.[3]

Before the first American Folk Blues Festival crossed the Atlantic in 1962, some of the fans caught up in the folk revival in England and the United States began to focus their attention on old blues recordings.[4] Added to the existing fan base of blues enthusiasts, this new cohort of collectors and listeners grew into a sizeable audience—big enough to support tours of Europe between 1949 and 1958 by several acoustic blues performers: Lead Belly (Huddie Ledbetter), Josh White, Lonnie Johnson, Big Bill Broonzy, and the duo Brownie McGhee and Sonny Terry. David Evans wrote, "Studies . . . confirm that the growing transatlantic White audience for contemporary Black blues performers grew from musical influences of the folk revivalists and an alternative youth culture based on rhythm and blues and rock 'n' roll."

Electric blues arrived in 1958. Singer and electric slide player Muddy Waters and his regular pianist Otis Spann toured England in 1958, backed by British "trad" (traditional) jazz musicians including the popular Chris Barber Band. Waters and Spann's volume startled both English audiences and the older musicians on stage with them; but the new sound influenced younger musicians in Barber's band such as guitarist Alexis Korner and harmonica player Cyril Davies. Soon club owner Harold Pendleton and his manager John Gee instituted a rhythm and blues night at London's Marquee Club for which audiences queued up down Wardour Street.[5]

In Germany, jazz historian and television producer Joachim-Ernst Berendt proposed the concept of a touring group of American blues musicians that would draw crowds. The UK Blues Federation wrote, "Jazz had become very popular, and rock and roll was just gaining a foothold, and both genres drew influences directly back to the blues. Berendt thought that European audiences would flock to concert halls to see them in person."[6]

Booker's opportunity to bring his brand of country blues to audiences in Europe and Great Britain was made possible by Willie Dixon, a Chicago-based bass player and songwriter from Vicksburg, Mississippi. Booker's daughter Irene Kertchaval recalled that her father and Dixon had become friends during Booker's recording trips to Chicago.[7]

In the late 1950s, it had become hard for Chicago's blues musicians to find work in their city. The scarcity of demand led Dixon to team up with pianist/singer Memphis Slim (John Len Chatman) so that they could back up each other's gigs. Dixon recalled, "It got to the point where it was . . . just one night a week in Chicago, so Memphis Slim and I said we got to get out of here."[8] In 1960, an Israeli club owner visiting Chicago heard the duo and booked them into her club in Haifa. Once the Americans were overseas, they wrote to German promoter Horst Lippmann, who reached them in Paris, where they were backing up the conga line at Les Trois Mailletz nightclub.[9] According to Dixon, he and Memphis Slim pitched Lippman and his partner Fritz Rau on the idea of a larger European blues show. Persuaded by the audiences Dixon and

Memphis Slim were drawing, Lippmann and Rau asked the Americans to help them recruit enough blues musicians to make up a package tour. Dixon took the lead. Lippmann was surprised by his good fortune:

> I didn't know Willie was kind of a father figure in Chicago blues since he produced Muddy Waters, Howlin' Wolf, and Sonny Boy Williamson. I was not so much familiar that he was a great songwriter and some of the songs Muddy Waters and Howlin' Wolf had been doing actually came from the pen of Willie Dixon. I found that out later so that was actually the biggest surprise I had with the blues, to find a man like Willie Dixon, who as a musician, singer, producer, and songwriter was really the right person.[10]

The first American Folk Blues Festival consisted of a series of twenty-five performances in England and Europe extending through most of October 1962.[11] Hoping to appeal to a variety of enthusiasts, Lippmann and Rau asked Dixon and Memphis Slim to include both electric and acoustic performers in the touring company. The two musicians were able to recruit vocalist Helen Humes; electric guitarists T-Bone Walker and John Lee Hooker; Sonny Terry and Brownie McGhee; and drummer Armand "Jump" Jackson.

Humes was one of the last of the great female blues vocalists. T-Bone Walker's single-note guitar solos and chording influenced B. B. King, among many others. Detroit's John Lee Hooker played passionate blues with a boogie groove that influenced young white bands such as Alan Wilson's Canned Heat. During the tour, Dixon introduced performers during the stage shows as well as playing bass, and Jump Jackson joined Dixon in the rhythm section. After the tour, Memphis Slim emigrated to Paris, and was treated with considerable respect. In 1971, I heard him in person at Les Trois Mailletz, where he was introduced as "le premier chanteur de blues americain"—in English, "the leading American blues singer."

Horst Lippmann (born March 17, 1927) was a jazz drummer. The son of a German hotel owner, Lippmann played in a jazz club in Frankfurt even as the music was banned during the 1940s. A knowledgeable musician, he also contributed articles to one of the first German jazz magazines. His career moved in the direction of concert promotion. After World War II, he helped found the German Jazz Federation, which organized concert tours of West German jazz clubs. He put together the German Jazz Festival in Frankfurt in 1953.

Though the two men were only three years apart in age, Lippmann's future business partner Fritz Rau (born March 9, 1930) came to music later. Graduating with a law degree from the eminent University of Heidelberg, he worked as a court clerk and in a law firm. He began to help with the management of a Heidelberg jazz club, Cave 54, and promoted a successful jazz concert at Heidelberg Town Hall in December 1955.

The concert brought him to the attention of Horst Lippmann, who hired Rau to help arrange tours of Europe by Jazz at the Philharmonic—a group tour of American jazz musicians organized by American promoter Norman Granz. The two men began to work together and established the concert agency Lippmann + Rau.[12] Their partnership coincided with an increasing interest in American jazz and blues in Great Britain and Europe. With their involvement in the package tours of jazz musicians organized by Granz, Lippmann and Rau saw an opportunity to organize and promote similar tours of "folk" (loosely defined to mean American roots music) and blues musicians. David Evans writes: "Beginning in 1962, blues festivals, modeled on successful folk and jazz festivals, offered European and White American audiences increased access to Black blues artists' live performances. . . . The [American Folk Blues Festival] artists also reached millions through appearances on European radio and television broadcasts."[13] Evans contrasts Europe and Great Britain's increased familiarity with American blues performers through the AFBF tours and accompanying media coverage with the limited stage time given to Black blues musicians by the two largest American festivals: the Newport Jazz Festival, which began in 1954, and Newport Folk Festival that started in 1959. The word "blues" does not appear in the names of either festival. Though running two or three days, these festivals "billed only a few Black performers as featured performers, although blues songs were a staple in the repertoire of the largely White revivalist-scene performers in the early 1960s."[14]

The audience at Manchester in 1962—the first venue for the festival in England—included Mick Jagger, Keith Richards, and Brian Jones of the Rolling Stones, and guitarist Jimmy Page, who later put together Led Zeppelin. Attending later festivals in London were Eric Burdon, Eric Clapton, and Steve Winwood.[15] The festivals directly influenced a generation of young British musicians with an interest in blues, and were significant contributors to the repertoire of the groups lumped together in the musical "British Invasion" of the United States.

As would happen again in 1976, when Booker flew to Boston for a five-night residency at a jazz and blues club, he experienced a deep personal loss just before touring with the American Folk Blues Festival in 1967. The sister he was closest to died. Booker rarely talked about his siblings, but when Professor Fred J. Hay asked him if anyone in his family besides his father played music, he talked about his sister Estelle:

> Yeah, my sister. My sister Etta, she played guitar. She could sing, I'm telling you the truth. She fell dead in '67. I was getting ready to go overseas. So she went up to check on her son's house. He was in some part of . . . Indiana. And she went up there to check the house to see if nobody had bothered it. And so, she turned around and coming back she must a had a heart attack; she done fell dead.[16]

Lippmann and Rau's American festival tours turned a number of American blues musicians into international performers. When Booker said from the stage of the 1968 Memphis Country Blues Festival that he felt he was not as well-known in the city as he deserved to be, he mentioned that he toured Europe the previous October. His inclusion in the 1967 American Folk Blues Festival roster was the first of four times he played before audiences in Europe and Great Britain. He toured with the AFBF twice more, in 1970 and 1972.

Booker touched a number of lives on his overseas trips. Gary Atkinson was one such person. Gary called my attention to a film of Booker performing in Copenhagen on November 7, 1970. Danish television carried the concert. Fourteen and a half minutes of footage are available online. Booker sits in a wooden chair in front of a vocal microphone, with a second microphone placed in front of his National Duolian steel guitar.[17] The film offers a rare glimpse of Booker on stage in a formal setting. Two different posters advertised the 1970 tour as the American Blues and Gospel Festival and the American Negro Blues Festival.

In Copenhagen, Booker wears a dark suit and light dress shirt, set off by his "Texas" string tie. He plays four numbers: "Gibson Hill," "Poor Boy," "Lighthouse (on the Sea) Blues," and "Blues All Under My Pillow." Spliced together, the first three are from the concert's first set, and the fourth is Booker's last number in the second set. With the exception of "Poor Boy," played with the guitar on his lap sliding a steel rod across the strings, he keeps the same medium boogie tempo going. His large right hand strums up and down like a metronome—guitar picks on his thumb and forefinger. Relaxed and clearly enjoying himself, he is *performing*. Ending "Gibson Hill" with a string of slide notes, he flashes the audience a big grin. During "Lighthouse Blues," he exhorts himself: "Take your time and play it good now!" The lyrics to "Blues Under My Pillow" sound improvised like those of his "sky songs." Before leaving the stage, he tells the audience, "I got to go now. My brother, he sleeps so much. I've got to go wake him up. He's in there [backstage] snoring like a goat."

Gary Atkinson attended the 1970 American Folk Blues Festival tour in Leicester, England, on Sunday, November 1. He told me about the Copenhagen concert footage because it was taken only six days after the Leicester show. He was fourteen, living with his parents in the village of South Cave, eighteen miles west of the town of Hull, where he was born. He was a fourth year student at the South Hunsley School in Welton, East Yorkshire. He was a serious blues fan. His father took him to the concert at De Montfort Hall in Leicester. Before the show, he met harmonica players Sonny Terry and Shakey Horton as they walked from their bus to the hall. He was looking for Bukka White:

> I had written to him a few weeks prior to the show, but I had no response from him. At fourteen, it did not occur to me that Bukka was on the road and had probably not received my letter, asking if I could meet him on the evening of the show I was going to attend. Indeed, it was only by pure luck that I did get to meet him after the show. He gave me a pencil-written note which he had already written and was going to send me, which simply read "In looking for you last night, we had a good time, from Bukka White." I still have it, after all these years, with pride of place in a scrap book.[18]

"Bukka greeted me like a long-lost friend," he recalled, "even though he hadn't seen me before in his life. [He wore a] huge, grinning smile and seemed genuinely pleased to see me. Like Sonny Terry, he was amazed that a young boy from 'way overseas, in England' knew all about him." Gary Atkinson went on to become the managing director of Document Records, founded in Austria and now based in Scotland. Document advertises itself as "the world's largest catalogue of vintage blues, jazz, boogie-woogie, gospel, old-time country and more. . . ." The company's mission is to assemble complete sets of 78 rpm recordings by artists in these genres and repackage their music on CDs.

After staying home in 1971, the musicians of the American Folk Blues Festival returned to Europe in 1972 for two separate month-long tours in March and October. Booker was part of the October tour, which opened at London's Rainbow Theatre, played four dates in Germany, and gave a final concert in the spacious Salle Pleyel concert hall in Paris. Promoter Horst Lippmann recorded the October 18 and 26 concerts in Lünen in northwest Germany (October 18) and at Circus Krone Bau in Munich (October 26), where the Beatles had played in June 1966. Two songs from Booker's performances, "Getting Ready" and "Aberdeen Mississippi Blues," were included in the compilation *American Folk Blues Festival '72*.

The American Folk Blues Festival appearances sometimes led to other opportunities for the musicians. On October 27, 1972, the day after an AFBF concert in Munich, independent producer Peter Gleissner recorded an album with Booker at Munich's Union Studio. Not surprisingly, Booker was tired. He limited his playing to six numbers, which he stretched out to fill the album. His guitar playing was shaky, and he stumbled on some lyrics. Two other AFBF musicians were in the studio, but the only accompaniment was provided by German harmonica player Gerhard "Gary" Engbarth, who played on one number, "Stone." Titled *Baton Rouge Mosby Street*, the album was released in 1972 by the German label Blues Beacon, which was founded in 1971 by Matthias Winckelmann and Horst Weber for the specific purpose of making albums with American blues musicians who performed in Europe. Other blues artists on the label were Robert Pete Williams and Little Brother Montgomery.

Booker's visibility on the 1967, 1970, and 1972 American Folk Blues Festival tours enhanced his standing among British and European blues enthusiasts, who sought him out on both sides of the Atlantic. In July 1971, when a false report that Booker had died reached Max Jones, principal jazz writer for the British publication *Melody Maker*, Jones eulogized him:

> It is interesting to note that his 1940 recordings were what Sam Charters referred to as "the last of the classic Delta recordings to be released on the commercial market."
>
> If White had made nothing else, he would be revered by blues fanciers as a patriarch figure on a par with Patton, Son House and Skip James. But in fact he was rediscovered in '63 and launched a new recording career. . . .
>
> His death removed from the lists a true giant of Mississippi folksong, one of the last living legends of country blues.[19]

Alive and on tour in 1972, Booker was interviewed by a French television reporter (probably on March 3 when the AFBF performed in Paris) for the trendy cultural program *Pop 2*. Broadcast on December 2, the segment set the scene with a montage of photos of rural Mississippi, Black field workers, the workers' shacks, and the front entrance to Parchman Farm. The interview gave viewers a rare glimpse into Booker's skills as a storyteller. Sitting with his National steel guitar cradled between his knees, he slowed down his rapid-fire speech for the French interviewer, used hand gestures such as finger-pointing and opening his palms, and tapped on his breastbone to signify sincerity. Much of the interview was devoted to the circumstances of his discovery in 1930 by talent scout Ralph Lembo. When asked whether he ever had met Charley Patton, he responded, "I never seen him, but I met his brother. [In those days] I was too young to go out at night. . . ."[20]

In December 1972, Italian blues enthusiasts Lucio Maniscalchi and Gianni Marcucci spent twelve days in Memphis recording a number of the area's blues musicians: Laura Dukes, John "Piano Red" Williams, Dewey Corley, Mose Vinson, Sleepy John Estes with Hammie Nixon, and Bukka White. In the notes to one of the two albums that were produced, Marcucci recalled what it was like to work with Booker in Memphis:

> When we arrived at his house, Bukka White had just finished eating, and when we asked him to record his blues songs, he explicitly told us that he wanted to be paid, repeatedly claiming that he would play for us for a very low price (20 dollars) only because Hammie Nixon and Sleepy John Estes were with us. Five of the blues songs recorded in chronological order at the December 22nd session (seven in total) were selected to be issued on this compilation. The style of these songs belong[s] to the so-called "Delta Blues" genre, of which Bukka White is one of the few living representatives.
>
> When striving to transcribe the lyrics, we often had to face a remarkably intermittent conversational style from which emerged such main themes as detachment [death], drinking and love that have always underpinned his blues; altogether absent here . . . is the theme of imprisonment, which repeatedly occurs during and after the time he served at Parchman Farm.[21]

The notes accompanied *Tennessee Blues Vol. 1*, released in 1975, which showcased Laura Dukes, Piano Red, and Booker. Booker's five songs were "Aberdeen [Mississippi] Blues," "I Ain't Got a Little Bed," "All Night

Long," "Cross the River," and "Please!" Released in 1974, *Blues Oggi* was a compilation featuring all seven of the artists. Booker's two songs were "I'm Getting Ready" and "Brownsville, Tennessee."

The two Italian albums documented for European record buyers a mid-1970s Memphis scene where musicians would encourage and accompany one another. As the result of staying true to his music for almost sixty years, Washington White of Chickasaw County, Mississippi, had become an internationally known performer.

ON MARCH 12, 1974, PROFESSOR F. JACK HURLEY, WHO FIRST INTERviewed Booker in 1966, set up an informal session in the musician's apartment. Since Hurley and White had kept in contact for eight years, the session sounds informal and relaxed. Booker was in excellent form, recording seven songs. Two of them were new.

On "Black Spider Climbing," the lyrics ask what it signifies to see a black spider "webbing" down a man's wall. The twin instruments of Booker's voice and guitar intertwine to create a single effect. After each of several verses, Booker plays a series of four or five identical guitar riffs that represent the spider "webbing" down.

The second new song, "The M & O Line," sounds like a sky song, with Booker improvising lyrics, but also is organized like a traditional blues. The Mobile and Ohio Railroad was the company that employed his father and ran through Houston. The singer is a railroad man who returns home to discover that his wife has left him and taken their son with her:

> Oh boy it hurt me so bad
> When I heard that old M & O blow
> What hurt me so bad
> When I heard that old M & O blow
> You could hear that old M & O blowing in the morning
> And you wouldn't know what was going on
> I went home that night
> And [my] next door neighbor told me my baby was gone.

Booker's guitar playing on "The M & O Line" is ominous, and his voice sounds as if the singer inhabits the railroad man's lament. In 1974, when I interviewed jazz pianist and songwriter Mose Allison, he told me that as he toured the world, he heard a similar sadness in the music of every culture. He called this quality “the universal lament.”[22] I think “The M & O Line” is an example of what Allison had in mind.

The other five numbers are more familiar to listeners. They are “Ballin’ the Jack,” “Brownsville, Tennessee,” “Miss Mary and Miss Magdalene,” “Bukka’s Jitterbug Swing,” and “Kansas City Black Bottom.”

In early 1975, Booker would make one more trip across the Atlantic to Europe.

Chapter Twenty-Seven

BREMEN 1975

FROM THE EXPOSURE HE HAD RECEIVED ON THE AMERICAN FOLK Blues Festival tours, Booker came into focus for British and European blues enthusiasts as an authentic Mississippi blues musician who had made historic records, but still had enough energy and enthusiasm to engage a contemporary audience. His solo performance in Bremen, Germany, on March 11, 1975, would confirm this, but almost did not take place.

The idea for the performance occurred to a young concert producer who was in the audience when the AFBF came to the Hamburg Musikhalle on March 14, 1972. Volker Steppat had grown up in Bremen during the country's postwar occupation. He recalled, "When I was a small kid in the early Fifties, there was still a very special atmosphere, with ruins in the cities wherever you went. At the same time, American music broadcast by the American Armed Forces Network was influencing taste and lifestyle. I used to listen to the AFN as mom listened to it, and [to] Radio Bremen, which was part of the German public radio network."[1]

Bremen's original radio station had gone on the air in 1924. Renamed Radio Bremen, it broadcast its first program of American music on December 23, 1945, with help from an American military band. The station's first jazz program was broadcast on February 12, 1946, and the American military government continued to operate the station until April 6, 1949. Listening to Radio Bremen as he grew up, Volker became fascinated with American blues and jazz. His interest in American music led to a successful career.

In the early 1970s, Steppat worked as a freelance curator and producer of music for the city of Bremen, in tandem with the jazz and popular music department of Radio Bremen. He set up a series of concerts for the city called "Forum Junge Musik" (Young Music Forum), which presented artists from most genres other than classical. This led to receiving a phone call from the bank Sparkasse Bremen in 1974. The bank "wanted to offer something hip for their younger customers," he recalled, "so we decided to start a series called Sparkasse in Concert as fast as possible, beginning in October of that year."[2]

Around the same time, German blues promoter Siegfried A. "Ziggy" Christmann began to put together a solo tour for Booker White to take place during the fall.[3] When Steppat was contacted by Christmann, he seized the opportunity to bring the musician to Bremen as the first performer in the Sparkasse series. The venue for the series was Aula der OPD (Postaula), an education center for postal service workers. The building held a state-of-the-art concert hall seating more than four hundred. Volker thought the hall would be ideal for a live recording.

He and Ziggy Christmann agreed on Tuesday, October 22, as the date for Bremen concert. As the date approached, Volker prepared the necessary promotional materials. Posters, flyers, and tickets had already been printed when, "on very short notice," Booker called Christmann to cancel the tour.[4] He said that his partner, Leola Morris, had suffered a stroke, and he needed to stay in Memphis to take care of her. Volker had to postpone the first Sparkasse concert until November 4, when he was able to book a suitable replacement. A progressive Pink Floyd–influenced group from Paris, Gong, opened the new venue.

The cancellation was a setback, but Volker was determined to present Booker at the Postaula concert hall. "I did not want to give up, and contacted him a few months later," he said. "We decided to bring him over just for the period of a week." He and Booker communicated by telephone and letter to set up the trip, and rescheduled the concert for Tuesday, March 11, 1975. "We were really happy that it worked out," Steppat said. "We would fly him in, fly him out and have a great time with him."[5]

On Sunday, March 9, Booker departed from Memphis to Chicago, then flew from Chicago to Frankfurt, Germany, where he caught a flight to Bremen. From the day of his arrival on March 10, Booker was treated like a celebrity, Volker recalled. He met Booker at the airport and drove him to the Übersee Hotel, where he would stay for five nights.

Steppat went so far as to hire "a very nice and sophisticated person," Walter Pauly, to be Booker's personal assistant during his stay. Booker's only commitment on the day of his arrival was an interview with a reporter from Bremen's leading newspaper, *Weser Kurier*. At noon the next day, photographer Jochen Mönch took Booker on a walk around the medieval section of Bremen, known as the Schnoor, to photograph him with the historic center as a backdrop.

In one photo, Booker leans back against a brick wall between an antique door and window. He appears relaxed—hands in the pockets of his suit jacket, and legs casually crossed. Leaning next to him is the case for his National steel guitar, covered with travel stickers. Booker wears a fedora hat. His overcoat and business suit, and the shine of his well-polished black shoes, are true to the sartorial advice he gave to the young B. B. King: "Always dress like you are going to the bank." His nod to informality is wearing a favorite string tie with his dress shirt. The image stands in sharp contrast to the colorful 1960s shirts and vest he wore when performing in the United States.

On March 11, the evening of the concert, a German television crew from WDR (Westdeutscher Rundfunk) in Cologne was on hand to tape the performance for German public television. Recording supervisor Peter Schulze and engineer Dietram Köster recorded the concert for the album. The concert was a success. More than four hundred people attended, filling the Postaula concert hall.

When Arne Schumacher attended the concert, he was an eighteen-year-old fan of British blues musicians like Peter Green. As a student in the middle of exams, he arrived late:

> I wasn't really prepared for the very different experience that I had to adjust to walking into a Bukka White concert. It was rough and seemed somehow archaic. One guy on a big stage, no wild showmanship, just pure music and sound. What captured and amazed me was that this man obviously was one with his playing and his songs, that the music was just coming out of him. I had never seen and felt anything comparable in a concert before.[6]

Today Arne is a freelance journalist in Bremen, having worked full-time as a music journalist before becoming an editor and producer at Radio Bremen. He recalled, "It was only a few months later, when I bought the LP with the accompanying book . . . that I really learned to appreciate what I had seen and heard that night at the Postaula."

The reviews were almost reverential. Under the headline "Criticism Was Blasphemy," reporter Felix Feucht covered Booker's performance for *Bremer Nachrichten*, the sister newspaper of *Weser Kurier*:

> To write about Bukka White critically would be almost blasphemy. With him it is not about craftsmanship, about polished, about show. He plays as he lives, straightforwardly, as he tells his

> little stories in the dialect of the Delta, which is difficult to understand. He has never been successful in the broad sense of the word, except for the fact that he was singled out from among his nameless peers by fortunate circumstances (such as his recruitment for a European tour in the 1960s). So he reeled off his program at the Postaula cheerfully and calmly—"Relax," he also recommended to his listeners—a bit carefree, too, which an almost 70-year-old can confidently do. Radiate calm.

Once described as a man who had been hardened by life,[7] Booker responded to being treated well in Germany. "He was open. He was really nice. He was a real gentleman. He was always dressed sharp," Volker Steppat recalled. "He was never alone except for the time he wanted to be. We looked after him. It was really cool. We went for meals and beer and sometimes something a little stronger than beer. . . . It was a different situation [from the American Folk Blues Festival] that he could stay here for all of the days except going to Hamburg."

When I asked Volker if he drove Booker back to the airport himself, he became thoughtful. "It's always important to pick up the artist, driving to a hotel that was close by. He stayed in a nice city hotel. I'm always saying what would the world be without music? Shitty and gray. So we have to do something for them. We've been blessed having a chance to invite all these great artists."

Steppat was the rare promoter who would answer a question about what Booker was paid. Booker received 2,300 Deutsche Marks (about $880 in American dollars) for making the record, and $1,500 in American dollars for the week in Germany. The bank, Bremen Sparkasse, pressed only two thousand copies of the album, accompanied by a 68-page book that included song lyrics, a transcription of Booker's onstage remarks at Postaula, photographs of Booker in the Schnoor district, and archival photos of Black life in Mississippi.

Two years later, water flooded the cellar where copies of the album were stored, and it has become a collectors' item. "All our notes from the tour were gone," Steppat said. "The records were completely done. There are only one thousand copies around the world."

In 2019, an independent record label in Los Angeles released the Sparkasse concert on compact disc, justifying its bootleg CD with the claim that the original vinyl album had received only "limited release."

Chapter Twenty-Eight

CHANGES

THE ARC OF A MAN'S LIFE CAN CHANGE WITH UNNERVING SPEED. Both good and bad things can happen in what seems almost like the same time. To paraphrase the opening sentence of a well-known Charles Dickens novel, the year 1976 was the best of times and worst of times for Booker.

Through its first five months, 1976 promised to be a good one. On Thursday, May 27, the number one song in the United States was "Silly Love Songs" by Wings,[1] but regular radio listeners in Chickasaw County might have tuned in to a different type of music on Houston station WCPC. Station owner-manager Robin Mathis was conducting an on-air interview with Booker that included live performances of his songs.

Houston mayor Harry G. Robinson had proclaimed May 27 to be Bukka White Day—one of the most important events of Chickasaw County's Bicentennial Week. Robin Mathis was chairman of the celebratory week, which was taking place six weeks in advance of the bicentennial of the United States on July 4. During the interview, Mathis asked Booker how he felt about returning to Houston after so many years. The normally garrulous musician was almost speechless. He described what he felt as "nervous excitement" before conceding that he could not put the feeling into words. A professional radio man, Mathis avoided the medium's worst predicament—dead air—by reminding Booker that he had said the previous day that he felt like a man who had won "ten acres and a house."

The interview with the station owner called attention to the musician's return to his home town, and publicized a free concert that evening in Courthouse Square. According to the Houston *Times Post*, Booker was guest of honor at "a concert of secular music"—a minor error, because one group sang gospel songs.[2] Published after the concert, the article's headline read "Blues Singer Bukka White Returns

Home for Festival," and reported that Booker "performed several blues numbers before a large audience on the north side of the courthouse."[3]

The concert began at 7:00 p.m. with a flatbed trailer for a stage. Sharing the program with Booker were singer-guitarist John Arnold of Grenada, who performed a tribute to Mississippi native Jimmie Rodgers, the "Blue Yodeler" of the 1930s; a local bluegrass group called the Hayloft Orchestra; and Dr. W. L. Stabler and Arthur Vinson with the Crusaders Choir. The choir's performance was cut short by rain, but not before the ubiquitous Robin Mathis presented Booker with a proclamation from Mayor Robinson, honoring Booker as a son of Houston, born November 12, 1909.

The Houston Booker had left when he was quite young was now proud of him because "Mr. White has been recognized worldwide as one of the finest blues artists of this century . . . has spread goodwill throughout the nation and abroad . . . [and] we in the Houston area are inspired by his enjoyable music and valid art form." It must have been deeply satisfying to Booker that Houston had invited him back. He claimed that he had returned to the city only once after leaving at age nine.[4]

A color photograph in the files of the Chickasaw County Historical Society captures Booker playing slide style on his familiar National Duolian steel guitar. He is wearing a pinkish-red blazer and red socks. His right hand is in mid-picking stroke, and his mouth is open as he strains to put over a lyric. Seated on a folding metal chair of the kind one might see at a school picnic, he wears sunglasses and a black hat. Known through most of his adult life as a snappy dresser, Booker's wardrobe reflected the patriotic sentiments of the week.

Standing next to the stage behind Booker is a boy of about nine, taking in the performance. The boy is wearing a red shirt, red pants, and a tan jacket. Booker and the boy wear matching red clothing that complements the red, white, and blue bunting hanging from the front edge of the stage. Though the snapshot is uncredited, it is something of an historic document. It captures what may have been Booker's last public performance.

Perhaps it was around the time of his "day" in Houston that Booker paid a surprise visit to members of his family who lived near Aberdeen, Mississippi. His granddaughters Sandra and Donna White came home from school one afternoon to find a stranger with a guitar sitting on their front steps. The stranger stood up and announced that he was Big

Daddy. The girls looked at each other. *Big Daddy! Wasn't he the one who was a famous musician?*[5]

Booker stayed overnight, playing music until midnight. Neighbors who heard he was in town came over to visit. Sandra remembered him singing "Shake 'Em On Down" over and over, and recalled the memorable lyrics to "When Can I Change My Clothes," about a convict feeling trapped in his prison uniform. During the evening, Booker asked Sandra to bring him shots of whiskey, paying her five dollars for each one. He left the next morning.

Just weeks after Booker was honored in Houston, he boarded a flight to Boston, where he was scheduled to perform from Monday, June 28, through Sunday, July 4, at a small jazz and blues club twenty-six miles north of the city.[6] In the 1970s, Sandy's Jazz Revival in Beverly, Massachusetts, was building its reputation by presenting a blend of young talent and stars who were past their prime. On the way up were performers like teenage jazz drummer Terri Lyne Carrington and the Rhode Island band Roomful of Blues with guitarist Duke Robillard. Toward the end of their careers, but still drawing audiences, were blues singer Helen Humes and electric guitar pioneer Aaron "T-Bone" Walker. Jazz violinist Joe Venuti and his counterpart on jazz harmonica, Toots Thielemans, played Sandy's more than once. Tenor saxophone star Stan Getz performed one night. Arriving at the club two hours late, Getz was given a public scolding by the feisty Rose Berman, who founded the club in 1933 with her husband, Samuel. After Samuel's death in 1954, Rose managed the club before turning the job over to her son Sanford, nicknamed Sandy.

With his hipster beard and deadpan face, Sandy Berman was a fixture at the club, standing by the front door to collect the cover charge. He had a sense of humor about it. When a patron failed to recognize him outside the club, Sandy prodded his memory by putting out his right hand, palm up, and saying "Five dollars."

Berman was notorious for introductions that went too long. *Boston Globe* jazz critic Ernie Santosuosso called them "Homeric." The club's news releases were hyperbolic. The advance release for Booker's engagement quoted Sandy as saying, "When you talk about the blues, 'Bukka' White is the man who has done it all. A figure of legendary importance who has influenced artists in all fields of music. His songs have become hits for Bob Dylan, the Rolling Stones, Tom Rush, and Mose Allison."[7]

Allison wrote his own wry take about the Mississippi Penal Farm at Parchman titled "Parchman Farm," but did not sing Booker's much earlier "Parchman Farm Blues." Expanding the length of Booker's career, the release boasted, "Through the years he has played with such greats as Bessie Smith and the father of the Memphis blues, W. C. Handy." Both performers preceded Booker's arrival in Memphis by decades. As Sandy often did, he called me at the *Salem Evening News* to badger me until I committed to reviewing the performance. My wife and I had an eight-month-old son. I said I would try.

Devoted blues fans David Little and Peter Riley were excited about this rare New England appearance by an historic blues musician.[8] Dave was twenty-one and Peter was twenty-two. They were "consumed" with their love of blues and jazz. In 1973 they began driving from Newburyport, Massachusetts, south to Beverly and Boston to see classic blues and jazz musicians such as Roosevelt Sykes and Betty Carter at Sandy's, and big blues names like Muddy Waters, Howlin' Wolf, and John Lee Hooker at clubs in Boston and Cambridge: the Jazz Workshop and Paul's Mall in the same building on Boylston Street, and the Speakeasy on Norfolk Street in Cambridge.

Dave carried with him a paperback copy of Paul Oliver's *The Story of the Blues* so that he could ask musicians to sign near their pictures. When Dave and Peter saw a newspaper advertisement for Bukka White at Sandy's, they were thrilled. They believed Booker had known one of the originators of Delta blues, Charley Patton.

The two friends left two hours before show time to get a good seat. At the club, they took a table next to the stage and sipped Coca-Cola. Their excitement increased until Sandy stepped onto the low stage to announce that the show was cancelled. He told the waiting audience that Booker had suffered a heart attack and was hospitalized. Disappointed, Dave and Peter assumed the hospital was in Boston. "We drove back to Newburyport, passing the Beverly Hospital on the way," Dave recalled. "One of us suggested that it was too bad Bukka hadn't made it to Beverly. We could just visit him in the hospital." They went home.

Only when Sandy called at the end of the week did I remember that Booker had been scheduled to play at his club. Sandy told me that Booker was "feeling bad" when he met him at the airport, and was now in the intensive care unit at Beverly Hospital.[9] I later learned that Sandy delegated picking up Booker at the airport to a young blues musician from Bainbridge Island, Washington, named TJ Wheeler, who met Booker at the 1973 New Orleans Jazz and Heritage Festival. By 1976, TJ had moved to Rumford, Maine.

That spring, after Wheeler told Berman that he should bring Booker White to his club, Sandy called Booker at home in Memphis to set up the five-night engagement. Since my notes from 1976 said that the club owner had met Booker at the airport, I asked TJ what he recalled. "I picked Bukka up at the airport by myself," TJ wrote in an email, "and was shocked to see him arrive in a wheelchair. I also took him to the hospital."[10]

Upon learning that Booker was hospitalized, I had called Beverly Hospital for an update. These were simpler times when hospitals would tell a local reporter about a patient's condition over the phone. Booker was listed in good condition in the intensive care unit. He had given the hospital his address as 867 Mosby Street in Memphis, and his age as sixty-six. If I had time, I would have written a brief item for that day's paper. A Mississippi blues musician being hospitalized in Beverly was news.

I followed up after the July 4 holiday weekend, and still have my notes. Booker "had a stroke . . . regain[ed] normal functioning . . . [was in] good condition . . . making progress."[11] Doctor Alvan C. Schwartz was in charge of his care. On July 4, Booker was transferred to the hospital's rehabilitation unit after spending eight days in the ICU. He remained in the rehabilitation unit until his discharge. When I learned from Sandy that Booker was about to be discharged, I called Doctor Schwartz's office to ask if Booker was well enough to have a visitor, and went to see him on July 29.

Booker was in his hospital bed. The back of the bed had been raised so he could sit. He had the room to himself. I introduced myself, telling him that I was a newspaper reporter who had planned to cover him at the club. I said that I had attended the benefit Sandy staged at the club the previous Saturday, July 24.

On what Booker hoped would be his last day in the hospital, I was a complete stranger who wanted something from him, not a medical person who could help him get out of the hospital. The hospital's public relations director, Grace Sawyer, told me that when he was admitted, "He simply wanted to go home. He didn't know he had the stroke until he got up in the plane and began to feel dizzy."[12]

When I mentioned the benefit, Booker's interest perked up. He allowed that he did give interviews when he was back home, but was accustomed to being paid for them. In 1976 many reporters were influenced by the investigative reporting that led to President Nixon's resignation. Woodward and Bernstein did not pay their sources. I told

Booker that my paper was small and could not afford to pay him. He considered this for a moment. "The Bible says it's better to give than to receive," he decided, and gave me permission to use my tape recorder.

What followed was a free-ranging interview in which Booker took the lead. I knew almost nothing about him, so asked basic questions such as where he was born, and follow-up questions to better understand his answers. After thirty-five minutes, medical social worker John Root came to the door to ask Booker how he was feeling.[13] Booker responded:

> I'm doing fine. I'm giving him some interview here. I like to turn him down, though. And I got to thinking about it, you know. I'm in the hospital, he come to see me, and was up there [at the club] Saturday, that night when they was making that [benefit], and the Bible says it's better to give than to receive a lot of the time, and that commenced to thinking upon my mind, so I got freely—I'm really giving, you know.

"He's been generous," I said. Root told Booker he would come back. What I didn't know was that Root had vital information for Booker about his discharge from the hospital, scheduled for the next morning. As Booker's medical social worker, Root was his lifeline to follow-up medical care in Memphis.

When Root came back to the room, he told Booker that he had reservations about discharging him. Booker responded that he felt "all right." Root stated the reason he was concerned— the previous evening, Booker had fallen forward in a wheelchair—but Booker still wanted to return home. "Yeah, I done come a long way," he said, referring to his rehabilitation. "No, I wouldn't jump up and say I'm able to go playing baseball. No, I ain't—I couldn't do that, but I know with my feeling I can be on that plane for three hours 'cause I can be in this bed sitting."

Root pointed out that the trip would take seven hours—an optimistic estimate. Doctor Schwartz was on vacation. The physician covering for him had said that Booker could leave the hospital, but Booker's nurse—who was off that day—was worried about his ability to make the journey. Soon the social worker introduced a subject that provoked intense discussion: the availability of follow-up medical care in Memphis. Having earlier offered to turn off the tape recorder, which Root said was unnecessary, I stepped outside when the conversation became more personal. It was months before I listened to the tape. The subject of Booker and Root's conversation took me by surprise. I had no idea that de facto segregation was still the reality in Memphis in 1976.

JOHN ROOT: There's only one other thing and that's, uh . . . I talked to the Baptist Hospital, and I talked to a whole number of different people, and I finally talked to the outpatient, and they said people from Memphis use the John Gaston and that it's for the people from the county or something. I didn't understand why she said . . . but she didn't have a card for you. You've never been to the outpatient there?

BOOKER WHITE: Yeah, I've been there for, you know . . .

ROOT: You were in-patient once. Did you go to the outpatient department at all?

WHITE: Naw, I don't guess I did. I just went there and signed and . . .

ROOT: Yeah, how long did they keep you?

WHITE: They didn't keep me. They just give me treatment. They didn't keep me.

ROOT: You went to the emergency [room]?

WHITE: No. No. While I was in the hospital, they kept me at John Gaston, and I fell out with John Gaston because you go there in the morning, you might not get waited on 'til tomorrow.

ROOT: Yeah.

WHITE: 'Cause see, everybody just . . . bunches of people around there fell out with John Gaston and would go to the Baptist, you see.

ROOT: What is the Baptist, anyway?

WHITE: Well, they just two different hospitals, you know.

ROOT: They said they didn't take people from Memphis. Is it in Memphis?

WHITE: Yeah, it's in Memphis, right across the street from the John Gaston. . . .

ROOT: See, because I don't know what to do. I mean, should I make an appointment at the Gaston?

WHITE: Well, you can do it.

ROOT: Because they wouldn't make an appointment for you at the Baptist; they said you're not supposed to go there. You're supposed to go to the Gaston. And, uh, we'll see . . . if you want to, when you get down there, though, try to get over to the Baptist yourself, you could do that.

WHITE: Well, now they might tell me like they told you 'cause they know I live there—been living there for a mighty long . . .

ROOT: But you went there, and you got in before so maybe you can do it again. How long ago was that, do you remember?

WHITE: Oh, that's been, I don't know . . . that's been about three or four years ago.

ROOT: That was the only time you went?

WHITE: Yeah.

ROOT: To the Baptist? Just once?

WHITE: First time . . . first time, uh huh.

ROOT: So you've only been there once.

WHITE: And they just writ me a prescription.

ROOT: That's wrong! I don't agree with that at all. I mean, I . . . you . . . people can go to any hospital they want.

WHITE: Well, I'd a thought you ought to.

ROOT: I don't know why they said that, but, you know, talking long distance, you can't do much.

WHITE: No, you can't.

ROOT: But, if you want to go there, I would go there first.

WHITE: Well, that's the b . . . you get the best treatment there.

ROOT: Yeah.

WHITE: See, I went there for this deal, and they give me a shot in this shoulder and give me two tablets, and I was walking like a man been shot with a .45, and I laid in the bed there, I think I laid there about an hour—let that stuff go through me. Then I got up and they writ me a 'scription down to their druggist—you know, the hospital has a druggist—and I went and got some pills. I didn't want to mess with no shot. I wouldn't take no shot. And it burnt me to death up there. And when I came back, I went to John Gaston and was telling them about it 'cause at the beginning I started with them 'cause I was in the hospital there, and they said the pill was too strong, and they commenced to giving me—put me back on them shots, you know. Them shots never did stop the hurtin'.

The insulin shots were for Booker's diabetes. He took pills for low blood pressure. At Beverly Hospital, he experienced some dizziness. The night before I visited, he had refused to get on an examination table because on the previous occasion "getting off that table . . . had my side hurting. It don't do me good on that thing. You know, I just had a faint spell up there when he went to examine me." The two men agreed on a resolution.

> ROOT: Okay, well, I will make an appointment for you at the Gaston.
> WHITE: Yeah, you do that.
> ROOT: As an outpatient. And then if you want to go, when you get there, try to get over to the Baptist.
> WHITE: See over there first.
> ROOT: Yeah, but I'll have the appointment at least, so that . . .
> White: Monday?
> ROOT: Well, I'll tell you, but I would like to have it for Monday.
> WHITE: Yeah, that's what I'm sayin'. Course I ain't too far from there—two blocks and a half. [I have my] old lady to call there, and they got a . . . well, I said, they got a car . . .

Side one of the tape ended. When John Root said I could return to the room, I flipped the tape and tried to pick up the interview—unaware of the emotional impact on Booker of the conversation that had taken place. After two questions, it was clear that Booker was too tired to continue. I thanked him and left, thinking that he was on the road to recovery. A photograph of him smiling, taken to accompany my newspaper article, seemed to confirm his improving spirits.

Beverly Hospital discharged Booker in the morning of Friday, July 30, so that Sandy Berman could drive him to Boston's Logan Airport in time to board a flight to Memphis. Featuring New England folksinger Tom Rush, the benefit concert had raised a thousand dollars. Rush agreed to appear because he had combined Booker's train songs under the title "Panama Limited" on one of his early albums.

Sandy Berman told me that he sent two hundred dollars to Booker's wife in Memphis, and gave the remaining eight hundred to him at the airport. "I didn't want to give all the money to him right away because I was afraid he'd pack up and go home," he said. No wonder Booker wanted money for the interview. He was broke. On the way to the airport, Booker told Berman that he had "a lot of things to write songs about."

After stopping at a drugstore to fill Booker's prescriptions, the club owner and musician arrived at Logan, where they ran into a group of people from Houston, Mississippi, who were on their way to a homecoming. "Bukka. Bukka," the travelers exclaimed, "is that you?" An

American airline attendant helped Booker change his ticket for a seat on the Memphis-bound plane. It was a rainy, miserable day to be traveling in a wheelchair. Booker was very weak. "I practically had to carry him on the plane," Berman said.

On the day I visited Booker, hospital spokesperson Grace Sawyer shared with me that Booker flew to Massachusetts with a tragic loss on his mind. Four weeks before he left Memphis, his stepdaughter was murdered outside the Harlem House restaurant, about two blocks from where Booker and Leola lived. According to Irene Kertchaval, the oldest daughter from Booker's marriage to Emma L. White in 1944, the victim's name was Presilla.[14] Irene spelled the name for me. Presilla was Leola's daughter. "The night she died, she was walking in the alley almost to Dad's house when her boyfriend shot and killed her," Kertchaval said. "Dad and Leola heard the shots and ran out to discover her already dead." Blues researcher Bob Eagle was able to find the story.

On June 3, 1976, the Memphis *Commercial Appeal* reported that a man fired shots at Mrs. Priscilla G. Taylor, 32, behind the Harlem House restaurant near the corner of Poplar Avenue and Ashland Street. One shot struck Mrs. Taylor in the back, killing her. Separated from her husband, she was living with Booker and Leola at 867 Mosby Avenue, Apartment 17. She left two sons and two daughters.[15] Her violent death was on Booker's mind enough that he told his caregivers about it.

After I had interviewed Booker, the hospital called Leola to tell her that Booker would be discharged the next morning, and someone needed to meet him at the airport. A nurse would be with him on the flight home.

Chapter Twenty-Nine

HOME TO LEOLA

TIME AT HOME WITH LEOLA MORRIS WAS EXACTLY WHAT BOOKER needed to restore his health. Leola had taken care of him since shortly after they met. At that time, his apartment was on St. Paul Avenue, and she lived just five minutes away on Orleans Avenue. When he would see her on the street, he would strike up a conversation about her cooking. One day he asked her if he bought something to eat, would she cook for him? When she allowed that she would, they went to the store together to buy greens. This was the beginning of their relationship.[1]

In late June, Booker had not been feeling well. He told Leola that he felt "drunkified." She urged him to postpone his trip to Massachusetts, but he assured her that he would feel better once he was on the plane. A friend drove him to Memphis International Airport, and he boarded the plane without a problem, realizing something was wrong only after the plane landed in Boston and flight attendants instructed the passengers to prepare to disembark. Inside the terminal, blues musician TJ Wheeler waited as all the other passengers emerged from the exit ramp. He was shocked to see a nurse pushing Booker down the ramp in a wheelchair.

In Memphis, Leola had begun to worry because she hadn't heard from Booker, who made a point of calling her when he arrived at his destination. The nurse who wheeled Booker off the plane told TJ that he needed to take him to a hospital. Perhaps after conferring with club owner Sandy Berman by phone, Wheeler decided to drive Booker thirty-two miles north to the hospital in Beverly, Massachusetts, when Boston hospitals would have been closer.

TJ stayed with Booker for three days and nights, reporting his condition to Leola every other night until Booker was well enough to speak with her himself. What she heard over the phone must have been upsetting because the effects of the stroke required him to have speech therapy. Booker stayed in the hospital for a month, spending the first eight days in the intensive care unit and the rest of his time there on the rehabilitation floor. Fortunately, he was being treated at an excellent community hospital.

After returning to Memphis, where he could eat Leola's home cooking and have plenty of time to rest, Booker began to feel better. He even said to Leola that he thought he might be able to go back on the road—but that was not to be. Even as he recovered from the stroke and managed his diabetes, he began to feel worse.

When musician John Battaglia visited the Mosby Avenue apartment in November, Booker told Battaglia that he just had gotten out of the Memphis City Hospital (also called the John Gaston) and was feeling weak. In February 1977, when photographer Andy Yale stopped by to see him after learning that he was sick, Booker was confined to a hospital bed that had been moved into the apartment. Yale photographed Booker leaning on an elbow, turning his body so that he could face the camera, and smiling.

As Leola had done throughout his illness, she took responsibility for Booker's home care. She tried to keep him comfortable as his body began to fail him. Toward the end, he told her that he was losing control of his systems. He died at 3:00 a.m. on Saturday, February 26, 1977. Leola recalled that even after he died, he looked as if he were still alive. She called one of Booker's granddaughters to let his family know, and signed a release so that his body could be taken to the city morgue.

The Southern Funeral Home gave the Memphis *Commercial Appeal* information on Booker's survivors and funeral arrangements. A twelve-paragraph obituary appeared the next day in the *Commercial Appeal* on the page that carried death notices. The headline read "Famed Artist of the Blues, Bukka White, 89, Dies." Accompanying the obituary was a formal-looking photograph of Booker wearing a bow tie. Customarily, the funeral home would supply the newspaper with a photo from the family. Much of the obituary was devoted to Booker's accomplishments as a musician, but it also included biographical details: "White recalled that he left home at the age of 9 and started rambling, first in Mississippi but later in St. Louis and Chicago." The anonymous obituary writer described his music:

> His songs exhibited such an understanding of human nature that one writer called him the best folk poet he'd ever met. . . . His guitar playing (he used mainly a steel-bodied National guitar) had a raw quality with the stress on a train-like rhythm. His voice was primitive, like the best of his contemporaries yet uncommonly strong, causing his songs to have a startling authority about them.[2]

The obituary reported that Booker was survived by three daughters, two sons, a sister, twenty-seven grandchildren, and thirteen great-grandchildren. His funeral service was arranged for Thursday, March 3, at 1:00 p.m. in the Mt. Gilliam Missionary Baptist Church, with burial to follow in New Park Cemetery. Leola told Andy Yale that Booker had attended Baptist services while living in Memphis.[3] His surviving sister was Mrs. Lattie C. Parker of Gary, Indiana. His daughters were Mrs. Henrietta Williams of Schertz, Texas; Mrs. Irene Kertchaval of Harvey, Illinois; and Miss Beulah White of Chicago. Sons were David Lee White of Memphis, and Will Arthur White of Aberdeen, Mississippi.

A simple headstone marks Booker's grave in the New Park Cemetery. The inscription reads "Booker W. White, 1909–1977, Loved by All." As in other areas of the musician's life, accounts of his final arrangements vary. In 2002, when I mentioned to B. B. King that Booker thought highly of his guitar playing, B. B. paused to take in the compliment. "I never knew that," he said. "I never knew where he died. You're telling me something I didn't know. I think I was overseas." Yet in one of my conversations with Booker's daughter Irene Kertchaval, she told me that B. B. had paid for her father's headstone.[4] Both could be true.

Booker was laid to rest among other now-historic Memphis musicians. Also in the New Park Cemetery are the graves of gospel composer Rev. William Herbert Brewster Sr. ("Move On Up a Little Higher"); five of the founding members in the city's two most famous rhythm and blues groups, Booker T. & the MG's and the Bar-Kays (Carl Lee Cunningham, Al Jackson Jr., Phalon Jones, Jimmy King, and Lewie Steinberg); hit recording artist Johnny Ace ("Pledging My Love"), disc jockey and entertainer Rufus Thomas Jr. ("Walking the Dog"), and soul singer James Carr ("The Dark End of the Street").[5]

In the 1970s, it took time for news of Booker's passing to reach us. I may have learned of his death from the pages of *Rolling Stone*. My first reaction was one of surprise. When I visited Booker in Beverly Hospital, he had seemed like a patient who was getting better. I had gone back to my newspaper to write an article that appeared on the front page under the headline "'Bukka' White goes back home to Memphis."[6] Next to the article was a photograph of a smiling Booker being attended to by a nurse:

> BEVERLY—The round-faced man with the guitar and black derby hat propped next to his Beverly Hospital bedside was telling the

> story of his life when medical social worker John Root stopped by the room.
>
> "How you doing?" asked Root.
>
> "Real well, I think," said Booker "Bukka" White, who, at 66, is a true living legend in a field of music known as the blues.
>
> Root reminded White that he was still showing a little dizziness when he sat up—the after-effects of a stroke White suffered on an airplane to Boston June 27—and that this might give him trouble on the long trip back to his home in Memphis, Tenn.
>
> "That don't bother me," said the musician. "I'll feel a whole lot better there because I'll be home and won't have things weighing on my mind. Here I've got things weighin' on my mind."
>
> "I know how you feel," said Root, and together the two men began to get down to the details of planning White's return to Memphis—a trip he made this weekend.

Clearly I believed that Booker was making a recovery. My initial surprise at news of his death turned into something like shock when I realized he had lived only seven months from the day we met. Not in the article, I recalled, was Root telling Booker that he wished he would stay in the hospital a little longer. When Booker was discharged, the doctor in charge of his care was on vacation.

Looking back on my notes, I am not sure that I was aware Booker was about to be discharged. I may have learned that when he met with John Root. From the article, it was clear that Booker wanted to go home. It's also clear from the article and my tape recording of Booker's meeting with Root that the medical social worker had concerns about whether his patient was fit to make the trip. Yet Booker was discharged on Friday, July 30, into the care of Sandy Berman, the nightclub owner who brought him to Massachusetts.

Berman called me at the newspaper on Monday, August 2, to give me the details of Booker's departure. Once at the airport, Berman said, "A young Black bellhop took good care of him through changing his ticket and getting him onto the plane."[7] Booker was taken aboard the Alleghany aircraft in a wheelchair.

Memphis had a history of segregated hospital care. In 1931, a study of the United States Veterans Administration Hospital in Memphis "found that blacks received inferior treatment." In their 1981 book *Beale Black & Blue*, journalists Margaret McKee and Fred Chisenhall amplified on the finding:

> So that the white nurse would not have to use the same toilet as the black maid, one toilet and washroom were provided for all the Negro patients on a ward where there were provisions for three. Certain types of treatment were refused the black patients; some doctors indicated that prescribed hospital treatment was too good for a black man. Nurses made black patients come to them for temperature and pulse rate checks instead of their going to the patients.
>
> Along with the attitude that such treatment was all blacks deserved was the feeling that it was no more than they expected.[8]

In 1976, the Baptist Memorial Hospital in Memphis consisted of three buildings holding 2,000 beds; yet "the Baptist" would not let John Root make an appointment for his patient, maintaining instead that a Memphis resident should be seen at the City of Memphis Hospital, also known as "the Gaston" after a wealthy donor. In no uncertain terms, Booker told Root that he did not want to go to the Gaston, but Root apparently had no alternative if he wanted to arrange a follow-up visit for Booker.

Later, when I listened to my tape and heard Booker and Root go back and forth about the appointment, I understood why Booker's mood had spiraled downward the afternoon of our interview. He was aware of the level of care he could expect at the Gaston, and it was unacceptable to him. As the reporter who interviewed a minister familiar with the city's Black hospitals wrote in 2019, "Jim Crow laws meant if you were African American and sick, you went to John Gaston Hospital, or you went to Collins Chapel, or you stayed home and hoped you'd get better."[9]

In hindsight, there are questions about Booker's diagnosis and treatment. At Beverly Hospital, he was treated for stroke and diabetes. In Memphis seven months later, the causes of his death were identified as cardiopulmonary arrest, acidosis, hepatorenal syndrome (a serious complication of advanced liver disease),[10] and widespread neoplastic disease (tumor). The approximate interval between the onset of cardiopulmonary arrest and his death was given as two weeks.

Once Booker returned to Memphis, he was hospitalized at the John Gaston at least twice. When Andy Yale photographed Booker during his February 1977 visit, Booker was wearing a hospital wrist band. Yale said that he had visited Booker only days before he died. From Yale's 1982 interview with Leola Morris, it sounds as if Booker died at home, but the death certificate lists the hospital. Perhaps he was pronounced dead there.

As someone who spent time with Booker in Beverly Hospital, I am puzzled that no one on the hospital staff said anything about his having a tumor. If the hospital was aware of a malignancy, the subject surely would have come up in Booker's meeting with John Root. It would appear that the hospital did not look further than the stroke symptoms; and Booker would have told the medical staff about his diabetes. In regard to his final seven months in Memphis, there is no information from his visitors or Leola Morris that would suggest that he received additional treatment for the stroke, or any treatment for cancer. The conclusion is unavoidable: Booker would have received a higher level of medical care if was a white person.

Chapter Thirty

BOOKER'S LEGACY

OVER THE COURSE OF MY RESEARCH, I CAME TO BELIEVE THAT DURING Booker White's second musical career from 1963 to 1976, he was not perceived to be as "serious" a blues musician as others who had been rediscovered. A person who spent time with Booker soon after his rediscovery recalled thinking that he was more like a "raunchy uncle" than a wise old bluesman. Some of this perception may have stemmed from the fact that he was younger and healthier than the others. When Booker was 58, Mississippi John Hurt was 71, Son House was 61, and Skip James was 62. Hurt was frail, House was an alcoholic, and Skip James had been treated for cancer. Booker chased women.

In early interviews, blues enthusiasts sometimes seemed to have as much interest in Booker's recollections of other bluesmen as in Booker himself. He was asked whether he had met House, Robert Johnson, Charley Patton, and lesser known musicians. When Booker mentioned offhand in spring 1964 that his friend Lillie Mae Glover had seen Son House in Memphis, three young white men jumped into a car and drove to Tennessee to locate the musician. The report was inaccurate, so they drove back north to find House in Rochester, New York.

In 2017, the year after Bob Dylan received the Nobel Prize in Literature, Harvard professor of classics Richard F. Thomas published a serious study of the correspondences between Dylan's lyrics and the Greek and Roman classics. He called the book *Why Bob Dylan Matters.* Demonstrating to readers that the subject of a book was worth their attention had become something of a trend. Dylan does not have a problem in that area. My brief search turned up almost 150 titles.

This book, on the other hand, is the first full-length biography of Booker White. Since White was an influence on Dylan, who chose to record "Fixin' To Die Blues" for his first album, I would like to end the book by offering some thoughts on why Booker White matters.

When I met Booker in 1976, he mattered to me personally because his hospitalization in Massachusetts presented me with the chance to interview an authentic Mississippi blues musician who was a contemporary of the mysterious Robert Johnson. Sharing an interest in blues with several college friends, I had listened to their copy of Johnson's 1961 album on Columbia many times. I thought that interviewing Booker would be a rare opportunity to learn about the Mississippi Delta and the vanished days when Black men and women who wrote songs and played guitar were making historic records.

I believe Booker continues to matter because there is a quality in his music that keeps drawing musicians and other listeners to him. Here are several examples.

Recorded in 1937, Booker's "Shake 'Em On Down" was a highly original composition that was covered by several other blues musicians soon after he recorded it. In 1970 the British group Led Zeppelin appropriated some of the song's structure and lyrics and called their version "Hats Off To (Roy) Harper," the final cut on *Led Zeppelin III*. To evoke the blues, Robert Plant sang over Jimmy Page's droning slide guitar.

In 1992, Recoil—a side project of Alan Wilder of Depeche Mode—recorded "Electro Blues for Bukka White."[1] Mixing Booker's speaking and singing voices with a staccato electronic dance rhythm, "Electro Blues" begins with a vocal sample of Booker intoning "saddle up my black mare" from his remembrance of Charley Patton on *Mississippi Blues Vol. 1 Bukka White*. What follows is his refrain "Must I holler / Must I shake 'em on down?" Underneath Booker's vocal samples, the dance rhythm fades as he continues talking about Patton.

Booker's music was an influence on the rising generation of blues players. The young blues artist Corey Harris, who is Black, included his rendition of "Bukka's Jitterbug Swing" on his debut album *Between Midnight and Day* (1995). White blues musician Kenny Wayne Shepherd covered Booker's "Aberdeen Mississippi Blues" for his debut album *Ledbetter Heights* (1996). It became a hit single. On tour, Shepherd played the song slide-style on a National Resolectric guitar in the spirit of Booker's National Duolian playing.[2]

In 2016, guitarist and songwriter Rory Block recorded the album *Keepin' Outta Trouble* as a tribute to Booker and his music. The album was one of a series that Block dedicated to older blues performers, and was personal to her because she met Booker in 1965 at a New York club. In her notes to the CD, she wrote, "His face was like a painting. He exuded awesome power and intensity. He had a huge presence even though he was not a tall man. Clearly he'd been down a thousand roads."[3]

After being given the opportunity to play Booker's 1933 National Duolian guitar while on tour in the United Kingdom in 2001, blues musician and songwriter Eric Bibb was inspired to write "Booker's Guitar." It became the title song of an album. As with most things Booker, there was more to the story.

In 1976 Booker had given the guitar to Keith Perry, a British newspaper photographer who took pictures of him backstage at the 1967 American Folk Blues Festival concert in Newcastle, England. Encouraged by AFBF performer Brownie McGee, Perry sent Booker black-and-white prints of the photographs. When Booker responded with a handwritten letter, Perry made a tape of Booker's early recordings and sent it to him in Memphis.[4] Booker had not heard some of them for years.

After an exchange of letters and transatlantic telephone calls, the two men became friends. Perry wrote to Booker, "If you ever hear of a guitar similar to yours up for sale in the States, I'd be very interested to know about it." In late April 1976, after buying a new National steel instrument, Booker sent his old guitar to Perry in England for the cost of shipping and insurance.[5]

Booker had called the guitar "Hard Rock." Perry made a point of photographing Hard Rock in the hands of famous musicians who passed through Newcastle, from skiffle legend Lonnie Donegan to Mark Knopfler of Dire Straits. Perry photographed B. B. King admiring what writer Peter Daniels dubbed "the Holy Relic" on April 19, 1984. After Eric Bibb's performance at the Newcastle Opera House on May 10, 2001, Perry offered to bring the guitar to Bibb's hotel so that he could play it.[6]

Bibb was moved. "Spiritually, the experience of playing Booker White's guitar took my personal connection to country blues to another level," he wrote in the notes to *Booker's Guitar*. "It actually felt like an initiation and a benediction. I felt the time was right to offer a handmade tribute to the music and musicians of a bygone era. . . . The arrival of Booker's guitar was the sign I'd been waiting on for years."[7]

In March 2019, Keith Perry put the instrument up for auction in Wiltshire, England, where it sold for £93,000, including buyer's fees (US$121,000). Luke Hobbs, head of the guitar department at Gardiner Houlgate auctioneers, recalled, "We had interest from a few parties. One in the room and a couple in the U.S. The winner is a collector of National guitars, and this was one that 'he had to have' and did." The buyer remains anonymous.[8]

Another reason that Booker mattered to me in 1976 was that he was like a messenger from the past. The man and his music shared a history that reached back to the enslavement of Black people. As a young boy, Booker heard about life and music in "slavery time" from people who had experienced the cruel conditions—and survived.

I have a vivid memory of Booker recalling "slavery time" on the afternoon before he left Beverly Hospital. I stood at the foot of his hospital bed, facing him as he sat up, with my portable tape recorder on a table next to him. As Booker spoke, I felt as if I were looking through the wide end of a telescope toward the small end—a telescope in reverse—where hazy images of the people he described appeared and disappeared amid stark surroundings. I was spellbound.

When Booker's medical social worker, John Root, came to the door, the spell was broken. Booker was anxious to hear from Root because he was anxious be discharged the following morning to fly back to Memphis. At the hospital, his care team was not sure that he was well enough to make the ten-hour trip. For my part, I realized that I would never come this close again to *feeling* the roots of the blues.

In April 2002, I interviewed B. B. King about his cousin. Booker often spoke of this relationship in his interviews. Sometimes he included a story about giving B. B. his first guitar. As always, the King of the Blues was on the road when I managed to catch up with him by telephone. I was teaching journalism in Virginia as he was resting in a hotel in Portsmouth, New Hampshire, before an evening performance at the Hampton Beach Casino. His office in Las Vegas had referred me to his road manager, Sherman Darby, who allowed me ten minutes of his boss's time.

Speaking in a tired monotone quite different from his genial stage persona, King set the record straight about Booker's first guitar and showed emotion only when he learned something new about his cousin's opinion of him. Here is our conversation:[9]

DAVID JOHNSON: I interviewed Bukka White in 1976. He said he was related to you.

B. B. KING: He was my second cousin. He and my mother were first cousins.

JOHNSON: I recently spoke with Irene Kertchaval, who said when you were young, you lived for a time with her family in Memphis.

KING: [She's] his daughter. I was younger. [But] I was a man when I came from Mississippi. I lived with him for about six weeks. But she was too little to know about it.

JOHNSON: When you spent time with him in Memphis, how old were you?

KING: When I spent time, I was in my twenties. I used to see him before that up until I was nine. He used to come around to my family. My mother died when I was nine. So I was between six and nine years old when he came around.

JOHNSON: He said that he gave you your first guitar. Is that true?

KING: That's not true. He helped me get a job while I was living with him—a job where he worked. During that time, he wasn't playing. It was after he had been popular and got out of the business. We worked at the Newberry Equipment Company. We made tanks, like fuel tanks that go under the ground for service stations.

JOHNSON: Did he take an interest in you?

KING: His only playing would be like a weekend or going to a party. He didn't do it for money. He sometime would let me go with him. I never noticed him taking any interest in me playing or that sort of thing. I was crazy about him. He used to always tell me if you were going to be a blues singer, always dress like you were going to the bank to borrow money—you know, not to be slouchy. When he wasn't working, you couldn't tell he was a blues player.

JOHNSON: He dressed up?

KING: It wasn't like he wore a coat and tie all the time. He was always well dressed.

JOHNSON: So it sounds like you took an interest in him.

KING: Yes. I liked the way he played. He played bottleneck. I didn't try to play like him. I still can't play bottleneck. But I enjoyed hearing him play and sing.

JOHNSON: He told me he thought highly of your guitar playing, too.

KING: I never knew that. [Pause] I never knew where he died. You're telling me something I didn't know. I think I was overseas.

JOHNSON: One of his managers said Bukka White was a very difficult man. What do you think?

KING: I don't know about his management or anyone he may have worked with. I liked him. I didn't know anything about his difficulty with management. Managers can have their own ways. He was always fun to be around, to me. I always enjoyed being around him. He joked, told stories . . . I loved to hear him talk. When he used to come around to see us when I was small, he would always bring candy. He was always joyful. He got in trouble once. I think he killed a person in self-defense, but they still gave him time.

JOHNSON: How do you think Bukka White should be remembered?

KING: Booker White . . . I think he should be remembered as a pretty good guitarist and that his singing was superb of the kind of singing that he did, too. He was one of the engineers along with Big Bill Broonzy and all of those guys. He just didn't continue after he couldn't make any money. I look at him as I would the early guys like Bill Broonzy, like Charley Patton, like all those guys. To me he held his own.

I agree with B. B.'s description of Booker as one of the historic "engineers" of the blues, but the King of the Blues may have underestimated his cousin's guitar playing. Readers can learn more about Booker's impressive repertoire of guitar techniques and tunings in the article that follows.

HALFWAY THROUGH OUR INTERVIEW, BOOKER EXPLAINED HOW HE came to learn what conditions were like in slavery times. He said, ". . . some of the guys were wise enough to hold [memories] in their head where they could tell a young pants . . . where it would go down in history, you know. Just like youre doing that nowsomething happen to you, somebody else will carry that on cause somebody else will understand it. . . ."[11] Because Booker took the time to share his recollections from a hospital bed, I believe he wanted people to come to understand his life.

Born on a sharecropper's farm in Mississippi around 1905, Booker came of age in a time and place that historians of the American South consider to be the most oppressive since the abolition of slavery. His chances of being lynched were greater than his chances of becoming a well-known musician who toured Europe. Seventy years later, in 1975, he played before a full house at the Postaula concert hall in Bremen, Germany, where he had been invited to give a solo performance that was released on a record album. It was his fourth trip to Europe since 1967. In 1990 he was inducted into the Blues Hall of Fame.

After beginning my research into Booker's life in earnest in 1991, I began writing this book in 2017. Six years of focusing on the events of his life, his mistakes and successes, convinced me that Booker was unusually resilient and persistent. Through many changes in circumstance, he stayed true to his music. What he achieved is significant. He matters.

Appendix

BOOKER WHITE'S EXTRAORDINARY GUITAR PLAYING

JAS OBRECHT

EVEN ON HIS EARLIEST RECORDS, BOOKER WHITE DEMONSTRATED AN extraordinary knowledge of guitar tunings, playing positions, and slide guitar techniques. Making his recording debut for Victor in May 1930, he performed "The New 'Frisco Train," "The Panama Limited," and two gospel tunes in an E♭ version of Vestapol (open-E) tuning. During "The Panama Limited," he effectively used the slider on his fretting hand's little finger to imitate the sounds of airbrakes, a train whistle, and a ringing bell. At his next session, for Vocalion in 1937, White tuned to the open-G "Spanish" tuning for "Pinebluff Arkansas" and then played "Shake 'Em On Down" in the E position of standard tuning. The guitar phrasing and falsetto vocals of "Pinebluff Arkansas" echoed Robert Johnson's "Cross Road Blues."

Seventeen months later, recording for the Library of Congress while an inmate at Camp No. 10 at the State Penitentiary at Parchman, Booker revealed yet another tuning—the "cross-note" (E minor) heard on "Sic 'Em Dogs On"—played with the rollicking, metronomic rhythm that would become his trademark. After completing that take, he retuned to Spanish for a propulsive version of "Po' Boy." Decades later Booker was filmed playing this song, conjuring a sound similar to his first recorded version. This black-and-white footage shows him playing with his National resophonic guitar in the lap-style position favored by Hawaiian musicians. White's left hand holds a long metal bar that's about twice the thickness of a standard screwdriver. As he glisses the strings, he often gives the bar a little shake after hitting his intended pitch, heightening the song's tension. He anchors his fretting hand's ring and little fingers on the face of his guitar and plucks the strings with his thumb, index, and middle fingers. As he plays, he keeps time with his whole body, his guitar bouncing on his knees in time to the music. On most of his records, though, White played slide with his guitar held in the standard playing position, and with a metal slider on his little finger. Precious few guitarists during the 78 era recorded in all three open tunings—Vestapol, Spanish, and cross-note.[1]

The full range of Booker's guitar knowledge became apparent during March 1940, when over the course of two days he recorded a dozen sides for Vocalion and OKeh. It's a testament to White's creativity that he composed most of the songs after arriving in Chicago for the session. Accompanied by Washboard Sam, he began on March 7 with his guitar in a lower-than-usual version of standard tuning. He played "Black Train Blues" in the A position, "Strange Place Blues" in G position, the jailhouse lament "When Can I Change My Clothes" in E position, and then moved back to playing in the G position for "Sleepy Man Blues," which has melodic similarities to Leroy Carr's "In the Evening" and Robert Johnson's "Love in Vain." White next tuned to cross-note for "Parchman Farm Blues" and then performed the slide tune "Good Gin Blues" in Spanish tuning.

On the second day of his 1940 sessions, his guitar once again in a low-pitched variation of standard tuning, White played "High Fever Blues" in the C position and "District Attorney Blues" in E position. He then rekeyed to Spanish for "Fixin' To Die Blues." He retuned to cross-note for the final three songs that day, the superlative slide tunes "Aberdeen Mississippi Blues," "Bukka's Jitterbug Swing," and "Special Stream Line." The thumbed bass, chugging rhythms, and bottleneck swipes of "Bukka's Jitterbug Swing" built like a steam locomotive on a downhill run, while his bottlenecking on "Special Stream Line" effectively imitated train sounds. Few guitarists—then or today—have exhibited such a propulsive quality in their playing.

NOTES

CHAPTER ONE: MISSISSIPPI 1910

1. Harley Hill Floyd, *A Short History of Chickasaw County Mississippi* [*sic*], (Houston, MS: Chickasaw County Historical and Genealogical Society, 1985), 10–11.

2. Bob Eagle and Eric S. LeBlanc, "Bukka White," *Blues: A Regional Experience* (Santa Barbara, CA: Praeger, 2013), 111–12.

3. Dick Flohil, "Bukka T. White: The Man from Houston Mississippi," *Coda: Canada's Jazz Magazine* 8, no. 11 (January 1969): 3.

4. Jeff Todd Titon, *Early Downhome Blues: A Musical and Cultural Analysis* (Urbana: University of Illinois Press, 1977), 7.

5. Neil R. McMillen, *Dark Journey: Black Mississippians in the Age of Jim Crow* (Urbana: University of Illinois Press, 1989), 112.

6. Booker White, interview with the author, July 29, 1976.

7. "The Mississippi Poll Tax," *New York Times*, February 2, 1891, 1.

8. Diane McWhorter, *Carry Me Home: Birmingham, Alabama, the Climactic Battle in the Civil Rights Revolution* (New York: Simon & Schuster, 2001), 35.

9. McMillen, *Dark Journey*, 36.

10. Booker White interview, 1976.

CHAPTER TWO: EARLY YEARS

1. Houston *Times-Post*, January 30, 1936, as reported on FindAGrave.com, https://www.findagrave.com/memorial/41000761.

2. 1880 United States Census.

3. Kellee Blake, "'First in the Path of the Firemen': The Fate of the 1890 Population Census, Part 1," *Genealogy Notes* 28, no. 1 (Spring 1996), https://www.archives.gov/publications/prologue/1996/spring/1890-census-1.html.

4. Marriage affidavit filed on January 21, 1898, Chickasaw County Circuit Clerk.

5. 1910 United States Census.

6. F. Jack Hurley and David Evans, "Bukka White," in *Tom Ashley, Sam McGee, Bukka White: Tennessee Traditional Singers*, ed. Thomas G. Burton (Knoxville: University of Tennessee Press, 1981), 147.

7. Hurley and Evans, 147.

8. Booker White, as quoted in Bruce Cook, *Listen to the Blues* (New York: Scribner's, 1973), 127–28.

9. Eric Arnesen, *Brotherhoods of Color: Black Railroad Workers and the Struggle for Equality* (Cambridge: Harvard University Press, 2001), 2.

10. Arnesen, 2.

11. Hurley and Evans, "Bukka White," 157.

12. Hurley and Evans, 157.

13. Booker White, as quoted in Hurley and Evans, "Bukka White," 157.

14. Hurley and Evans, "Bukka White," 157.

15. Hurley and Evans, 157–58.

16. Jas Obrecht, "Blues with a Feeling: The Great Slidemen," *Guitar Player* 28, no. 8, August 1994, 65ff.

17. Booker White interview, July 29, 1976.

18. Bo Basiuk, "Interview with Bukka White—August 1975," *Blues Magazine* 2, no. 6 (December 1976), 26.

19. John Battaglia, interview with the author, December 14, 2020.

CHAPTER THREE: A BOY IN GRENADA

1. Hurley and Evans, "Bukka White," 158.

2. Hurley and Evans, 158.

3. Hurley and Evans, 158.

4. *1928 Handy Railroad Atlas of the United States* (Milwaukee: Kalmbach Publishing, undated), 26. This is a reprint of *Handy Railroad Maps of the United States*, Rand McNally & Company, 1928.

5. Lewis Johnson, interview with the author, March 9, 2023.

6. Booker White, 1964 Cambridge tapes, Jackson-Christian Collection, American Folklife Center, Library of Congress. Used by permission.

7. 1890–1900 property transactions, Deeds Room, Grenada County Courthouse, 45–46.

8. 1890–1900 property deeds, Deeds Room, Grenada County Courthouse, 213.

9. Lewis Johnson interview, March 9, 2023.

10. Booker White, "Memphis Blues," John Quincy Wolf Collection, Lyon College, https://home.lyon.edu/wolfcollection/blues.htm#bukka.

11. David Evans, email to the author, March 3, 2018.

CHAPTER FOUR: BETWEEN TWO WORLDS

1. McMillen, *Dark Journey*, 31.

2. Julius Lester, "'Mr. White, Take a Break,' an Interview with Booker (Bukka) White by Julius Lester," *Sing Out! The Folk Song Magazine* 18, no. 4 (October–November 1968), 61.

3. Lester, 45, 61.

4. Roberta Richards, "The Legendary Bukka White," *Blues Magazine* 2, no. 6 (December 1976), 40.

5. Richards, 40.

6. John Fahey, "Fish," *How Bluegrass Music Destroyed My Life* (Chicago: Drag City, 2000), 197–213.

CHAPTER FIVE: THE ST. LOUIS STORY

1. David Evans, "Booker White," *Nothing but the Blues*, Ed. Mike Leadbitter (London: Hanover, 1971), 248–49.

2. F. Jack Hurley, interview with Booker White, December 5, 1967.

3. Fred J. Hay, *Goin' Back to Sweet Memphis: Conversations with the Blues* (Athens: University of Georgia Press, 2001), xxxiii.

4. Paul Garon and Gene Tomko, *What's the Use of Walking If There's a Freight Train Going Your Way? Black Hoboes and Their Songs* (Chicago: Charles H. Kerr Publishing, 2006), 91–92.

5. Hurley and Evans, "Bukka White," 161.

6. Hurley and Evans, 161.

7. Dick Flohil, "Bukka T. White: The Man from Houston Mississippi," 3.

8. Flohil, 3.

9. Flohil, 3.

10. Fred J. Hay, email to the author, March 27, 2023.

11. Hay, *Going Back to Sweet Memphis*, xxxiii.

12. Hay, 5.

13. Hay, 6–7.

14. Hay, 8.

15. Hay, 9.

16. Margaret McKee and Fred Chisenhall, *Beale Black & Blue: Life and Music on Black America's Main Street* (Baton Rouge: Louisiana State University Press, 1981), 122.

17. McKee and Chisenhall, 122.

18. Larry Davis, email to the author, May 27, 2020.

19. Bo Basiuk, "Interview with Bukka White—Memphis, August 1975," *Blues Magazine* 2, no. 6 (December 1976), 20.

20. Basiuk, 26.

21. Basiuk, 26–27.

22. Richards, "The Legendary Bukka White," 28–30.

23. Richards, 38–40.

24. "Po' Boy" is a song that was identified with Booker.

25. Richards, "The Legendary Bukka White," 38–39.

26. Richards, 39.

27. David Evans, email to the author, May 2022.

28. Hay, *Goin' Back to Sweet Memphis*, 9. The Dog was a colloquial name for the Yazoo and Mississippi Valley Railroad.

29. Bob Eagle, email to the Mississippi Blues Trail Writing and Research Team, July 21, 2009.

30. Richards, "The Legendary Bukka White," 40.

31. Adele Heagney, email to the author, April 19, 2023.

32. Adam Burns, email to the author, May 4, 2023.

33. Zorana Ivcevic Pringle, in conversation with the author, May 7, 2023.

CHAPTER SIX: TRYING TO SETTLE

1. Hurley and Evans, "Bukka White," 163.

2. Hurley and Evans, 163.

3. Hurley and Evans, 163–64.

4. Hurley and Evans, 164.

5. Research conducted by Bob Eagle and Ed Payne.

6. Hurley and Evans, "Bukka White," 164.

7. Stephen Calt, "The House Frolic: A Reminiscence by Booker White,"*78 Quarterly*, no. 8, 94.

8. Research by Bob Eagle.

9. Research by Bob Eagle.

10. Hurley and Evans, "Bukka White," 167.

11. Stephen Calt, "Booker White on Bullet Williams," *78 Quarterly*, no. 6, 83–85.

12. Calt, 84.

13. Calt, 84.

14. Calt, 84.

15. David Evans, "Booker White," in *Nothing but the Blues*, ed. Mike Leadbitter (London: Hanover Books, 1971), 248–55.

16. Evans, 249–50.

17. 1930 United States Census.

18. Godrich and Dixon, *Blues & Gospel Records 1902–1942*, 794.

19. Howard Rye, notes to *The Great Blues Harp Players (1927–1936)*, Document DOCD-5100, 1992.

CHAPTER SEVEN: MEMPHIS 1930

1. Booker White interview, 1976.

2. "History Page," City of Itta Bena website, http://ittabenams.homestead.com/historypage.html.

3. John M. Barry, *Rising Tide: The Great Mississippi Flood of 1927 and How It Changed America* (New York: Simon & Schuster, 1997), 192–93.

4. Barry, 206.

5. Barry, 200–201.

6. Thelma Collins, interview with the author, March 9, 2023.

7. Bo Prestidge, interview with the author, March 16, 2023.

8. T. DeWayne Moore, "Revisiting Ralph Lembo: Complicating Charley Patton, the 1920s Race Record Industry, and the Italian American Experience in the Mississippi Delta," *Association for Recorded Sound Collections Journal* 49, no. 2 (December 2018), 153–84.

9. Barry Mazor, *Ralph Peer and the Making of Popular Roots Music* (Chicago: Chicago Review Press, 2015), 13–14.

10. Mazor, 15.

11. Moore, "Revisiting Ralph Lembo," 160–61.

12. David Evans, email to the author, June 11, 2018.

13. Bob West and others, "Bukka White, interviewed by Bob West, Mike Duffy and John Ullman," *Blues & Rhythm*, No. 189 (May 2004), 4–7. The original interview was recorded in 1967 at radio station WRAB, Seattle, Washington.

14. Hurley and Evans, "Bukka White," 165.

15. Hurley and Evans, 165.

16. Hurley and Evans, 165.

17. Barry Mazor, email to the author, June 19, 2018.

18. Charters, *The Bluesmen*, 102.

19. Philip R. Ratcliffe, *Mississippi John Hurt: His Life, His Times, His Blues* (Jackson: University Press of Mississippi, 2011), 65.

20. Booker White interview, 1976.

21. Booker White interview, 1976.

22. Godrich and Dixon, *Blues & Gospel Records 1902–1942*, 785–86.

23. Ralph S. Peer, letter to L. L. Watson of RCA Victor Co., June 6, 1930. Letter courtesy of Barry Mazor and Peer Family Archives.

24. Godrich and Dixon, *Blues & Gospel Recordings*, 785.

25. Peer to Watson, 1.

26. Peer to Watson, 1.

27. Peer to Watson, 1.

28. Hurley and Evans note that folklorist Howard W. Odum "described similar 'train songs' from his fieldwork in northern Mississippi just after the turn of the century." Hurley and Evans, 167.

29. Eric Sackheim, *The Blues Line: A Collection of Blues Lyrics* (New York: Grossman Publishers, 1969), 240–41.

30. Peer to Watson, 1.

31. Peer to Watson, 1.

32. Paul Garon and Beth Garon, *Woman with Guitar: Memphis Minnie's Blues* (San Francisco: City Lights Books, 2014), 197.

33. Garon and Garon, 309–12.

34. Booker White, as quoted in Bruce Cook, *Listen to the Blues*, 128–29.

35. Garon and Garon, *Woman with Guitar*, 131.

CHAPTER EIGHT: RESTLESS AND ROAMING

1. Samuel B. Charters, *The Bluesmen* (New York: Oak Publications, 1967), 102.

2. Samuel B. Charters, *The Legacy of the Blues* (London: Calder & Boyars, 1975), 36.

3. Charters, *The Bluesmen*, 102–3.

4. Hurley and Evans, "Bukka White," 170.

5. Bruce Jackson, 1964 Cambridge tapes, Bruce Jackson–Diane Christian Collection, American Folklife Center, Library of Congress. Used by permission.

6. Leslie A. Heaphy, *The Negro Leagues, 1869–1960* (Jefferson, NC: McFarland, 2003), 375.

7. Microfilm maintained by the Church of Jesus Christ of Latter Day Saints, Salt Lake City, Utah, under the catalog heading UNITED STATES MILITARY RECORDS—WORLD WAR. Original cards at National Archives, Atlanta, Georgia. http://www.files.usgwarchives.net/.

8. Hurley and Evans, "Bukka White," 167.

9. David Evans, email to the author, July 24, 2020.

10. Bruce Cook, *Listen to the Blues* (New York: Scribner's, 1973), 81.

11. Cook, 83.

CHAPTER NINE: A WINDING ROAD

1. Hurley and Evans, "Bukka White," 168.

2. Hurley and Evans, 170.

3. Hurley and Evans, 169.

4. Paul Garon, *The Devil's Son-in-Law: The Story of Peetie Wheatstraw and His Songs* (Chicago: Charles H. Kerr, 2003), 5.

5. Booker White interview, 1976.

6. Godrich and Dixon, *Blues & Gospel Records*, 771.

7. Garon, *The Devil's Son-in-Law*, 26.

8. Hurley and Evans, "Bukka White," 170.

9. Eagle and LeBlanc, "Bukka White," 156.

10. Bruce Jackson, 1964 Cambridge tapes, Bruce Jackson–Diane Christian Collection, American Folklife Center, Library of Congress. Used by permission.

11. McKee and Chisenhall, *Beale Black & Blue*, 125.

12. McKee and Chisenhall, 125.

13. McKee and Chisenhall, 125.

14. Hurley and Evans, "Bukka White," 171.

15. Paul Oliver, *The Story of the Blues* (Philadelphia: Chilton, 1969), 121.

16. Hurley and Evans, "Bukka White,"172.

17. Godrich and Dixon, *Blues and Gospel Records*, 786.

18. Wardlow, "Bukka White: From Aberdeen to Parchman," 104.

19. Wardlow, 103.

20. Hurley and Evans, "Bukka White," 171.

21. Wardlow, "Bukka White: From Aberdeen to Parchman," 103.

22. Peter Guralnick, *Last Train to Memphis: The Rise of Elvis Presley* (Boston: Little, Brown & Company, 1994), 14.

CHAPTER TEN: ON PARCHMAN FARM

1. Federal Writers' Project, 407–8

2. Federal Writers' Project, 407–8.

3. Alyce Guthrie interview with the author, September 28, 2022.

4. Alan Lomax, "Music in Your Own Back Yard," *Alan Lomax: Selected Writings 1934–1997*, ed. Ronald D. Cohen (New York: Routledge, 2003), 49.

5. Lomax, "Music in Your Own Back Yard," 49.

6. Ed Kahn, "1934–1950: The Early Collecting Years," *Alan Lomax: Selected Writings 1934–1997*, ed. Ronald D. Cohen (New York: Routledge, 2003), 1; and Charles Wolfe and Kip Lornell, *The Life and Legend of Leadbelly* (New York: HarperCollins, 1992), 112–13.

7. John Lomax, *Adventures of a Ballad Hunter* (Austin: University of Texas Press, 2017), 134–35.

8. Lomax, 134.

9. Lomax, 136.

10. Lomax, 137.

11. Lomax, 137.

12. Alan Lomax, *The Land Where Blues Began* (New York: Pantheon, 1993), 257.

13. Alan Lomax, 258.

14. Alan Lomax, "'Sinful Songs' of the Southern Negro," *Southwest Review* 19, no. 2 (Winter 1934), 29.

15. David M. Oshinsky, *"Worse than Slavery": Parchman Farm and the Ordeal of Jim Crow Justice* (New York: Free Press, 1996), 128.

16. John Lomax, *Adventures of a Ballad Hunter* 142.

17. John Lomax, 143.

18. McKee and Chisenhall, *Beale Black & Blue*, 121.

19. Bruce Jackson, 1964 Cambridge tapes, Bruce Jackson–Diane Christian Collection, American Folklife Center, Library of Congress. Used by permission.

20. Hurley and Evans, "Bukka White," 174.

21. Ruby Terrill Lomax, "1939 Southern Recording Trip Fieldnotes" for May 23–25. https://www.loc.gov/resource/afc1939001.afc1939001_fn0001/?st=gallery.

22. Tom Freeland and Chris Smith, "That Dry Creek Eaton Clan," *Nobody Knows Where the Blues Come From* (Jackson: University Press of Mississippi, 2006), 144.

23. Samuel Charters, *The Legacy of the Blues*, 35.

24. Charters, 35–36.

25. Ed Pearl, interview with the author, July 2, 2009.

CHAPTER ELEVEN: BOOKER IN MEMPHIS

1. Registration Card D.S.S. Form 1, Serial No. 2973, Order No. 359. Research by Bob Eagle.

2. Hurley and Evans, "Bukka White," 169.

3. George Q. Flynn, "Selective Service and American Blacks During World War II," *Journal of Negro History* 69, no. 1 (1984): 14–25.

4. Registration Card D.S.S. Form 1 for "Men Born on or after February 17, 1947 and on or before December 31, 1921," Serial No. 902, Order No. 11907. Research by Bob Eagle.

5. Ellen Rogers, interview with the author, February 11, 2021.

6. McKee and Chisenhall, *Beale Black & Blue*, 128.

7. Alyce Guthrie interviews.

8. Howard Upton, "James M. Newberry," *Tulsa Letter*, Petroleum Equipment Institute, January 18, 1985.

9. "About," Petroleum Equipment Institute, pei.org.

10. Ellen Rogers interview.

11. Information on James M. Newberry and the Newberry Equipment Company from interviews with Chris Long on May 25, 2019, and Ellen Rogers on February 11, 2021.

12. Alyce Guthrie interview, January 25, 2023.

13. B.B. King with David Ritz, *Blues All Around Me: The Autobiography of B. B. King* (New York: Avon, 1996), 101.

14. Leola Morris, interview with Andy Yale, September 1982. Copyright 1985 Andy Yale. Used by permission.

CHAPTER TWELVE: COUSIN RILEY

1. Charles Sawyer, *The Arrival of B. B. King* (New York: Doubleday, 1980), 34.

2. Sawyer, 35.

3. Bob Eagle, email to the Mississippi Blues Trail Writing and Research Team, February 25 ,2021.

4. Mary Katherine Aldin and Peter Lee, from interviews by Jim O'Neal, Rose Clayton, Bill Ferris, Suzanne Steel, Mark Newman, and Bob Eagle, "B. B. King," *Living Blues* 80 (May–June 1988), 11.

5. Aldin et al., "B. B. King," 11.

6. Sawyer, *The Arrival of B. B. King*, 36–37.

7. Sawyer, vii.

8. Sawyer, 50–52.

9. B. B. King with David Ritz, *Blues All Around Me: The Autobiography of B. B. King* (New York, Avon, 1996), 92.

10. Aldin et al., "B. B. King," 11.

11. King with Ritz, *Blues All Around Me*, 93.

12. King with Ritz, 98.

13. Aldin et al., "B. B. King," 13.

14. King with Ritz, *Blues All Around Me*, 98.

15. King with Ritz, 98.

16. King with Ritz, 99.

17. King with Ritz, 101–2.

18. In 2002, B. B. told me that Irene Kertchaval "was too little to know about it." She was about two when Cousin Riley arrived. She may have remembered the house as it was a year or two later.

19. King with Ritz, *Blues All Around Me*, 100.

20. King with Ritz, 100–101.

21. McKee and Chisenhall, *Beale Black & Blue*, 128.

22. McKee and Chisenhall, 128.

23. King with Ritz, *Blues All Around Me*, 102–3.

24. King with Ritz, 102.

25. King with Ritz, 102.

CHAPTER THIRTEEN: CHICAGO 1940

1. McKee and Chisenhall, *Beale Black & Blue*, 125.

2. Eleanor Roosevelt, "My Day," March 14, 1940, Eleanor Roosevelt Papers, George Washington University, https://www2.gwu.edu/~erpapers/myday/displaydoc.cfm?_y=1940&_f=md055527.

3. Bob Koester, "Lester Melrose: An Appreciation," *The American Folk Blues Occasional*, eds. Pete Welding and Chris Strachwitz (New York: Oak Publications, 1970), 58.

4. Koester, 58.

5. Hurley and Evans, "Bukka White," 177.

6. Hurley and Evans, 177.

7. Hurley and Evans, 178.

8. Mike Rowe, *Chicago Blues: The City and the Music* (New York: Da Capo Press, 1975), 20

9. David Evans, *Big Road Blues: Tradition and Creativity in the Folk Blues* (Berkeley: University of California Press, 1982), 27.

10. Peter Guralnick, *The Listener's Guide to the Blues* (New York: Facts on File, 1982), 36.

11. Guralnick, *The Listener's Guide to the Blues*, 36.

12. Hurley and Evans, "Bukka White," 178–79.

13. Evans, *Big Road Blues*.

14. Booker White interview, 1976.

CHAPTER FOURTEEN: MISTER MELROSE

1. Howard Reich and William Gaines, *Jelly's Blues: The Life, Music, and Redemption of Jelly Roll Morton* (Cambridge, MA: Da Capo Press, 2003), 73–74.

2. Lester Melrose, "My Life in Recording," *The American Folk Music Occasional*, eds. Chris Strachwitz and Pete Welding (New York: Oak Publications, 1970), 59.

3. Melrose, 59.

4. Melrose, 59.

5. Koester, "Lester Melrose," 58.

6. Koester, 58.

7. David Deutsch, dir., Arthur "Big Boy" Crudup, *Born in the Blues*, videocassette, 65 min., Shanachie VHS 1401, 1995. Copyright 1973 WETA-TV, Washington, DC.

8. Tammy L. Turner, *Dick Waterman: A Life in the Blues* (Jackson: University Press of Mississippi, 2019), 145.

9. Turner, 146.

10. Hurley and Evans, "Bukka White," 186.

CHAPTER FIFTEEN: TIMES OF TRANSITION

1. Melrose, "My Life in Recording," 60.

2. Brian Ward and Patrick Huber, *A & R Pioneers: Architects of American Roots Music on Record* (Nashville: Country Music Foundation, Vanderbilt University Press, 2018), 118.

3. Evans reader's report, September 3, 2023.

4. Hurley and Evans, "Bukka White," 178.

5. Jim O'Neal, notes to *Tampa Red, Guitar Wizard,* RCA Records AXM2-5501, 1975.

6. Evans reader's report, September 3, 2023.

7. O'Neal, notes to *Tampa Red.*

8. Paul Oliver, "Tub, Jug Washboard Bands," *Blues Off the Record: Thirty Years of Blues Commentary* (New York: Hippocrene Books, 1984), 37.

9. Robert Dixon and John Godrich, *Recording the Blues* (New York: Stein and Day, 1970), 96.

10. Julius Lester, "Mr. White, Take a Break," *Sing Out!* 18, no. 4 (October–November 1968), 61.

11. Lester, 61.

12. Lester, 61.

13. Meili Powell, BlackPast.org, https://www.blackpast.org/african-american-history/orange-mound-memphis-1890/.

14. Powell, BlackPast.org.

15. Irene Kertchaval, interview with the author, 2009.

16. Program of service, Emma Lee White, October 5, 2009. Courtesy of Irene Kertchaval.

17. Beulah Faye (White) Anderson, interview with the author, March 29, 2019.

18. Irene Kertchaval interview, 2009.

19. Henrietta Williams, interview with the author, August 14, 2020.

20. Irene Kertchaval, interview with the author, July 21, 2017.

21. 1950 United States Census.

22. Bob Eagle, email to the author, October 23, 2022.

23. *Commercial Appeal,* March 28, 1952, 44.

24. *Commercial Appeal,* April 12, 1952, 33.

25. Ellen Rogers interview, 2021.

26. F. Jack Hurley, interview with the author, November 16, 2018.

27. Inmate photograph, Shelby County Sherriff's Office, 1952.

28. Conversation with attorney Barbara L. Dean, Memphis Housing Authority General Counsel, November 17, 2020.

29. Shelby County General Court index, Booker T. White, defendant, and Memphis Housing Authority, complainant, Volume 53, docket number 067921, division 4.

CHAPTER SIXTEEN: AUTHENTIC BLUES

1. Roger House, *Blue Smoke: The Recorded Journey of Big Bill Broonzy* (Baton Rouge: Louisiana State University Press, 2010), 148.

2. House, 149.

3. House, 149.

4. House, 153–54.

5. John Godrich and Robert M. W. Dixon, *Blues & Gospel Records 1902–1942* (London: Storyville, 1969), 336.

6. Pete Welding, "The Rise of Folk-Blues," *Down Beat* 28, no. 19 (September 14, 1961), 15–16.

7. Welding, 16.

8. Paul Oliver, *Blues Fell This Morning: The Meaning of the Blues* (New York: Horizon Press, 1960), xvii–xviii.

9. Gayle Dean Wardlow, "Knocking on Doors for 78s: Buying Race Records in the South," *Chasin' That Devil Music: Searching for the Blues* (Milwaukee: Back Beat Books, 1998), 10–16. Originally published in *Victrola and 78 Journal*, no. 9 (Summer 1996), 9–14.

10. Wardlow, 10–11.

11. Welding, "The Rise of Folk-Blues," 16.

12. Welding, 17.

13. Welding, 17.

14. Welding, 17.

15. Philip R. Ratcliffe, *Mississippi John Hurt: His Life, His Times, His Blues* (Jackson: University Press of Mississippi, 2011), 120–31.

16. Ratcliffe, 121.

17. Tom Hoskins, letter to Alex Haley, February 12, 1982, quoted in Ratcliffe, 124.

18. Bruce Jackson, 1964 Cambridge tapes, Bruce Jackson–Diane Christian Collection, American Folklife Center, Library of Congress. Used by permission.

19. Dixon and Godrich, *Recording the Blues*, 98–99.

20. Dixon and Godrich, 99.

CHAPTER SEVENTEEN: 1963'S NOT 1962

1. ED Denson, "The Re-Discovery of Bukka White," *Blues Magazine* 2, no. 6 (December 1976), 7.

2. Claudio Guerrieri, *The John Fahey Handbook*, 2nd ed. (Claudio Guerrieri, 2022), 6.

3. Steve Lowenthal, *Dance of Death: The Life of John Fahey, American Guitarist* (Chicago: Chicago Review Press, 2014), 25.

4. ED Denson, email to the author, April 16, 2010.

5. Robert Gordon, email to the author, November 28, 2022.

6. "Roland Janes," Memphis Music Hall of Fame, https://memphismusichalloffame.com/inductee/rolandjanes/.

7. Don Crawford, "Blues Singer Rediscovered in South," *Daily Californian*, November 22, 1963.

8. John Fahey, notes to *Mississippi Blues Vol. 1 Bukka White*, Takoma Records B1001, 1964.

9. Ralph J. Gleason, "Digging Up Some Oldtime Favorites: Blues Singer Bukka White Rediscovered," from the *Boston Globe*, December 1, 1963. Courtesy of Claudio Guerrieri.

10. John Fahey, letter to Samuel Charters, November 1963. Courtesy of the John Fahey Trust and the Samuel and Ann Charters Archive of Blues and Vernacular African American Musical Culture, Archives & Special Collections, University of Connecticut Library.

11. ED Denson, "The Re-Discovery of Bukka White," *Blues Magazine* 2, no. 6 (December 1976), 12.

12. "Roland Janes," Memphis Music Hall of Fame.

CHAPTER EIGHTEEN: BOSTON 1964

1. Tom Rush, notes to *Tom Rush*, LP, Elektra Records EKS-7288, 1965.

2. John McPhee, *Time*, November 23, 1962.

3. Phil Spiro, email to the author, November 9, 2018, and Peter Guralnick, email to the author, May 23, 2023.

4. *The Broadside of Boston* 3, no. 4 (April 15, 1964), 19.

5. Peter Guralnick, email to the author, May 18, 2023.

6. David Evans, email to the author, July 5, 2020.

7. Peter Guralnick, email to the author, May 19, 2023.

8. Phil Spiro, email to the author, October 18, 2018.

9. Phil Spiro, email to the author, November 9, 2018.

10. Alan Wilson, "Learn Delta Blues," advertisement, *The Broadside of Boston* 3, no. 4 (April 15, 1964).

11. Alan Wilson, "Bukka White, Master of the Blues Lyric," *The Broadside of Boston* 3, no. 4 (April 15, 1964), 3.

12. Wilson, 3.

13. Rebecca Davis, *Blind Owl Blues: The Mysterious Life and Death of Blues Legend Alan Wilson* (Rebecca Davis, 2013), 37.

14. Bruce Jackson, email to the author, April 13, 2023.

15. Bruce Jackson, 1964 Cambridge tapes, Bruce Jackson–Diane Christian Collection, American Folklife Center, Library of Congress. Used by permission.

16. Jackson, 1964 Cambridge tapes.

17. Booker White and others, from handwritten notes to Booker's interview with Laurie Forti, Alan Wilson, and Phil Spiro, April 1964. Courtesy of David Evans. Note-taker unknown.

18. Interview transcript courtesy of David Evans.

19. Evans, email to the author, July 5, 2020.

20. Bruce Jackson, 1964 Cambridge tapes, Jackson-Christian Collection, American Folklife Center, Library of Congress. Used by permission.

21. ED Denson, email to the author, March 4, 2021.

22. Phil Spiro, email to the author, October 18, 2018.

CHAPTER NINETEEN: SKY SONGS

1. Rachael Rifkin, "Berkeley Flashback: The Crunchy Munchy Man," *California Magazine*, April 13, 2017, https://alumni.berkeley.edu/california-magazine/online/berkeley-flashback-crunchy-munchy-man.

2. Scott Krafft, "Foreword—The Berkeley Folk Music Festival & the Folk Revival on the US West Coast—an Introduction," https://sites.northwestern.edu/bfmf/foreword/.

3. Denson, email to the author, March 4, 2021.

4. Chris Strachwitz, email to the author, August 18, 2019.

5. Chris Strachwitz interview, March 6, 2018.

6. Chris Strachwitz, notes to Bukka White, *Sky Songs, Volume 1* and *Sky Songs, Volume 2*, Arhoolie Records F1019 and F1020, 1965.

7. Strachwitz, email, August 18, 2019.

8. Strachwitz, email.

9. Strachwitz email.

10. Strachwitz, notes to *Sky Songs, Volume 1* and *Sky Songs, Volume 2*.

11. Strachwitz notes.

12. Chris Strachwitz, undated conclusion of March 6, 2018, interview.

13. Chris Strachwitz notes.

14. Strachwitz notes to *Sky Songs*.

15. Bruce Pingree, conversation with the author, November 21, 2017.

16. Strachwitz interview, March 6, 2018.

17. David Evans discusses this process in *Big Road Blues: Tradition and Creativity in the Folk Blues* (University of California Press, 1982).

18. John Kane, author of *Pilgrims of Woodstock*, Red Lightning Books, 2019, in conversation with the author, April 28, 2023.

CHAPTER TWENTY: UNCERTAIN PROSPECTS

1. Dick Waterman, *Between Midnight and Day: The Last Unpublished Blues Archive* (San Rafael, CA: Insight Editions, 2004), 76–79.

2. Steve Cushing, *Pioneers of the Blues Revival* (Urbana: University of Illinois Press, 2014), 78.

3. Dick Waterman, interview with the author, March 3, 2021.

4. Irene Kertchaval interview, July 2018.

5. *New York Times*, February 5, 2019.

6. *New York Times*, February 5, 2019.

7. Ronald D. Cohen, *Rainbow Quest: The Folk Music Revival and American Society, 1940–1970* (Amherst: University of Massachusetts Press, 2002), 247.

8. Letter courtesy of Scott Barretta. Used with the permission of Irene Kertchaval.

9. Ed Pearl, interview with the author, July 2, 2009.

10. Jill A. Edy, for The Editors of *Encyclopedia Britannica*.

11. Bernie Pearl, email to the author, March 13, 2019.

12. William Riverside, notes to Buffy Sainte-Marie, *Many a Mile*, LP, Vanguard Records VSD-79171, 1965.

13. *Festival: Folk Music at Newport, 1963–1966*, Murray Lerner, MLF Productions, Criterion Collection (DVD Edition), September 2017.

14. Eric Sackheim and Jonathan Shawn, *The Blues Line* (New York: Grossman, 1969), 232.

15. John Fahey, *How Bluegrass Destroyed My Life: Stories by John Fahey* (Chicago: Drag City, 2000), 199.

16. Ed Pearl, email to the author, April 19, 2010.

17. Booker White interview, 1976.

CHAPTER TWENTY-ONE: RIVER CITY VENUES

1. David Evans, notes to Bukka White, *1963 Isn't 1962*, CD, Genes GCD 9903 (1994), 4.

2. Ronald D. Cohen, *A History of Folk Music Festivals in the United States: Feasts of Musical Celebration* (Lanham, MD: Scarecrow Press, 2008), 70–71.

3. William Bearden, *Memphis Blues: Birthplace of a Tradition* (Charleston, SC: Arcadia, 2006), 53.

4. Bengt Olsson, *Memphis Blues* (London: Studio Vista, 1970), 22.

5. Olsson, 15.

6. Dewey Corley and Willie Borum recollections, quoted in Olsson, 15.

7. Willie Borum recollection, quoted in Olsson, 15.

8. Olsson, *Memphis Blues*, 20.

9. 1950 United States Census.

10. David Evans reader's report, September 3, 2023.

11. John M. Hubbell, "The Blues Silence a D. J. Who Knew Them Well," *New York Times*, August 3, 2008.

12. Robert Gordon, *It Came from Memphis* (Nashville: Third Man, 2020), 83.

13. Jim Dickinson, *I'm Just Dead, I'm Not Gone* (Jackson: University Press of Mississippi, 2017), 133.

14. Memphis Music Hall of Fame, https://memphismusichalloffame.com.

15. Alan Lightman, *Screening Room* (New York: Pantheon, 2015), 72

16. Chris Wimmer, quoted in Robert Gordon, *It Came from Memphis*, 117.

17. Gordon, *It Came from Memphis*, 128.

CHAPTER TWENTY-TWO: FOLK FESTIVALS

1. Robert Palmer, writing as Bob Palmer, "Memphis Revisited," *Blues World*, no. 25 (October 1969), 5–6. Originally published in *Changes*.

2. Palmer, 6–7.

3. Palmer, 7–10.

4. "Nathan Beauregard," Mt. Zion Memorial Fund, https://mtzionmemorialfund.com/project/nathan-beauregard/.

5. Palmer, "Memphis Revisited," 7.

6. *Commercial Appeal*, July 28, 1966, 15.

7. Dean Pope, "1,000 Hear Blues Sung in Old Style," *Commercial Appeal*, July 31, 1966, 40.

8. *Commercial Appeal*, July 28, 1966, 15.

9. *Commercial Appeal*, July 28, 1966, 15.

10. Dorothy Beath, "Crowd Is Medley of Its Own at Hot, Cool Blues Festival," *Commercial Appeal*, June 4, 1967, 18.

11. Robert Jennings, "Blues Artists To Unwind Tonight," *Commercial Appeal*, July 20, 1968, 21.

12. Mike Vernon, interview with the author, August 1, 2018.

13. Stanley Booth, "Even the Birds Were Blue," *Rolling Stone*, April 16, 1970, 38.

14. *Memphis '69: The 1969 Memphis Country Blues Festival*, filmed by Gene Rosenthal, DVD produced for Fat Possum Records by Joe LaMattina, Bruce Watson, and Lisa LaMattina, FB 1693-9, 2019.

15. Booth, 36–37.

16. John Kane, conversation with the author, August 9, 2021.

17. *Memphis Commercial Appeal*, April 19, 1970, 147.

18. *Memphis Commercial Appeal*, October 9, 1970.

19. "1970 Festival of American Folklife," https://festival.si.edu/past-program/1970.

20. "1970 Festival of American Folklife," https://festival.si.edu/past-program/1970.

21. "Blues Session Is Called 'Success,'" *Memphis Commercial Appeal*, December 4, 1971.

22. "Annual Festival Calls Out Blues Stalwarts," *Memphis Commercial Appeal*, November 19, 1972, 2.

23. Rachel Lyons, email to the author, May 22, 2023.

24. Mike Vernon interview, August 1, 2018.

25. TJ Wheeler, *Blues Guy First 8 Chapters*, unpublished manuscript, 2007. Courtesy of TJ Wheeler.

26. Linzie Butler, interview with the author, May 10, 2023.

CHAPTER TWENTY-THREE: THE BLUES BUS

1. Arne Brogger, interview with the author, October 3, 2019.

2. Eugene Chadbourne, "Steve LaVere," AllMusic, https://www.allmusic.com/artist/steve-lavere-mn0000018737.

3. Arne Brogger interview, October 3, 2019.

4. Steve LaVere, letter to Arne Brogger, February 29, 1972. Courtesy of Arne Brogger.

5. Arne Brogger, interview with the author, March 5, 2021.

6. Robert Gordon, "Robert Johnson," *Memphis Rent Party* (New York: Bloomsbury, 2018), 67.

7. Steve LaVere, notes to *Memphis Blues Caravan Vol. I*, Memphis Archives 7008, 1994, 1–2.

8. Arne Brogger interview, October 3, 2019.

9. Arne Brogger interviews, October 3, 2019, and March 5, 2021.

10. Stephen C. LaVere, notes to *Memphis Blues Caravan Vol. I* and *Vol. II*, CD, Memphis Archives, 1994, 1–2.

11. Tour members recalled by Arne Brogger and David Evans.

12. Arne Brogger interview, March 5, 2021.

13. LaVere, notes to *Memphis Blues Caravan*, 2.

14. Stephen C. LaVere, notes to Bukka White's *Big Daddy* album, Biograph BLP-12049 -Stereo, 1974.

15. LaVere, notes to *Memphis Blues Caravan*.

16. Arne Brogger, email to the author, April 12, 2018.

17. Arne Brogger email.

18. Arne Brogger email.

19. B. B. King, interview with the author, fall 2002.

CHAPTER TWENTY-FOUR: BOOKER AND FURRY

1. Arne Brogger interview, October 3, 2019.

2. Written by the Mississippi Blues Trail Writing and Research Team for Lewis's marker in Greenwood, Mississippi, where he was born.

3. Robert Gordon, "Preface," *Memphis Rent Party*, 1–2.

4. Brogger interview, October 3, 2019.

CHAPTER TWENTY-FIVE: COAST TO COAST

1. Barry Melton, interview with the author, April 30, 2020.

2. Barry Melton interview.

3. David Evans reader's report, September 3, 2023.

4. Ronald D. Cohen, *A History of Folk Music Festivals in the United States* (Lanham, MD: Scarecrow Press, 2008), 71.

5. George Wein, *Myself Among Others: A Life in Music* (Cambridge, MA: Da Capo Press, 2003), 332.

6. Wein, 334.

7. Nelson George, from documentary about *The Blues*, Canadian Broadcasting Corporation, January 1966, https://www.cbc.ca/television/fromthevaults/the-day-the-blues-came-to-town-1.4903425.

8. McKee and Chisenhall, *Beale Black & Blue*, 128.

9. Paul Rishell, conversation with the author, March 11, 2017.

10. "A History of the Seattle Folklore Society," http://www.seafolklore.org/wp/about-sfs/history-of-sfs/.

11. "Bukka White—1967 Interview by Bob West, Mike Duffy, and John Ullman," *Blues & Rhythm*, No. 189 (May 2004), 4–7.

12. "Bukka White—1967 Interview by Bob West, Mike Duffy, and John Ullman," 4–7.

13. Dates are approximate from music downloads available on the Web.

14. Booth, *Dance with the Devil*, 130.

15. Wolfgang's Concert Streaming, https://www.wolfgangs.com/music/bukka-white/audio/20053297-10315.html?tid=4806967.

16. Booth, *Dance with the Devil*, 131.

17. Booth, 131.

18. Wein, *Myself Among Others*, 45.

19. Wein, 98.

20. Wein, 313.

21. Wein, 320.

22. Michael Taft, email to the author, March 5, 2008.

23. Peter Goddard, "No Mariposa like this one: Dylan, Lightfoot, Young, Mitchell," *Toronto Star*, July 15, 1972.

CHAPTER TWENTY-SIX: TRANSATLANTIC

1. Ed Pearl interview, July 2, 2009.

2. Mark H. Makin, email to the author, May 20, 2020.

3. Makin, email to the author.

4. David Evans, "Blues: Chronological Overview," *African American Music: An Introduction* (New York: Routledge, 2006), 110.

5. John Gee, interview with the author, summer 1971.

6. UK Blues Federation, https://www.ukblues.org/history-of-british-blues-american-folk-blues-festival/.

7. Irene Kertchaval, interview with the author.

8. Willie Dixon and Don Snowden, *I Am the Blues* (London: Quartet Books, 1995), 115.

9. Dixon and Snowden, 125–26.

10. Dixon and Snowden, 127.

11. Stefan Wirtz, "American Music," https://www.wirz.de/music/afbf.htm.

12. "Horst Lippman," Wikipedia, https://en.wikipedia.org/wiki/Horst_Lippmann.

13. David Evans. "Blues: Chronological Overview," *African American Music: An Introduction*, 111.

14. Evans, "Blues: Chronological Overview," 111.

15. "American Folk Blues Festival," Wikipedia, https://en.wikipedia.org/wiki/American_Folk_Blues_Festival.

16. Hay, *Goin' Back to Sweet Memphis* 15.

17. "American Folk Blues Festival discography," Stefan Wirz' American Music website, https://www.wirz.de/music/afbf.htm.

18. Gary Atkinson, email to the author, June 7, 2020.

19. Max Jones, *Melody Maker*, July 1971.

20. *Pop* 2 program on French television, December 2, 1972. https://archive.org/details/pop-2-pop-deux-emission-du-08011972-au-15121973.

21. Gianni Marcucci, notes to *Tennessee Blues Vol. 1*, LP, Albatros VPA 8240, 1975.

22. Mose Allison, interview with the author, 1974.

CHAPTER TWENTY-SEVEN: BREMEN 1975

1. Volker Steppat interview, June 3, 2020.
2. Volker Steppat interview.
3. Volker Steppat, email to the author, June 24, 2021.
4. Volker Steppat, email to the author, May 20, 2021.
5. Volker Steppat email.
6. Arne Schumacher, email to the author, April 24, 2023.
7. McKee and Chisenhall, *Beale Black & Blue*, 119.

CHAPTER TWENTY-EIGHT: CHANGES

1. Hot 100 chart, *Billboard*, May 22, 1976, https://www.billboard.com/charts/hot-100/1976-05-22/.
2. "Blues Singer Bukka White Returns Home for Festival," *Times Post*, 1.
3. "Blues Singer Bukka White Returns Home for Festival," 1.
4. Bukka White interview, 1976.
5. Sandra Marble, undated interview with Mississippi Blues Trail Writing and Research Team. Courtesy of Scott Barretta.
6. Steve Finkel, "Blues Great 'Bukka White' at Sandy's June 28–July 4," press release, June 1976.
7. Finkel, press release, June 1976.
8. David Little, email to the author, June 29, 2020.
9. Author's notes from July 2, 1976.
10. TJ Wheeler, email to the author, March 4, 2021.
11. Author's notes from July 2, 1976.
12. Author's notes from July 29, 1976.
13. Author's notes.
14. Irene Kertchaval, email to the author, December 31, 2009.
15. "Gunshot in Back Fatal to Woman," *Commercial Appeal*, June 3, 1976, 10.

CHAPTER TWENTY-NINE: HOME TO LEOLA

1. Leola Morris, interview with Andy Yale, 1982. Copyright 1985 Andy Yale. Used with permission.
2. "Famed Artist of the Blues, Bukka White, 69, Dies," Memphis *Commercial Appeal*, February 27, 1977.
3. Leola Morris interview with Andy Yale, 1982. Copyright 1985 by Andy Yale. Used with permission.
4. B. B. King interview with the author, fall 2022. Three concert listings for January–March 1977 on the Web site Concert Archives (https://www.concertarchives.org/bands/bb-king?year=1977) indicate that B. B. was in the United States.

5. "Famous Memorials in New Park Cemetery," Find a Grave, https://www.findagrave.com/cemetery/16314/famous-memorials?page=1#sr-167272694.

6. David W. Johnson, "'Bukka' White goes back home to Memphis," *Salem Evening News*, August 2, 1976, 1.

7. Sandy Berman, from my typewritten notes, Monday, August 2, 1976.

8. McKee and Chisenhall, *Beale Black & Blue*, 71.

9. Mike Matthews, "Hospital that treated African Americans decades ago wants to make a comeback," WATN-TV ABC24, April 19, 2019, https://www.localmemphis.com/article/news/local/hospital-that-treated-african-americans-decades-ago-wants-to-make-a-comeback/522-06a7840f-8dc6-47b4-a54d-745c7d7677ad.

10. "Hepatorenal Syndrome (HRS): Diagnosis, Treatment & Symptoms," Cleveland Clinic, https://my.clevelandclinic.org/health/diseases/23399-hepatorenal-syndrome.

11. Booker White interview, July 29, 1976.

CHAPTER THIRTY: BOOKER'S LEGACY

1. Recoil, "Electro Blues for Bukka White," *Bloodline*, Sire/Reprise 9 26850-2, 1992.

2. Kenny Wayne Shepherd, "Aberdeen," *Ledbetter Heights*, 1995, https://www.kennywayneshepherd.net/.

3. Rory Block, album notes to *Keepin' Outta Trouble: A Tribute to Bukka White*, Stony Plain Records SPCD1393, 2016.

4. Peter Daniels, *The Legend of Booker's Guitar* (United Kingdom: Peter Daniels, 2014), 92–94.

5. Daniels, 101.

6. Daniels, 135–41.

7. Eric Bibb, album notes to *Booker's Guitar*, Telarc TEL-31756-02, 2010.

8. Luke Hobbs, email to the author, May 30, 2022.

9. B. B. King interview with the author, April 27, 2002.

APPENDIX: BUKKA WHITE'S EXTRAORDINARY GUITAR PLAYING, BY JAS OBRECHT

1. Booker's slide playing in Vestapol and cross-note seems to owe a lot to one-string playing. This resemblance is discussed in David Evans, "Afro-American One-Stringed Instruments," *Western Folklore* 29, no. 4 (October 1970), 229–45 (reprinted in *Afro-American Folk Art and Crafts*, ed. William Ferris [Boston: G. K. Hall, 1983], 181–96). Booker played a one-stringed instrument as a child, which was common in his part of the South prior to World War II.

DISCOGRAPHY

Barbecue Bob. *Chocolate to the Bone*. Yazoo 2005, 1992.

Bibb, Eric. *Booker's Guitar*. Telarc TEL-31756-02, 2010.

Blackwell, Scrapper. *The Virtuoso Guitar of Scrapper Blackwell*. Yazoo 1019, 1991.

Blind Blake. *The Essential Blind Blake*. Classic Blues CBL 200035, 2002.

Block, Rory. *Keepin' Outta Trouble: A Tribute to Bukka White*. Stony Plain SPCD1393, 2016.

Broonzy, Big Bill. *Complete Recorded Works . . . Vol. 7*. Document DOCD-5129, 1992.

Broonzy, Big Bill. *Do That Guitar Rag, 1928–1935*. Yazoo 1035, 1991.

Broonzy, Big Bill. *Good Time Tonight*. Columbia CK 46219 1990.

Carter, Bo. *Twist It Babe, 1931–1940*. Yazoo 1034, 1992.

Charters, Samuel, compiler. *Blues Roots/Chicago—The 1930s*. Smithsonian Folkways RBF 16, 2007.

Charters, Samuel, compiler. *The Country Blues*. Smithsonian Folkways Archival RF 1, 2006.

Charters, Samuel, compiler. *The Jug Bands*. RF 6, 1973.

Collins, Sam. *Jail House Blues*. Yazoo 1079, 1990.

Davis, Rev. Gary. *Harlem Street Singer*. Soul Jam 600878, 2016.

Dukes, Laura, Piano Red, Bukka White. *Tennessee Blues, Vol. 1*. Albatros VPA 8240, 1975.

Estes, Sleepy John. *I Ain't Gonna Be Worried No More, 1929–1941*. Yazoo 2004, 1992.

Fahey, John. *On Air*. T&M 034, 2005.

Fuller, Blind Boy. *Untrue Blues*. Catfish KATCD 109, 1998.

Gordon, Jimmie. *1934–1938 The Remaining Titles*. Old Tramp OTCD-01.

Guy, Buddy. *The Very Best of Buddy Guy*. Rhino R2 70280, 1992.

Harris, Corey. *Between Midnight and Day*. Alligator ALCD 4837, 1995.

Hopkins, Lightnin'. *The Very Best of Lightnin' Hopkins*. Rhino R2 79860, 2000.

House, Son. *The Complete Library of Congress Sessions*. Travelin' Man TM CD 02, 1990.

House, Son. *Father of the Folk Blues*. Columbia CS 9217, 1965.

House, Son. *The Original Delta Blues*. Columbia/Legacy CK 65515, 1998.

House, Son. *Son House and the Great Delta Blues Singers 1928–1930*. Document DOCD-5002, 1990, 2000.

House, Son. *Special Rider Blues: The 1930–1942 Mississippi and Wisconsin Recordings*. Soul Jam 600885, 2016.

Howlin' Wolf. *Memphis Days: The Definitive Edition, Vol 1*. Bear Family BCD 15460, 1989.

Hurt, Mississippi John. *Avalon Blues: The Complete 1928 OKeh Recordings*. Columbia/Legacy, CK 64986, 1996.

James, Elmore. *The Best of Elmore James*. Great American Music CD-GA-552, 2009.

Jefferson, Blind Lemon. *Complete Recorded Works . . . Vol. 1*. Document DOCD-5017, 1991.
Jefferson, Blind Lemon. *Texas Blues*. Complete Blues SBLUECD 502X, 2007.
Johnson, Blind Willie. *The Complete Willie Johnson*. Columbia/Legacy C2K52835, 1993.
Johnson, Blind Willie. *Dark Was the Night*. Columbia/Legacy CK 65516, 1998.
Johnson, Lonnie. *Hot Fingers*. Catfish KATCD 110, 1998.
Johnson, Tommy. *Canned Heat 1928–1929*. Document DOCD 5001, 2000.
Johnson, Robert. *The Complete Recordings*. CD, Columbia C2K 46222, 1990.
King, B. B. *The Best of B. B. King*. Virgin 09463-30904-2-2, 1994.
King, B. B. *Live at the Regal*. MCA MCAD 11646, 1997.
Lewis, Furry. *Good Morning Judge*. Fat Possum FB80374-2, 2003.
Lewis, Furry. *His Best 22 Recordings 1927–1929*. Wolf WSE 101 CD, 2004.
Lewis, Furry. *In His Prime, 1927–1928*. Yazoo 1050, 1991.
Furry Lewis, Bukka White, and Friends. *Party! At Home*. Arcola A CD 1001, 2001.
Furry Lewis, with Bukka White and Gus Cannon. *On the Road Again*. Adelphi/Genes GCD 9918, 1999.
Lomax, Alan, producer. *Blues in the Mississippi Night*. United Artists UAL 4027, 1959.
Lipscomb, Mance. *Texas Songster*. Arhoolie CD 306, 2000.
McClennan, Tommy. *Complete Recordings . . . Vol. 1*. Document DOC-CD 5669, 2002.
McDowell, Fred. *Delta Blues*. Arhoolie F-1021, 1964.
McDowell, Fred. *You Gotta Move*. Arhoolie CD 304, 1989.
McDowell, Fred. *Shake 'Em On Down*. Fat Possum FP 1149-2, 2010.
McMullan, Hayes. *Everyday Seem Like Murder Here*. Light in the Attic LITA 152, 2010.
McTell, Blind Willie. *Blind Willie McTell 1927–1940*. Real Gone RGMCD237, 2007.
Memphis Jug Band. *Complete Recorded Works . . . Vol. 3*. Document DOCD-5023, 1991.
Memphis Minnie. *Blues Classics* BC-1, 1964.
Memphis Minnie. *The Essential Recordings*. Primo PRMCD 6108, 2010.
Memphis Minnie and Kansas Joe. *In Chronological Order, Vol. 1*. Document DOCD 5028, 1991.
Memphis Slim. *The Folkways Years, 1959–1973*. Smithsonian Folkways SFW CD, 2000.
Mississippi Sheiks. *Honey Babe Let the Deal Go Down: The Best of the Mississippi Sheiks*. Columbia/Legacy CK65709, 2004.
Oliver, Paul, compiler. *Blues Fell This Morning: Rare Recordings of Southern Blues Singers*. Philips BBL 7369, 1969.
Oliver, Paul, compiler. *The Story of the Blues*. Columbia CG 30008 (reissue of CBS 66218, M 63572, M 63573, 1969).
Owens, Jack, and Bud Spires. *It Must Have Been the Devil*. Testament TCD 5016, 1995.
Patton, Charley. *The Definitive Charley Patton*. Catfish, KATCD 180, 2001.
Petway, Robert. *Mississippi Blues, Vol. 3: The Complete Recordings of Robert Petway (1941–1942)*. Document DOCD-5761, 2002.
Philips, Washington. *I Am Born to Preach the Gospel*. Yazoo 2003, 1991.
Recoil. *Bloodline*. Sire/Reprise 9 26850-2, 1992.
Rush, Tom. *Tom Rush*. Elektra EKS 7288, 1965.
Sainte-Marie, Buffy. *Many a Mile*. Vanguard VSD-79171, 1965.
Shepherd, Kenny Wayne. *Ledbetter Heights*. Giant 24621-2, 1995.
Smith, Bessie. *The Anthology*. Not Now Music NOT2CD342, 2010.

Spivey, Victoria. *The Essential Victoria Spivey*. Classic Blues CBL 200014, 2001.

Stokes, Frank. *Complete Victor Titles with Alternate Takes*. Document DOCD-5013, 2011.

Stokes, Frank, and Dan Sane. *The Beale Street Sheiks 1927–1929*. Document DOCD-5012, 1990.

Sykes, Roosevelt. *The Honey Dripper*. Fabulous FABCD 130, 2002.

Sykes, Roosevelt. *Mr. Sykes Blues 1929–1932*. Riverside RM 8819, 1967.

Tampa Red. *Bottleneck Blues, 1928–1937*. Yazoo 1039, 1992.

Tampa Red. *Guitar Wizard*. RCA AXM2-5501, 1975.

Thomas, Henry. *"Ragtime Texas" Complete Recorded Works . . . 1927–1929*. Document DOCD 5665, 2000.

Various. *Afro-American Blues and Game Songs*. Rounder CD 1513, 1999.

Various. *Afro-American Folk Music from Tate and Panola Counties, Mississippi*. Rounder 18964-1515-2, 2000.

Various. *American Folk Blues Festival '62–'65*. Evidence ECD 26087-2, 1997.

Various. *American Folk Blues Festival '65*. L + R Records LR CD-2025, 1983.

Various. *American Folk Blues Festival '67*. L + R LR CD-2070, 1990.

Various. *American Folk Blues Festival '70*. L + R LR CD-2021, 1980.

Various. *American Folk Blues Festival '72*. L + R LR CD-2018, 1980.

Various. *American Primitive, Vol. 1: Raw Pre-War Gospel (1926–36)*. Revenant REV 206, 1997.

Various. *Before the Blues, Vol. 1: The Early American Black Music Scene*. Yazoo 2015, 1996.

Various. *Before the Blues, Vol. 2*, Yazoo 2016, 1996.

Various. *Before the Blues, Vol. 3*, Yazoo 2017, 1996.

Various. *Blues Oggi*. I Dischi del Sole DS 526/28, 1974.

Various. *Classic African American Songsters*. Smithsonian Folkways SFW 40211, 2014.

Various. *Classic Delta and Deep South Blues*. Smithsonian Folkways SFW 40222, 2018.

Various. *Classic Piedmont Blues*. Smithsonian Folkways SFW 40221, 2017.

Various. *Classic Railroad Songs*. SFW CD 40192, 2006.

Various. *Contemporary Guitar: Robbie Basho, John Fahey, Max Ochs, Harry Taussig, Bukka White*. Takoma 4M226, 2012.

Various. *Delta Blues—Vol. 1* (1929–1930). Document DLP 532, 1988.

Various. *The Devil's Music: The Soundtrack to the 1976 BBC TV Documentary Series*. Indigo/Sanctuary Records IGOTCD 2537, 2003.

Various. *East Memphis Music: The Hits from the Stax Era*. Almo Music EM 50009, 1984.

Various. *Giants of Country Blues, Vol. 1 (1927–1938)*. Wolf WSE 107 CD, 2000.

Various. *Guitar Wizards, 1926–1935*. Yazoo 1016, 1991.

Various. *Living Legends: Son House, Skip James, Bukka White, Big Joe Williams*. Verve Folkways FT-3010, 1967.

Various. *Lonesome Road Blues: 15 Years in the Mississippi Delta, 1926–1941*. Yazoo 1038, 1997.

Various. *Masters of the Delta Blues: The Friends of Charlie Patton*. Yazoo 2002, 1991.

Various. *Memphis Blues Caravan Vol I*. Memphis Archives MA 7008, 1994.

Various. *Memphis Blues Caravan Vol II*. Memphis Archives MA7009, 1994.

Various. *Memphis Masters: Early American Blues Classics, 1927–34*. Yazoo 2008, 2003.

Various. *Memphis Swamp Jam*. Blue Thumb BTS 6000, 1969.

Various. *The Mississippi Blues No. 1*. Origin Jazz Library OJL 5, 1963.

Various. *Mississippi Delta Blues Jam in Memphis Volume 2*. Arhoolie CD 386, 1993.

Various. *Mississippi Masters: Early American Blues Classics, 1927–1935*. Yazoo 2007, 1994.

Various. *OKeh Chicago Blues*. Epic 37318, 1982.

Various. *The Roots of Robert Johnson*. Yazoo 1073, 1990.

Various. *The Rough Guide to Jug Band Blues*. Rough Guides/World Music RGNET 1358CD, 2017.

Various. *Sic 'Em Dogs On Me*. Herwin H-201, 1972.

Various. *Spivey's Blues Cavalcade: Blues and More Blues!* Spivey LP 1015, 1970.

Various. *St. Louis Country Blues*. Document DOCD-5147, 1993.

Various. *Traveling Through the Jungle: Fife and Drum Band Music from the Deep South*. Testament TCD 5017, 1995.

Various. *The Unissued 1963* [American Folk] *Blues Festival*. Multimedia MIL 6105, 1999.

Various. *Wake Up Dead Man: Black Convict Worksongs from Texas Prisons*. Rounder 2013, 1975.

Various. *Windy City Blues: The Transition 1935–1953*. Nighthawk NH 101, 2017.

Waters, Muddy. *The Complete Plantation Recordings: The Historic 1941–1942 Library of Congress Field Recordings*. Chess/MCA MCD 09344, 1993.

Washboard Sam. *Complete Recorded Works . . . Vol. 3*. Document DOCD-5173, 1993 (2007).

Washboard Sam. *Completed Recorded Works . . . Vol. 4*. Document DOCD-5174, 1993.

Wheatstraw, Peetie. *Complete Recorded Works . . . Vol 2*. Document DOCD-5242, 1994.

Wheatstraw, Peetie. *Complete Recorded Works . . . Vol. 3*. Document DOCD-5243, 1994.

White, Bukka. *1963 Isn't 1962*. Genes GCD 9903, 1994.

White, Bukka. *The 1968 Memphis Country Blues Festival/The Complete Blues Horizon Sessions*. Sony BMG 82876851232, 2006.

White, Bukka. *Aberdeen, Mississippi Blues*. Sunset Boulevard SBR 7948, 2020.

White, Bukka. *Aberdeen Mississippi Blues: The Vintage Recordings (1930–1940)*. Document DOCD-5679, 2003.

White, Bukka. *Baton Rouge Mosby Street*. Blues Beacon 1932 119, 1972.

White, Bukka. *Big Daddy*. Biograph BLP-12049, 1974.

White, Bukka. *Memphis Hot Shots*. Blue Horizon S 7-63229, 1969.

White, Bukka. *Mississippi Blues, Vol. 1*. Takoma B1001, 1964.

White, Bukka. *Parchman Farm*. Columbia C 30036, 1970.

White, Bukka. *Sky Songs, Vol. 1*. Arhoolie F 1019, 1965.

White, Bukka. *Sky Songs, Vol. 2*. Arhoolie F 1020, 1965.

White, Bukka. *Sparkasse in Concert Country Blues*. Sparkasse I/75, 1975

White, Bukka. *Worried Blues*. Fat Possum, 2017.

White, Bukka, and Skip James. *Live at the Café au Go Go 1965*. Rock Beat ROC-CD 3251, 2014.

Wilkins, Robert. *The Original Rolling Stone*. Yazoo 1077, 1989.

Williams, Big Joe. *Big Joe Williams*. Grammercy, 2003.

Williams, Big Joe. *Complete Recorded Works . . . Vol 1*. Document BDCD-6003, 1991 (2007).

Williams, George. "Touch Me Light Mama," "Frisco Leaving Birmingham (take 2)," "The Escaped Convict (take 2)," "Middlin' Blues." *Great Blues Harp Players (1927–1936)*. Document DOCCD-5100, 1992.

Williams, George. "Touch Me Light Mama." *Harmonica Masters*, Yazoo 2019, 1996.

Wolfe, Carl, and others. *W. C. Handy's Beale Street: Where the Blues Began*. Inside Sounds/Inside Memphis ISC-0516, 2, 2003.

ADDITIONAL RECORDINGS OF BOOKER WHITE

Seven songs recorded March 12, 1974, by F. Jack Hurley. Courtesy of Professor Hurley and Dr. David Evans.

Radio interview on WCPC in Houston, Mississippi, recorded May 27, 1976, by station manager Robin Mathis. Courtesy of Melanie Munlin.

VIDEOGRAPHY

The American Folk Blues Festival 1962–1966 (Volume One). Produced by David Peck and John Kanis for Reelin' in the Years Productions; Janie Hendrix and John McDermott for Experience Hendrix. HIP-O Records, B0000750-09, 2003.

The American Folk Blues Festival 1962–1969 (Volume Three). Produced by David Peck and John Kanis for Reelin' in the Years Productions; Janie Hendrix and John McDermott for Experience Hendrix. HIP-O Records, B0002397-09, 2004.

Born in the Blues (Arthur "Big Boy" Crudup). Directed by David Deutsch. Shanachie VHS 1401, 1995. Copyright 1973 WETA-TV, Washington, DC.

Devil Got My Woman: Blues at Newport 1966. Vestapol Productions 13049, 2001.

Festival: Folk Music at Newport, 1963–1966. Directed by Murray Lerner. MLF Productions. The Criterion Collection, 2017.

Legends of the Country Blues Guitar, Volume Two. Vestapol 13016, 2001.

Memphis '69: The 1969 Memphis Country Blues Festival. Directed by Gene Rosenthal (1969), and Joe LaMattina for Fat Possum Records. FB 1693-9, 2019.

Son House and Bukka White: Masters of the Country Blues. Yazoo 500 (DVD), 2000.

BIBLIOGRAPHY

1928 Handy Railroad Atlas of the United States (Milwaukee: Kalmbach Publishing, undated), 26 (reprint of *Handy Railroad Maps of the United States*, Rand McNally, 1928).

Aldin, Mary Katherine, and Peter Lee. "B. B. King." *Living Blues* 19, no. 3 (May–June 1988).

Anderson, Annye C., with Preston Lauterbach. *Brother Robert: Growing Up with Robert Johnson*. New York: Hachette, 2020.

"Annual Festival Calls Out Blues Stalwarts." *Commercial Appeal*, November 19, 1972.

Arnesen, Eric. *Brotherhoods of Color: Black Railroad Workers and the Struggle for Equality*. Cambridge: Harvard University Press, 2001.

Basiuk, Bo. "Interview with Bukka White—August 1975." *Blues Magazine* 2, no. 6 (December 1976).

Basiuk, Bo. "Interview with Bukka White—Part 2." *Blues Magazine* 3, no. 1 (February 1977).

Bearden, William. *Memphis Blues: Birthplace of a Tradition*. Charleston, SC: Arcadia, 2006.

Beath, Dorothy. "Crowd Is Medley of Its Own at Hot, Cool Blues Festival." *Commercial Appeal*, June 4, 1967.

Beaumont, Daniel. *Preachin' the Blues: The Life and Times of Son House*. Oxford: Oxford University Press, 2011.

Berlin, Ira. *Many Thousands Gone: The First Two Centuries of Slavery in North America*. Cambridge, MA: Belknap Press, 1998.

Berlin, Ira, Marc Favreau, and Steven F. Miller, eds. *Remembering Slavery: African Americans Talk about Their Personal Experiences of Slavery and Emancipation*. New York: New Press, 1996.

"BH Rehabilitation." Beverly (Massachusetts) Hospital, 1976.

Bibb, Eric. Notes to *Booker's Guitar*, Telarc TEL-31756-02, 2010.

Blake, Kellee. "'First in the Path of the Firemen': The Fate of the 1890 Population Census, Part 1." *Genealogy Notes* 28, no. 1 (Spring 1996). https://www.archives.gov/publications/prologue/1996/spring/1890-census-1.html.

Block, Rory. Notes to *Keepin' Outta Trouble*, Stony Plain Records, SPCD 1393, 2016.

Bloome, Deirdre, and Christopher Muller. "Tenancy and African American Marriage in the Postbellum South." *Demography* 52, no. 5 (October 2015).

"Blues Session Is Called 'Success.'" *Commercial Appeal*, December 4, 1971.

"Blues Singer Bukka White Returns Home for Festival." (Houston, Mississippi) *Times Post*, June 3, 1976.

Bokelman, Marina, and David Evans. *Going Up the Country: Adventures in Blues and Fieldwork in the 1960s*. Jackson: University Press of Mississippi, 2022.

Booth, Stanley. "Blues Boy." *Rhythm Oil: A Journey through the Music of the American South.* New York: Pantheon, 1991.

Booth, Stanley. *Dance with the Devil: The Rolling Stones and Their Times.* New York: Random House, 1984.

Booth, Stanley. "Even the Birds Were Blue." *Rolling Stone* (April 16, 1970).

Booth, Stanley. *Red Hot and Blues: Fifty Years of Writing about Music, Memphis, and Motherf**kers.* Chicago: Chicago Review Press, 2019.

Bukka White. The Blues Collection, part 23. London: Orbis Publishing, 1994.

"Bukka White—1967 Interview by Bob West, Mike Duffy, and John Ullman." *Blues & Rhythm,* no. 189 (May 2004).

Calt, Stephen. "The House Frolic: A Reminiscence by Booker White." *78 Quarterly* no. 8.

Calt, Stephen. *I'd Rather Be the Devil: Skip James and the Blues.* New York: Da Capo, 1994.

Calt, Stephen (writing as Cal Stephens). "Booker White on Bullet Williams." *78 Quarterly* no. 6.

Calt, Stephen, and Gayle Wardlow. *King of the Delta Blues: The Life and Music of Charlie Patton.* Newton, NJ: Rock Chapel Press, 1988.

Chafe, William H., Raymond Gavins, and Robert Korstad, eds. *Remembering Jim Crow: African Americans Talk about Life in the Segregated South.* New York: New Press, 2001.

Charters, Samuel B. *The Bluesmen.* New York: Oak Publications, 1967.

Charters, Samuel B. *The Country Blues.* London: Michael Joseph, 1959.

Charters, Samuel B. *The Legacy of the Blues.* London: Calder & Boyars, 1975.

Cheseborough, Steve. *Blues Traveling: The Holy Sites of Delta Blues,* 3rd ed. Jackson: University Press of Mississippi, 2009.

Cohen, Ronald D. *A History of Folk Music Festivals in the United States: Feasts of Musical Celebration.* Lanham, MD: Scarecrow Press, 2008.

Cohen, Ronald D. *Rainbow Quest: The Folk Music Revival and American Society, 1940–1970.* Amherst: University of Massachusetts Press, 2002.

Congress, Richard. *Blues Mandolin Man: The Life and Music of Yank Rachell.* Jackson: University Press of Mississippi, 2001.

Cook, Bruce. *Listen to the Blues.* New York: Scribner's, 1973.

Cowley, John, and Paul Oliver, eds. *The New Blackwell Guide to Recorded Blues.* Oxford: Blackwell, 1996.

Crawford, Don. "Blues Singer Rediscovered in South." *Daily Californian,* November 22, 1963.

Cushing, Steve. *Pioneers of the Blues Revival.* Urbana: University of Illinois Press, 2014.

Dance, Helen Oakley. *Stormy Monday: The T-Bone Walker Story.* Baton Rouge: Louisiana State University Press, 1987.

Daniels, Peter. *The Legend of Booker's Guitar.* United Kingdom: Peter Daniels, 2014.

Davis, Francis. *The History of the Blues.* New York: Hyperion, 1995.

Davis, Rebecca. *Blind Owl Blues: The Mysterious Life and Death of Blues Legend Alan Wilson.* Rebecca Davis, 2013.

De Vise, Daniel. *King of the Blues: The Rise and Reign of B. B. King.* New York: Atlantic Monthly Press, 2021.

Denson, ED. Notes to *Mississippi Blues Vol. 1.* Takoma Records B1001, 1964.

Denson, ED. "The Re-Discovery of Bukka White." *Blues Magazine* 2 no. 6 (December 1976).

Dickinson, Jim. *I'm Just Dead, I'm Not Gone.* Jackson: University Press of Mississippi, 2017.

Dixon, Willie, and Don Snowden. *I Am the Blues: The Willie Dixon Story*. London: Quartet Books, 1989.

Dregni, Michael. "Hard Traveled: Booker White's 1933 National Duolian." *Vintage Guitar* 30, no. 11 (September 2016).

Eagle, Bob, and Eric S. LeBlanc. *Blues: A Regional Experience*. Santa Barbara, CA: Praeger, 2013.

Epstein, Dena J. *Sinful Tunes and Spirituals: Black Folk Music to the Civil War*. Urbana: University of Illinois Press, 1977.

Equal Justice Initiative. *Lynching in America: Confronting the Legacy of Racial Terror*. Montgomery, AL: Equal Justice Initiative, 2017.

Evans, David. *Big Road Blues: Tradition and Creativity in the Folk Blues*. Berkeley: University of California Press, 1982.

Evans, David. "Blues: Chronological Overview." *African American Music: An Introduction*. New York: Routledge, 2006.

Evans, David. "Booker White." *Nothing but the Blues*, ed. Mike Leadbitter. London: Hanover Books, 1971.

Evans, David. Notes to Bukka White, *1963 Isn't 1962*. CD, Genes GCD 9903, 1994.

Evans, David. *Tommy Johnson*. London: Studio Vista, 1971.

Fahey, John. "Fish." In *How Bluegrass Music Destroyed My Life*. Chicago: Drag City, 2000.

Fahey, John. Notes to Bukka White, *Mississippi Blues Vol. 1*. LP, Takoma Records B1001, 1964.

"Famed Artist of Blues Dies, Bukka White, 89." *Commercial Appeal*, February 27, 1977.

Federal Writers Project. "Mississippi Past and Present." *Mississippi: A Guide to the Magnolia State*. New York: Viking, 1938.

Ferris, William. *Blues from the Delta*. Garden City, NY: Anchor/Doubleday, 1978.

Finkel, Steve. "Blues Great 'Bukka White' at Sandy's June 28–July 4." News release, June 1976.

Flohil, Dick. "Bukka T. White: The Man from Houston Mississippi." *Coda: Canada's Jazz Magazine* 8, no. 11 (January 1969).

Floyd, Harley Hill. *A Short History of Chickasaw County Mississippi, Vol. 1*. Houston, Mississippi: Chickasaw County Historical Society, 1985.

Flynn, George Q. "Selective Service and American Blacks During World War II." *Journal of Negro History* 69, no. 1 (1984).

Folklore Productions, the First Fifty Years. Santa Monica: Folklore Productions, 2007.

Ford, Robert. *A Blues Bibliography: The International Literature of an African-American Genre*. Bromley, Kent, UK: Paul Pelletier, 1999.

Freeland, Tom, and Chris Smith. "That Dry Creek Eaton Clan." *Nobody Knows Where the Blues Come From*. Jackson: University Press of Mississippi, 2006.

Garon, Paul. *The Devil's Son-in-Law: The Story of Peetie Wheatstraw & His Songs*. Chicago: Charles H. Kerr, 2003.

Garon, Paul, and Beth Garon. *Woman with Guitar: Memphis Minnie's Blues*. San Francisco: City Lights Books, 2014.

Garon, Paul, and Gene Tomko. *What's the Use of Walking If There's a Freight Train Going Your Way? Black Hoboes and Their Songs*. Chicago: Charles H. Kerr Publishing, 2006.

Gear, Robert. "The National Guitar." *Sing Out!* 20, no. 5 (May–June 1971).

Gioia, Ted. *Delta Blues: The Life and Times of the Mississippi Masters Who Revolutionized American Music*. New York: W. W. Norton, 2008.

Gleason, Ralph J. "Digging Up Some Oldtime Favorites: Blues Singer Bukka White Rediscovered." *Boston Globe*, December 1, 1963.

Goddard, Peter. "No Mariposa Like This One: Dylan, Young, Mitchell." *Toronto Star*, July 15, 1972.

Gordon, Robert. *Can't Be Satisfied: The Life and Times of Muddy Waters*. Boston: Little, Brown, 2002.

Gordon, Robert. *It Came from Memphis*. Nashville: Third Man, 2020.

Gordon, Robert. "Robert Johnson." *Memphis Rent Party*. New York: Bloomsbury, 2018.

Gray, Michael. *Hand Me Down My Travelin' Shoes: In Search of Blind Willie McTell*. Chicago: Chicago Review Press, 2009.

Green, Roger, ed. *The Train*. Oxford: Oxford University Press, 1992.

Guerrieri, Claudio. *The John Fahey Handbook*, 2nd ed. Claudio Guerrieri, 2022.

Gunn, Jennie, John Gunn, and Carroll Gunn. *The Life of Mary Shepard: Queen of the Legendary Club Ebony*. Oxford, MS: Gunn Books, undated.

Guralnick, Peter. *Last Train to Memphis: The Rise of Elvis Presley*. Boston: Little, Brown, 1994.

Guralnick, Peter. *The Listener's Guide to the Blues*. New York: Facts on File, 1982.

Gussow, Adam. "W. C. Handy and the 'Birth' of the Blues." *Southern Cultures* 24, no. 4 (Winter 2018).

Hamilton, Marybeth. *In Search of the Blues*. New York: Basic Books, 2008.

Handy, W. C., ed. *A Treasury of the Blues: Complete Words and Music of 67 Great Songs from Memphis Blues to the Present Day*. New York: Charles Boni, 1940.

Harris, Sheldon. *Blues Who's Who: A Biographical Dictionary of Blues Singers*. New Rochelle, NY: Arlington House, 1979.

Harrison, Daphne Duval. *Black Pearls: Blues Queens of the 1920s*. New Brunswick, NJ: Rutgers University Press, 1988.

Hay, Fred J. *Goin' Back to Sweet Memphis: Conversations with the Blues* (Athens: University of Georgia Press, 2001).

Heaphy, Leslie A. *The Negro Leagues, 1869–1960*. Jefferson, NC: McFarland, 2003.

Hoffsomer, Donovan L. *Railroads of the Trans-Mississippi West*. Plainview, TX: Wayland College, 1974.

Hopper, Columbus B. "The Conjugal Visit at Mississippi State Penitentiary." *Journal of Criminal Law, Criminology, and Police Science* 53, no. 3 (September 1962).

House, Roger. *Blue Smoke: The Recorded Journey of Big Bill Broonzy*. Baton Rouge: Louisiana State University Press, 2010.

Hurley, F. Jack, and David Evans. "Bukka White." *Tom Ashley, Sam McGee, Bukka White: Tennessee Traditional Singers*. Knoxville: University of Tennessee Press, 1981.

Irons, Peter. *White Men's Law: The Roots of Systemic Racism*. Oxford: Oxford University Press, 2022.

Issac Harrington obituary. (Houston, Mississippi) *Times Post*, January 30, 1936, as reported on Find a Grave. https://www.findagrave.com/memorial/41000761.

Jackson, Bruce. "Newport: The Who, What, Where, When, Why and How of America's Biggest, Most 'Successful,' Most Controversial Folk Festival." *Sing Out!* 16, no. 4 (September 1966).

Jackson, Bruce. *The Story Is True: The Art and Meaning of Telling Stories*. Philadelphia: Temple University Press, 2007.

Jackson, Bruce. *Wake Up Dead Man: Afro-American Worksongs from Texas Prisons*. Collected and edited by Bruce Jackson. Cambridge: Harvard University Press, 1972.

Jennings, Robert. "Blues Artists to Unwind Tonight." *Commercial Appeal*, July 20, 1968.

Johansen, Bruce E. *The Native Peoples of North America: A History*. Brunswick, NJ: Rutgers University Press, 2005.

Johnson, David W. "'Bukka' White goes back home to Memphis." *Salem Evening News*, August 2, 1976.

Johnson, David W. "'Fixin' To Die Blues': The Last Months of Bukka White." *Southern Cultures* 16, no. 3 (Summer 2010).

Jones, LeRoi (Amiri Baraka). *Blues People: Negro Music in White America*. New York: Harper Perennial, 2002.

Kahn, Ed. "1934–1950: The Early Collecting Years." In Ronald Cohen, ed., *Alan Lomax: Selected Writings 1934–1997*. New York: Routledge, 2003.

Keefe, Kevin P. "Rhythm of the Rails: From Country to Blues, American Roots Music Grew Up Along the Tracks, and Its Heart Was in Mississippi." *Trains* 77, no. 9 (September 2017).

King, B. B., with David Ritz. *Blues All Around Me: The Autobiography of B. B. King*. New York: Avon Books, 1996.

Koester, Bob. "Lester Melrose: An Appreciation." *The American Folk Blues Occasional*. New York: Oak Publications, 1970.

Kubik, Gerhard. *Africa and the Blues*. Jackson: University Press of Mississippi, 1999.

Lauterbach, Preston. *Beale Street Dynasty: Sex, Song, and the Struggle for the Soul of Memphis*. New York: W. W. Norton, 2015.

Leadbitter, Mike. *Nothing but the Blues*. London: Hanover Books, 1971.

Leadbitter, Mike, and Neil Slaven. *Blues Records: 1943–1946*. New York: Oak Publications, 1968.

Lester, Julius. "I Can Make My Own Songs." *Sing Out!* 15, no. 3 (July 1965). Interview with Son House.

Lester, Julius. "Mr. White, Take a Break." *Sing Out!* 18, no. 4 (October–November 1968). Interview with Booker White.

Leverentz, David. *Honor Bound: Race and Shame in America*. New Brunswick, NJ: Rutgers University Press, 2012.

Lightman, Alan. *Screening Room: Family Pictures*. New York: Pantheon, 2015.

Lomax, Alan. *Alan Lomax: Selected Writings 1934–1997*. New York: Routledge, 2003.

Lomax, Alan. *The Land Where Blues Began*. New York: Pantheon, 1993.

Lomax, Alan. "'Sinful' Songs of the Southern Negro." *Southwest Review* 19, no. 2 (Winter 1934).

Lomax, John. *Adventures of a Ballad Hunter*. Austin: University of Texas Press, 2017.

Lowenthal, Steve. *Dance of Death: The Life of John Fahey, American Guitarist*. Chicago: Chicago Review Press, 2014.

Mazor, Barry. *Ralph Peer and the Making of Popular Roots Music*. Chicago: Chicago Review Press, 2015.

McCormick, Robert "Mack." *Biography of a Phantom: A Robert Johnson Blues Odyssey*. Ed. John Troutman. Smithsonian Books, 2023.

McKee, Margaret, and Fred Chisenhall. *Beale Black and Blue*. Baton Rouge: Louisiana State University Press, 1981.

McMillen, Neil R. *Dark Journey: Black Mississippians in the Age of Jim Crow*. Urbana: University of Illinois Press, 1989.

McPhee, John. "Sybil with a Guitar." *Time*, November 23, 1962.

McWhorter, Diane. *Carry Me Home: Birmingham, Alabama, The Climactic Battle of the Civil Rights Revolution*. New York: Simon & Schuster, 2001.

Melrose, Lester. "My Life in Recording." *The American Folk Music Occasional*. New York: Oak Publications, 1970.

Mertz, Paul E. "Sharecropping and Tenancy." In Melissa Walker and James C. Cobb, eds., *The New Encyclopedia of Southern Culture, Volume 11: Agriculture and Industry*. Chapel Hill: University of North Carolina Press, 2008.

Mississippi Blues Trail marker "Bukka White." https://msbluestrail.org/blues-trail-markers/bukka-white.

"Mississippi Poll Tax, The." *New York Times*, February 2, 1891.

Mitchell, George. *Mississippi Hill Country Blues 1967*. Jackson: University Press of Mississippi, 2013.

Moore, T. DeWayne. "Revisiting Ralph Lembo: Complicating Charley Patton, the 1920s Race Record Industry, and the Italian American Experience in the Mississippi Delta." *Association for Recorded Sound Collections Journal* 49, no. 2 (December 2018).

Murray, Paul T. "Blacks and the Draft: A History of Institutional Racism." *Journal of Black Studies* 2, no. 1 (September 1971).

Nelson, Paul. "Newport: The Folk Spectacle Comes of Age." *Sing Out!* 14, no. 5 (November 1964).

Nelson, Paul. Notes to *Tom Rush*. LP, Elektra Records EKS-7288, 1965.

Nelson, Scott Reynolds. *Steel Drivin' Man: John Henry, the Untold Story of an American Legend*. Oxford: Oxford University Press, 2006.

Obrecht, Jas. *Early Blues: The First Stars of Blues Guitar*. Minneapolis: University of Minnesota Press, 2015.

Oliver, Paul. *Blues Fell This Morning: The Meaning of the Blues*. New York: Horizon Press, 1960.

Oliver, Paul. *Blues off the Record: Thirty Years of Blues Commentary*. New York: Hippocrene Books, 1984.

Oliver, Paul. *Screening the Blues: Aspects of the Blues Tradition*. New York: Da Capo, 1989.

Oliver, Paul. *The Story of the Blues*. Philadelphia: Chilton, 1969.

Olsson, Bengt. *Memphis Blues*. London: Studio Vista, 1970.

O'Neal, Jim, and Amy Van Slaven, eds. *The Voice of the Blues: Classic Interviews from Living Blues Magazine*. New York: Routledge, 2002.

Oshinsky, David M. *"Worse than Slavery": Parchman Farm and the Ordeal of Jim Crow Justice*. New York, Free Press, 1996.

Ottenheimer, Harriet Joseph. "The Blues Tradition in St. Louis." *Black Music Research Journal* 9, no. 2 (Autumn 1989).

Ottenheimer, Harriet Joseph. "Writing Cousin Joe: Choice and Control Over Orthographic Representation in a Blues Singer's Autobiography." Revision of paper presented to American Anthropological Association, 1997.

Palmer, Robert. *Deep Blues*. New York: Viking Press, 1981.

Palmer, Robert. "Memphis Revisited." *Blues World*, no. 25 (October 1969).

Pastras, Phil. *Dead Man's Blues: Jelly Roll Morton Way Out West.* Berkeley and Chicago: University of California Press and Center for Black Music Research, 2001.

Petrusich, Amanda. *Do Not Sell at Any Price: The Wild, Obsessive Hunt for the World's Rarest 78rpm Records.* New York: Scribner, 2014.

Pope, Dean. "1,000 Hear Blues Sung in Old Style." *Commercial Appeal,* July 31, 1966.

Porterfield, Nolan. *Last Cavalier: The Life and Times of John A. Lomax, 1867–1948.* Urbana: University of Illinois Press, 1996.

Powell, Meili. "Orange Mound, Memphis (1890–)." BlackPast.org (July 30, 2018). https://www.blackpast.org/african-american-history/orange-mound-memphis-1890/.

Rachlin, Harvey. *The Encyclopedia of the Music Business.* New York: Harper & Row, 1981.

Ratcliffe, Philip R. *Mississippi John Hurt: His Life, His Times, His Blues.* Jackson: University Press of Mississippi, 2011.

Reich, Howard, and William Gaines. *Jelly's Blues: The Life, Music, and Redemption of Jelly Roll Morton.* Cambridge, MA: Da Capo Press, 2003.

Richards, Roberta. "The Legendary Bukka White." *Blues Magazine* 2, no. 6 (December 1976).

Riesman, Bob. *I Feel So Good: The Life and Times of Big Bill Broonzy.* Chicago: University of Chicago Press, 2011.

Rifkin, Rachael. "Berkeley Flashback: The Crunchy Munchy Man." *California Magazine,* April 13, 2017.

Riverside, William. Notes to Buffy Sainte-Marie, *Many a Mile.* LP, Vanguard Records VSD-7917, 1965.

Rowe, Mike. *Chicago Blues: The City and the Music.* New York: Da Capo Press, 1975.

Rush, Tom. Notes to *Tom Rush.* LP, Elektra Records, EKS-7288, 1965.

Sackheim, Eric, and Jonathan Shawn. *The Blues Line.* New York: Grossman, 1969.

Sacre, Robert, ed. *Charley Patton: Voice of the Mississippi Delta.* Jackson: University Press of Mississippi, 2018.

Sawyer, Charles. *The Arrival of B. B. King.* New York: Doubleday, 1980.

Segrest, James, and Mark Hoffman. *Moanin' at Midnight: The Life and Times of Howlin' Wolf.* New York: Thunder's Mouth Press, 2004, 2005.

Shelton, Robert (writing as Stacey Williams). Notes to *Bob Dylan.* LP, Columbia Records CS 8579, 1962.

Shlaes, Amity. *The Forgotten Man: A New History of the Great Depression.* New York: Harper Collins, 2007.

Silber, Irwin. "Country Joe Unstrung." *Sing Out!* 18, nos. 2–3 (June–July 1968).

Strachwitz, Chris. Notes to Bukka White, *Sky Songs, Volume 1* and *Sky Songs, Volume 2.* LP, Arhoolie Records F1019 and F1020, 1965.

Titon, Jeff Todd. *Early Downhome Blues: A Musical and Cultural Analysis.* Urbana: University of Illinois Press, 1977.

Tracy, Stephen C. *Going to Cincinnati: A History of the Blues in the Queen City.* Urbana: University of Illinois Press, 1993.

Turner, Tammy L. *Dick Waterman: A Life in the Blues.* Jackson: University Press of Mississippi, 2019.

Unterberger, Richie. Notes to *Tom Rush.* CD, CCM 2312, Collectors' Choice, 2001.

Von Schmidt, Eric, and Jim Rooney. *Baby, Let Me Follow You Down: The Illustrated Story of the Cambridge Folk Years*, 2nd ed. Amherst: University of Massachusetts Press, 1994.

Wald, Elijah. *Escaping the Delta: Robert Johnson and the Invention of the Blues*. New York: Amistad, 2004.

Wald, Elijah. *Josh White: Society Blues*. Amherst: University of Massachusetts Press, 2000.

Ward, Brian, and Patrick Huber. *A & R Pioneers: Architects of American Roots Music on Record*. Nashville: Country Music Foundation and Vanderbilt University Press, 2018.

Wardlow, Gayle Dean. "Bukka White: From Aberdeen to Parchman." *Chasin' That Devil Music: Searching for the Blues*. San Francisco: Backbeat Books, 1998.

Waterman, Dick. *Between Midnight and Day: The Last Unpublished Blues Archive*. San Rafael, CA: Insight Editions, 2004.

Wein, George, with Nat Chinen. *Myself Among Others: A Life in Music*. Cambridge, MA: Da Capo Press, 2003.

Welding, Pete. "The Rise of Folk Blues." *Down Beat* 28, no. 19 (September 14, 1961).

Wheeler, TJ. "Blues Guy First 8 Chapters." Unpublished memoir courtesy of TJ Wheeler.

White, Booker. Letter to Israel Young. May 28, 1966. Courtesy of Scott Barretta.

White, Booker. Notes from BW interview with Laurie Forti, Phil Spiro, and Alan Wilson, Cambridge, Massachusetts, April 1964. Courtesy of David Evans.

White, Emma Lee. Funeral service program. New Life Church of God in Christ, Harvey, Illinois, October 5, 2009. Courtesy of Irene Kertchaval.

White, Willie Arthur (Sonnie). Celebration of life program. Jackson Memorial Chapel, Aberdeen, Mississippi, September 14, 1966. Courtesy of Sandra D. Marble.

Wilkerson, Isabel. *The Warmth of Other Suns: The Epic Story of America's Great Migration*. New York: Vintage Books, 2010.

Willis, John C. *Forgotten Time: The Yazoo-Mississippi Delta after the Civil War*. Charlottesville: University Press of Virginia, 2000.

Wilson, Alan. "Bukka White, Master of the Blues Lyric." *The Broadside of Boston* 3, no. 4 (April 15, 1964).

Wilson, Alan. "Learn Delta Blues." Advertisement. *The Broadside of Boston* 3, no. 4 (April 15, 1964).

Wolfe, Charles, and Kip Lornell. *The Life and Legend of Leadbelly*. New York: HarperCollins, 1992.

Work, John W., et al. *Lost Delta Found: Rediscovering the Fisk-Library of Congress Coahoma County Study, 1941–1942*. Nashville: Vanderbilt University Press, 2005.

INDEX

ABOUT THE AUTHOR

Photo by Joanna Eldredge Morrissey

DAVID W. JOHNSON IS A FORMER JOURNALIST AND COLLEGE TEACHER. He has written about rock, folk, and roots music since the 1960s. His article on the Carter Family, "Following the Valley Road to the Homeplace of American Music," was chosen for the anthology *Da Capo Best Music Writing 2004*. In 2013 the University Press of Mississippi published his biography of two old-time bluegrass musicians, *Lonesome Melodies: The Lives and Music of the Stanley Brothers*.

Having interviewed Booker "Bukka" White in 1976, Johnson jumped at the chance to write the first full-length biography of the musician. In July 2017, he took a research trip to Memphis, Tennessee, and the Mississippi counties where White was born and developed his style. The following year, the MacDowell Colony awarded him a fellowship to begin writing early chapters of the book. In 2020, he was asked by the National Recording Registry of the Library of Congress to write an essay on the Stanley Brothers' version of the gospel song, "Rank Stranger." He expanded the essay into an article that was published in 2021 in the *International Country Music Journal*.

Having written about the worlds of country music and blues, he hopes to set his next book in the 1970s rock scene in Boston and New York.

A 1968 graduate of Harvard College, Johnson holds a master's degree in communications from Boston University and a doctorate in English literature and criticism from Indiana University of Pennsylvania. He lives in Stratham, New Hampshire.